Struggling with God

An Introduction to the Pentateuch

MERCER
UNIVERSITY PRESS

Endowed by
TOM WATSON BROWN
and
THE WATSON-BROWN FOUNDATION, INC.

Struggling with God

An Introduction to the Pentateuch

by
MARK MCENTIRE

MERCER UNIVERSITY PRESS
Macon, Georgia USA
May 2008

Isbn 978-0-88146-101-5 Old pick number: MUP/P336

Struggling with God.
An Introduction to the Pentateuch.

Printed in the United States of America
First edition May 2008

The paper used in this publication meets the minimum requirements of American National Standard for Information Sciences—Permanence of Paper for Printed Library Materials, ANSI Z39.48-1984.

Library of Congress Cataloging-in-Publication Data

McEntire, Mark Harold, 1960-
Struggling with God : an introduction to the Pentateuch / by Mark McEntire. — 1st ed.
p. cm. — (A Mercer student guide)
Includes bibliographical references and indexes.
ISBN-13: 978-0-88146-101-5 (pbk. : alk. paper)
ISBN-10: 0-88146-101-6 (pbk. : alk. paper)
1. Bible. O.T. Pentateuch--Criticism, interpretation, etc. I. Title.
BS1225.52.M34 2008
222'.1061--dc22

2008000850

Contents

Tables

Preface

Why this Book?

During the past quarter century, about fifteen academic introductions to the Pentateuch in English have been produced.[1] This activity may have peaked in the 1990s with the highly regarded volumes by Joseph Blenkinsopp, Norman Whybray, and Terrence Fretheim, but a handful of introductions have already appeared in these early years of the twenty-first century. This situation demands an answer to the question, Why another book on the Pentateuch?"

Beyond obvious personal considerations, there are three major reasons for what I see as the need for this work. First, the field of Pentateuch studies is changing rapidly, and new introductory works are needed to address this shifting situation.

Second, the current books in this field often lack careful attention to the *literary* shape of each of the five individual books of the Pentateuch and of the whole. To date, the best attempt to address this important issue is Thomas W. Mann's excellent study, *The Book of the Torah: The Narrative Integrity of the Pentateuch*.[2] Mann's book was ahead of its time in its narrative focus, while also giving deserved attention to major historical issues that had arisen in the previous era. Still, major developments have taken place over the last two decades, and there is plenty of room for fresh work in this direction. Other books have attempted to follow the narrative shape of the Pentateuch with varying degrees of success. A common difficulty is maintaining the same level of attention to narrative issues beyond the books of Genesis and Exodus. This is an understandable phenomenon, therefore

---

[1]About ten other books, which either seem to address primarily a popular audience or are oriented toward a different purpose than providing a general introduction, have also appeared. Of course, many introductions to the Old Testament or to the whole Bible include some sort of introduction to the Pentateuch.

[2](Atlanta: John Knox Press, 1988).

great effort will be necessary in the second half of this book to maintain that focus.

A third and final reason for another book in this field is in this book's choice of intended audience, the undergraduate classroom. The best introductions currently available are aimed at seminary or graduate-school audiences. In addition, they do not look like textbooks. This present textbook, however, gathers information in tables, questions for reflection, and lists of key terms in each chapter in order to help both students and teachers in the undergraduate classroom as they struggle together to understand the books of Genesis, Exodus, Leviticus, Numbers, and Deuteronomy.

Plan of the Book

The following five chapters will treat each of the books of the Pentateuch in turn. Regardless of the history of formation of these books and their components, it has become obvious in our present context that the final form of each of the books deserves a privileged position. The discussion of each book will begin with an attempt to describe the broad contours of its literary shape in a section on its "literary landscape." Following this will be an examination of the major components of each book, which gives careful attention to the contents of that section and the role it plays in the book. It is not possible within the scope of a book like this to offer a thorough interpretation of all, or even most, of the texts in each book. Instead, the focus will be on the shape and function of larger complexes, with occasional closer readings which serve as important interpretive examples and demonstrate major issues. Deciding which passages in the Pentateuch are "most important" and deserving of more consideration is a subjective process and not all readers will agree with the relative attention given to various texts. It is always more important for an introductory textbook to point the reader in productive directions than to exhaust investigative possibilities, so the major point of discussion will always be the ongoing development of the larger Pentateuch narrative. More detailed discussions of certain texts are always intended to illustrate what might be possible with all texts.

While the primary focus of this book will be on literary issues related to the final form of the text, occasional attention will be given to historical-critical concerns. This is necessary for at least three reasons. First, more recent literary approaches were born out of the historical-critical era, and are still dependent on many of the ways of observing the text that arose in this period of biblical studies. Second, the body of Pentateuch scholarship still contains the results of the historical-critical era, and reading the Pentateuch in an academic context still requires conversance with this material. Third, historical-critical methods still have the ability to illustrate certain features of the text which may not otherwise be clearly visible. The value of any method of reading is not in its ability to provide definitive answers to its own questions, but in its capacity to direct our attention back to the text itself.

Tables appear throughout the book at points where this manner of presenting data seems efficient and helpful. In almost all of these cases, the material in the table should serve merely as an entry point to a more thorough investigation.

Near the end of each chapter, a section on history will appear. I agree with Joseph Blenkinsopp that an exploration of the literature must precede historical investigation or reconstruction of its origins and development.[3] Readers will soon discover that our historical conclusions are at best vague and provisional.

Each chapter will conclude with a list of key terms, some suggested questions for reflection, and a limited list of resources for further study. Some of these resources will be commentaries, which can provide a more thorough analysis of any particular text. Others are monographs or reference works, which identify and investigate major issues in a more comprehensive manner.

Unless otherwise noted, Bible translations in this book are my own. Because most quotations are brief, they may not differ much from other English translations, but in many cases I have leaned toward a more literal rendering of the Hebrew text in order to illustrate the point I am making. When word counts are provided, they always refer to the Hebrew text. For several reasons, such counts are often approximate. In cases of large counts, it is difficult to produce precise counts, and those published in various places are often slightly different. In other cases, there is some problem with the text that may cause the appearance of a word to be uncertain.

---

[3]Joseph Blenkinsopp, *The Pentateuch: An Introduction to the First Five Books of the Bible* (New York: Doubleday, 1992) 126. Blenkinsopp's introductory text is still a standard in the field and serves as a fine model in many ways for any attempt to introduce the Pentateuch, except for his decision, after two fine chapters on Genesis, to treat Exodus–Deuteronomy more thematically in two chapters that give insufficient attention to the distinct shape of these other four books. The aim of the present text is to be more accessible to a wider range of readers.

Finally, the discussion of texts throughout this book will assume the reader's familiarity with them, so this textbook is not a replacement for Genesis, Exodus, Leviticus, Numbers, and Deuteronomy. Readers will get the most out of this book if their Bible is open beside it.

Acknowledgments

Thanks are due to many people for their assistance in the preparation of this book. My family has been kind to me and supportive of my work throughout the completion of this project, as usual, and I grateful beyond words. I am indebted to Marc Jolley, director of Mercer University Press for approaching me about this project several years ago and encouraging me as I brought it to completion. The staff of the press has been extremely helpful, especially Edd Rowell, whose meticulous editing of the manuscript saved me countless blunders. My many colleagues at Belmont University, particularly those in the School of Religion, provide an atmosphere of abundant life and thought in which to work. In addition, Belmont University generously provided me with a sabbatical leave in the fall of 2006 during which I completed much of this project. During my leave the Graduate Department of Religion and the Divinity Library at Vanderbilt University provided generous resources for my research. Danny Mynatt of Anderson University offered very helpful insight on the organization of the first chapter. Finally, I had the great pleasure of working through this book in prepublished form with eighteen students in my Pentateuch class at Belmont University, and it was one of the greatest teaching experiences of my life. For all these I have listed and many others, I am most thankful.

Dedication

For My Children

Atticus and Claire

Chapter 1

Introduction: Reading the Pentateuch

The Problems and Prospects of Reading an Ancient Text

The first five books of the Bible are commonly referred to as the "Torah" in Jewish tradition and as the "Pentateuch" in Christian tradition. It does not take much reading in this part of the Bible to develop a sense of bewilderment. Like the rest of the Bible, the Pentateuch comes with no manual to tell us how to read it. The Pentateuch tells a continuous story from the creation of the universe in Genesis 1 to the death of Moses on Mount Nebo in Deuteronomy 34, but it tells the various parts of that story in such vastly different ways that readers have often been uncertain how to receive such a text. This problem is exacerbated by 2,000 years of tradition in Judaism and Christianity, in which individual texts from the Pentateuch have been extracted and used for wide-ranging purposes. These observations lead to some central questions that must be explored in an introductory book or course on the Pentateuch. Each of these larger questions will lead to many others.

(1) In what sense is the Pentateuch a coherent work of literature, to be read all the way through?
(2) What is the significance of the division into five books, and should these be read as five coherent works of literature?
(3) What is the relationship between the narrative and the legal portions of the Pentateuch?
(4) To what extent should the history of the development of the text be allowed to shape its interpretation, or should the final form always be normative?
(5) What is the role of the Pentateuch within the canonical traditions of the various faith communities that consider it sacred, and how should these communities receive and make use of the material in the Pentateuch?

The plan of the next several sections of this introductory chapter is to move primarily backwards through time in its presentation of what the

Pentateuch is and how it came into existence. The most significant advantage of this approach is that it begins with what is most certain—the content and organization of the Pentateuch in its present form—and moves toward what is least certain—issues of origin and authorship.

The Contents and Organization of the Pentateuch

Nobody knows at what point the five books of the Pentateuch, as they are now divided, began to be identified using names or titles. The way we use titles, like "Genesis" and "Exodus," makes it difficult to imagine a situation in which such titles did not exist. Ancient manuscripts do not have headings of any kind at the beginnings of any of the books, but the tradition of referring to books by the use of their initial words extends back into Judaism of ancient times. Table 1.1 provides an explanation of the names of the five books of the Pentateuch in Jewish tradition.

Table 1.1
The Hebrew Names of the Five Books

Bre'shiyt	the first Hebrew word in Genesis means "In (the) beginning"
Shemot	the second word in Exodus, meaning "Names," appears in the opening phrase, "These are the names."
Vayiqra'	the first word in Leviticus means "And he called (out)"
Bemidbar	the fourth word in Numbers, translated "in (the) wilderness," in the opening phrase, "And YHWH spoke to Moses *in the wilderness* of Sinai"
Debariym	the second word in Deuteronomy means "Words," and appears in the opening phrase "These are the words"

The current English names of the books have come into existence in different ways. *Genesis* is the Greek word for "beginning" and therefore is a translation of the Hebrew designation for the first book.

"Exodus" is a slightly altered Greek word (*exodos*) that means something like "departure," so it is a description of an important event in the book,[1] but does not correspond to the Hebrew name for the second book.

[1]A few Septuagint (LXX) manuscripts specify this event by adding *Aigyptou* to

"Leviticus" is derived from the Greek title, *Levitikon*. This title has no connection to the Hebrew name for the book. It is obviously related to the name of the tribe of Levi and the subsequent priestly group known as the Levites. Surprisingly, this priestly designation ("Levites") appears only four times in the book of Leviticus, all in 25:32-33. In contrast, related words appear about fifteen times in the preceding book of Exodus and more than sixty times in the following book of Numbers. The ordination of Aaron and his sons, members of the tribe of Levi, as the first priests (Leviticus 8—10) appears to be the governing feature in the development of this name.

The prominence of the taking of a census twice in the book of Numbers, in chapters 1 and 26, appears to have led to the development of the Greek title of the book, *Arithmoi* ("Numbers"). When the Bible was translated into Latin, this title was translated as *Numeri*, which of course led to the English title, "Numbers."

"Deuteronomy" is a slightly altered form of a Greek compound word meaning "second law" (*deuteronomion*). This seems to be a description of the bulk of the book's content, a series of speeches by Moses that revise, reiterate, and expand parts of the legal material presented in Exodus, Leviticus, and Numbers.

In Jewish tradition the Pentateuch is called "Torah," perhaps better translated as "Instruction" rather than "Law." The Torah is the first and most important of the three sections of the Hebrew scriptures. The Hebrew Bible is commonly named using the first letters of the Hebrew titles of the three sections: *Torah*, *Nebi'im* (Prophets), and *Ketubim* (Writings). Vowels are added to make the pronounceable acronym *TaNaK*.

It is not possible to say with certainty why the Pentateuch is divided into five books, each with separate designations or names. There is no inherent need for book divisions. The story told in the Pentateuch is continuous enough that it could be one large book, and in some sense it is treated that way. There has been much speculation about the physical limits of scroll length in ancient Israel. Liturgical synagogue scrolls today contain the entire Torah, but it is uncertain whether there were scrolls of this length in ancient times. It is possible that the Pentateuch became divided into five books because it was too long to copy onto a single scroll, but this proposal ultimately yields no helpful results.[2] It cannot be proven, and even if it

---

the superscription or title: *Exodos Aigyptou*, "Departure from Egypt."

[2]See the longer discussion of this issue in Blenkinsopp, *The Pentateuch*, 45-47.

could, this would still not explain why the books are divided in the places where they are. They are not close to being equal in length (see table 1.2).[3]

Subsequent chapters in this volume will argue that each of the books of the Pentateuch exhibit signs of careful literary design, which makes division of the five books by any simple procedure based upon mechanical considerations, such as ideal scroll length, seem highly unlikely.

Table 1.2

The Length of the Books of the Pentateuch

The group of Jewish scribes known as the Masoretes, who standardized the Hebrew text of *TaNaK* in the early Middle Ages, performed many tasks, including the addition of vowels and accent marks. While the specific numbering of chapters and verses came later, these scribes did count the verses of each book and provided the count at the end of each book. Here are the numbers of verses in each book along with the middle verse, another piece of statistical data provided by the Masoretes.

Genesis: 1534 verses, 27:40 is the middle verse
Exodus: 1209 verses, 22:27 is the middle verse
Leviticus: 859 verses, 15:7 is the middle verse
Numbers: 1288 verses, 17:20 is the middle verse
Deuteronomy: 955 verses, 17:10 is the middle verse

Our Access to the Text of the Pentateuch

We do not possess anything close to "original" copies of any of the books of the Bible, and this includes the Pentateuch. The Old Testament produced in most English versions of the Bible is based upon a manuscript known as the Leningrad Codex.[4] The Leningrad Codex is a full handwritten copy of

[3]Verse lengths vary, so a verse count is not always a precise means of comparing the relative lengths of texts, but for large bodies of text, like whole biblical books, average verse length will be relatively equal. Variances in chapter length may also provide imprecise comparisons of length, even of whole books. Comparisons of the length of the last four books of the Pentateuch to Genesis, based upon number of verses and number of chapters (in parentheses) yield the following: Exodus, 79% (80%); Leviticus, 56% (54%); Numbers, 84% (72%); Deuteronomy, 62% (68%).

[4]The word "codex" refers to the physical book form we are accustomed to, with

the Hebrew text of *TaNaK*. It was produced around the year 1000 CE, so the Leningrad Codex is approximately 1,000 years old, but this means it was written more than 1,000 years after the Pentateuch reached its final form. The only full manuscripts of the Pentateuch older than this are in the Greek manuscripts, such as Codex Vaticanus, Codex Sinaiticus, or Codex Alexandrinus, all of which were produced in the fourth to sixth centuries CE. These manuscripts represent the traditional translation of the Hebrew Scriptures into the Greek language, commonly referred to as the Septuagint (LXX). The books of the Pentateuch were likely translated into Greek during the third and second centuries BCE, so the production of these codices postdates the translation process by seven or eight centuries. It is obvious that the Hebrew text from which the Septuagint was translated was not exactly the same as the Hebrew text we have available today, though the differences in the Pentateuch are less severe than in most other parts of the Old Testament.[5]

This discussion reveals that our complete copies of the Pentateuch are far removed from the actual writing of the five books. Furthermore, because our oldest copies are all handwritten, they differ from each other, which requires that modern translators make decisions about which particular text to translate. Older, partial copies of the Hebrew text of the Pentateuch are present, of course, among the Dead Sea Scrolls. These scrolls were written around the beginning of the Common Era, some perhaps a century or so earlier. While they provide some useful information for translators and textual critics, their usefulness is limited because they constitute only a fraction of the text of the Pentateuch. Table 1.3 provides data regarding the Pentateuch among the Dead Sea Scrolls. While the biblical texts present in the Dead Sea Scrolls are not identical to the form found in the Leningrad Codex, the differences are relatively minor.

---

cut, stacked pages that have writing on both sides and are bound in some way. (From Latin *codex* [*caudex*], tree trunk; then a "book" originally made of waxed, inscribed, and bound wooden tablets.)

[5]The Greek text of the Pentateuch contains no lengthy additions to the books, such as those found in Esther and Daniel, nor any significant rearrangement or expansion of the material, such as in the book of Jeremiah. For more extensive information on the text of the Pentateuch, see Emanuel Tov, *Textual Criticism of the Hebrew Bible*, 2nd ed. (Minneapolis: Fortress Press, 2001).

Table 1.3

Books of the Pentateuch in the Dead Sea Scrolls

	Number of Scrolls[6]	Approximate % of Book Represented[7]
Genesis	15	20%
Exodus	17	65%
Leviticus	13	60%
Numbers	8	42%
Deuteronomy	27	71%

Slightly less than half of the verses in the Pentateuch are represented in whole or in part in any one of the Dead Sea Scrolls. The two most important conclusions that may be drawn from these data are that the first-century Jewish community that produced the scrolls had an intense interest in the Pentateuch and that the Masoretic Text, represented by the Leningrad Codex, was transmitted across ten centuries with reasonable accuracy.

Dating and Describing the Production and Canonization of the Pentateuch

Assigning dates to the various stages of development that led to the final form of the Pentateuch as a canonized text is a task that can only be performed in a tentative and approximate manner. The issues addressed in this section necessarily overlap with issues of authorship. Direct discussion of questions related specifically to authorship of the books of the Pentateuch will be deferred to the next section. In keeping with the plan of the

[6]James C. Vanderkam, *The Dead Sea Scrolls Today* (Grand Rapids MI: Eerdmans, 1994) 30-31. These are conservative numbers. It is often difficult to tell whether separate fragments came from the same or different scrolls. Some writers also include in such counts scrolls found at other sites in the Judean desert (such as Masada) which are believed to have originated in the same time period.

[7]These percentages are calculated from counting the verses that are represented in whole or in part in a reconstruction based on all of the scrolls combined. The percentage of actual words or letters represented would be somewhat lower than this. See Martin Abegg et al., *The Dead Sea Scrolls Bible: The Oldest Known Bible Translated for the First Time into English* (San Francisco: HarperSanFrancisco, 1999).

surrounding discussion, we will move backwards in time in this section, from what is most certain to what is least certain.

While there are references in the Old Testament itself to "the scroll/book (of the law) of Moses," such as in Joshua 8:31 or Ezra 6:18, there is no way to know to what sort of literary collections such passages refer. Furthermore, one would need to establish dates for these passages themselves in order to use them as the basis to establish a date for some form of the Pentateuch. There is common agreement that the reference in the prologue to the book of Sirach to "the Law and the Prophets and the other books" assumes an accepted Jewish canon in which the first two major sections had reached their current form, while the third section, the Writings, was still in a state of flux. This prologue comes from the middle of the second century BCE. The way in which the writer of the prologue uses this phrase indicates that his audience would have known exactly what he was talking about. Because such common understanding and usage take time, it is safe to conclude that by approximately 200 BCE "the Law," whether in Hebrew (*Torah*) or Greek (*Nomos*), referred to the first section of the Jewish canon, the Pentateuch as we now have it.

While it is almost certain that the Pentateuch was completed in its current form considerably earlier than 200 BCE, the arguments for establishing a date for its completion are complex and disputed. Recent scholarship has focused upon the period of the Exile and its aftermath, the sixth through fourth centuries BCE, as the highly productive period in which most of the biblical literature achieved its final form. This conclusion does not deny that many parts of the Bible, in both written and oral form, are many centuries older than this. William M. Schniedewind has recently produced an effective argument that places the beginning point of the production of the Pentateuch in the Josianic Reform of the late seventh century BCE.[8] He is not as clear and certain in establishing a date for the finished product of the Penta-

[8]This argument is based upon Schniedewind's development of the notion of "textualization," the growing investment of primary religious authority in written texts. See his discussion in *How the Bible Became a Book: The Textualization of Ancient Israel* (Cambridge UK: Cambridge University Press, 2004) 11-17. Schniedewind has clearly established that the idea of textuality is far more prominent in Deuteronomy than in the first four books of the Pentateuch. The association of Deuteronomy with the Josianic reform then forms the basis of his understanding that this was a generative period for the development of the Pentateuch (121-28).

teuch, but argues, primarily on economic grounds, against the common proposal that the period of the Babylonian Exile generated a large amount of literary activity.[9]

At a certain point the effort to use historical methods to establish dates for various stages in the production of the Pentateuch begins to offer diminishing returns. The argument that writing became important and began to claim significant authority before the Exile is convincing. That large steps toward the completion of what we think of as the books of the Pentateuch could have taken place is this period seems likely. Nevertheless, too many texts in the Pentateuch (Genesis 3:23, 4:12, 11:8, 27:42-45; Leviticus 26:1-39; Deuteronomy 5:33, 8:18-20, 29:28-29, 30:17-18) seem to assume the paradigm of expulsion from and return to the land to dismiss the exilic and early postexilic periods as the locus for the final shaping of the Pentateuch.

In summary, we can use approximate round numbers to present a reasonable scheme as follows:

600 BCE Disparate oral and written traditions begin to be drawn together into literary works similar to what we would recognize as the books of the Pentateuch.

400 BCE The Pentateuch reaches its final form and begins to achieve its status as a completed, unchangeable sacred text.

200 BCE The Pentateuch is firmly in position as the first of three sections of the Jewish canon.

Moses and the Authorship of the Pentateuch

Questions concerning the formation and canonization of the Pentateuch in the previous section eventually begin to raise and overlap with questions of authorship. The conclusions drawn at the end of the previous section obviously assume that Moses did not write the books of the Pentateuch in the form in which we have them. The presumption of Mosaic authorship of the Pentateuch is still prominent in many faith communities and requires some attention.

The traditional assumption that Moses wrote the books of Genesis through Deuteronomy appears to rely on three basic ideas. First, the Penta-

---

[9]Schniedewind, *How the Bible Became a Book*, 141-47. At another point Schniedewind assumes that Ezra "circulated and publicized the Book of the Torah in the early Second Temple period" (136).

teuch itself refers in vague fashion in five different places to Moses writing something. These five occasions are outlined in table 1.4.

Table 1.4
Moses and Writing in the Pentateuch

1. In Exodus 17:14, Moses is commanded by God to "write this, a remembrance, in the scroll. . . . " The following words indicate that what the text likely understands Moses to have written was an account of Joshua's battle against Amalek, which is reported in 7:8-13.
2. Exodus 24:4 says, "Moses wrote all the words of the LORD." While this passage does not indicate exactly what Moses wrote, the set of laws typically called the Covenant Code (Exodus 20:21–23:33) immediately precedes this report and is the most obvious potential referent.
3. Exodus 34:28 says, "And [Moses] wrote upon the tablets the words of the covenant, ten of the words." This report comes after Moses broke the initial tablets. Again, the text is not precise about what is written. The final phrase, "ten of the words," is awkward. Traditionally, it is taken as a reference back to the Ten Commandments in Exodus 20.
4. Deuteronomy 31:9 says, "Moses wrote this law and gave it to the priests, the sons of Levi, the ones carrying the Ark of the Covenant of the LORD." This report comes much later in the narrative of the Exodus. There is no clear indication of what was written. It is often understood as a reference to the collection of laws that comprise most of Deuteronomy 5–30. Deuteronomy 31:24 reports that, "Moses . . . finished writing the words of this law on a scroll."
5. Deuteronomy 31:22 says, "Moses wrote down this song on that day." This is a case where it seems most clear what Moses is writing. The poem that appears in Deuteronomy 32, commonly called the "Song of Moses," seems likely to be the written text to which this verse refers.

As the table above indicates, the idea of Moses producing written material is present in the Pentateuch itself, but it is not a precise or highly developed tradition. The tradition of Moses as a writer grows within the Bible and within Judaism after the biblical period. The notion that Moses wrote the entire Pentateuch in its final form is the end product of the development of this tradition. A clear statement of this conclusion in the Babylonian Talmud assigns all but the last eight verses, the account of

Moses' death, to Moses himself. It goes on to state that Joshua wrote the last eight verses, along with the book of Joshua.[10]

The second idea that has contributed to the assumption that Moses wrote Genesis through Deuteronomy is related to the first. It appears to have become standard practice to equate these books with Moses, in spoken and written language, as a matter of convenience. The origin of this habit is impossible to discern. Likewise, it is impossible to know whether this practice grew out of an assumption that Moses wrote these books or because of other factors, such as Moses' appearance as the main character in four of the five books, or the prominence of Moses' death at the end of Deuteronomy. The phrase, "scroll/book of the law of Moses" or just "the law of Moses," appears in Joshua 8:31, 32, 23:6, 1 Kings 2:3, 2 Kings 14:6, 23:25, 2 Chronicles 23:18, 30:16, Ezra 3:2, 7:6, Nehemiah 8:1, Daniel 9:11, 13, Luke 2:22, 24:44, John 7:23, Acts 13:39, 15:5, 28:23, 1 Corinthians 9:9, and Hebrews 10:28. In most of these cases it is unclear to what body of writing this phrase refers. In Nehemiah 8, Ezra reads "the scroll of the law of Moses." Nehemiah 8:3 says that he read "from the light [early morning] until the middle of the day." In the form we now have it, the Pentateuch contains 5,845 verses. Reading it in six hours would require maintaining a blistering pace of one verse every 3.7 seconds for the whole morning. Furthermore, Nehemiah 8:3 reports that the text was being interpreted by the priests as it was being read. Therefore, it is not possible that this text refers to the entire Pentateuch. More likely, it describes the public reading of the book of Deuteronomy. By the first century, when the New Testament was written, "the Law of Moses" or simply "Moses" was a shorthand way of referring to the books of Genesis through Deuteronomy.

The third underlying idea that has often supported the assumption of Mosaic authorship of the Pentateuch is the general sense in which writings become authoritative by being attached to authoritative personalities. This tendency can be seen in the gradual linking of all of the poems in the book of Psalms to David, the connecting of the other poetic books (Proverbs,

---

[10]This text is found in the tractate known as *Baba Bathra* in the Babylonian Talmud, a work that reflects rabbinic teachings from around the middle of the first millennium CE. The appearance of Joshua here is another case that reveals the tendency to assume that the main character of a biblical book or the person whose name has been traditionally attached to it was the author. For a more extensive discussion of this issue, see Alexander Rofé, *Introduction to the Composition of the Pentateuch* (Sheffield UK: Sheffield Academic Press, 1999) 11-13.

Ecclesiastes, Song of Songs) to Solomon, the production of pseudepigraphical works with the names of Enoch, Adam, and Ezra attached to them, and the linking of undesignated New Testament literature, such as Hebrews, to Paul. Of course, Moses is the main character in the Pentateuch, so it is natural to associate him with the book. The most significant narrative problem of the Pentateuch, understanding the relationship between the story material and the legal material, is also addressed by the gigantic figure of Moses, who is both liberator and lawgiver. Moses' dominant presence in the Pentateuch is easily transformed into assumptions about authorship. If the Pentateuch produces Moses, then perhaps it is natural to think that Moses produced the Pentateuch.

Critical Study of the Bible and the Authorship of the Pentateuch

One of the hallmarks of critical thinking is the rigorous examination of assumptions. Assumptions that are found to be lacking in evidentiary support, or which are contradicted by evidence, are rejected. With the rise of critical thought in the Enlightenment, many assumptions about the world were called into question and eventually rejected. The replacement of the Ptolemaic system (in which the earth is the center of the universe around which every other celestial body revolves) by the Copernican solar system (in which the sun is the center around which the earth and other planets revolve) is a classic case of critical thinking in which use of empirical evidence overcame long-held assumptions. The classic case in critical study of the Bible is the assumption of Mosaic authorship of the Pentateuch. Over the past three or four centuries, careful observation of the text of the Pentateuch has led to the common view that the Pentateuch is a composite work produced by many writers over a long period of time, using a wide variety of sources. In a few cases the Pentateuch itself appears to identify prior sources which provided some of its material. Some of these cases are listed in table 1.5.

Table 1.5
Other "Books" behind the Pentateuch

The word "book" appears in English translations of the Pentateuch a dozen or so times. This is typically a translation of the Hebrew word *sepher*. In the following examples, this word is translated as "scroll."[11]

(1) Genesis 5:1 introduces the genealogy of Adam with the phrase "This is the Scroll of the Generations of Adam." This may indicate that this and perhaps other genealogies in Genesis were taken from a collection of genealogies.
(2) In Exodus 17:14 God commands Moses to write down in a scroll the story of Joshua's battle against Amalek. This reference may acknowledge a written collection of battle stories.
(3) A more certain indication of a collection of war stories comes in Numbers 21:14 when Moses introduces a strange little geographical poem with the saying, "Therefore, it is said in the Scroll of the Wars of the LORD. . . ."[12]
(4) Deuteronomy 28-29 makes several references to what seems to be a book containing a collection of curses.

As the Enlightenment progressed, readers began to pay attention to more subtle details in the text of the Pentateuch that could be indicators of multiple authorship. Among the earliest writers to record such observations and raise questions about authorship and sources were Baruch Spinoza,

[11]To think of these as references to physical books, in codex form, is obviously an anachronism. It is far more likely that if these are references to physical objects, then they were scrolls, but people in the Ancient Near East also wrote on stone tablets and broken pieces of pottery, among other materials. Translations that use "book" in these passages do so in a metaphorical sense.

[12]Numbers 21:14 and Genesis 5:1 are two texts where the Pentateuch may provide something like titles of other written works to which it refers. This is more common in other parts of the Old Testament. Joshua 10:13 and 2 Samuel 1:18 both contain poems said to be taken from the "Scroll of Jashar." In Joshua 24:26 Joshua writes something in the "Scroll of the Law of God." 1 Kings 11:41 refers to the "Book of the Acts of Solomon." Numerous passages in 1 and 2 Kings refer to the "Scroll of the Annals of the Kings of Israel" (e.g., 1 Kings 14:19) and the "Scroll of the Annals of the Kings of Judah" (e.g., 1 Kings 14:29).

better known as a philosopher, whose *Tractatus Theological-politicus* was published in 1670, and a physician named Jean Astruc, whose primary work was done about a century later. One of the most obvious and important features that Spinoza and Astruc observed was the variation in divine names used in the Pentateuch. The most common designations by far are the unpronounceable name represented by the four consonants, YHWH, and the common noun *Elohim*. YHWH is usually translated, using all capital letters (routinely an initial capital-L plus small caps), as "LORD" in English Bibles; *Elohim*, which may approach the status of a title, is commonly translated as "God." These two designations can be used together, as in the YHWH *Elohim* ("LORD God") of Genesis 2:5. There are numerous other, less common, ways of referring to the deity. Table 1.6 offers a more thorough listing of these designations.

Table 1.6

Divine Designations in the Pentateuch[13]

YHWH	1,820 times (of 6,007 in the Old Testament)
Elohim	813 times (in various grammatical forms)
YHWH *Elohim*	Used in combination 21 times (12 in Genesis 2, 8 in Genesis 3, and Exodus 9:30)
'El	34 times
'Elyon	2 times (Numbers 24:14, Deuteronomy 32:8)
'El 'Elyon	4 times (all in Genesis 14)
'El Shaddai	6 times (5 in Genesis, 1 in Exodus)
'El Ro'i	1 time (Genesis 16:13)
'El 'olam	1 time (Genesis 21:33)
Yah	2 times (Exodus 15:2, 17:16)[14]

[13]Word counts of this sort are most easily obtained using Francis I. Anderson and Dean A. Forbes, *The Vocabulary of the Old Testament* (Chicago: Loyola Press, 1993).

[14]Of approximately 49 occurrences in the Hebrew Bible of this shortened divine name, approximately 43 appear in the book of Psalms, typically as part of the phrase *hallelu-yah* ("Praise the LORD"); the only other occurrences are in Isaiah (12:2; 26:4; 38:11[2]).

The use of this first and most obvious literary feature to argue for and delineate sources in the Pentateuch led to the use of many others as source criticism became more sophisticated.

A review of the history of historical-critical scholarship on the Pentateuch can result in a dizzying array of German names, complex theories, and strange abbreviations. Some of this complexity is necessary. This is a complex subject, and even ideas that have been essentially discarded have often served as the impetus for the next development. Some organizational principles established at the outset of such a review may help to keep these ideas under control. If the Pentateuch is a composite work, then there are two basic ways of thinking about how it developed into the form in which it now exists. These two ways can be distinguished by the basic nature of the components that one proposes were drawn together to form the Pentateuch.

For much of the critical era, the dominant idea was that multiple, continuous sources, each of which told Israel's story up to the arrival in Canaan, were combined in order to form the Pentateuch. This would account, for example, for the changing use of divine names and the appearance of two or more accounts of essentially the same story. These continuous sources now exist as "strands" within the Pentateuch, which exhibit different characteristics while operating together to tell this part of Israel's story. Within this "strand" category are many different hypotheses concerning the number, nature, extent, and date of the strands, some of which differ widely in their conclusions.

A second basic way of thinking about the composite development of the Pentateuch involves the relatively independent production of its major elements. The story of the ancestors, the story of the exodus, the wilderness accounts, the Sinai legislation, and the speeches of Moses in Deuteronomy may have all developed independently of one another. These "blocks" of tradition were then put together end-to-end with some minor connective elements to form the final Pentateuch. Again, hypotheses within this general "block" category may differ widely in terms of identifying, describing, and dating the blocks. The discussion to follow will be clearer if this basic sense of organization is kept in mind.

As mentioned earlier, observations related to potential sources for the Pentateuch began to appear in earnest in the late seventeenth century. Early attempts to outline the extent of sources, based primarily upon the use of the divine names, appeared in the eighteenth-century work of Jean Astruc and

Johann Eichorn.[15] The attempt to identify sources in the Pentateuch was addressed more systematically in the work of Wilhelm de Wette in the early to mid-nineteenth century, which established an important benchmark in the study of the Pentateuch. De Wette began his construction of a scenario of development with the assertion that the "book of the law" "found" by Hilkiah the high priest (1 Kings 22), which served as the program for Josiah's reforms during the late seventh century in Judah, was the book of Deuteronomy in an early form. De Wette detached the Pentateuch from Mosaic authorship and established Deuteronomy as the latest of the sources of the Pentateuch and proceeded to divide the remainder into three earlier sources. De Wette's work marked an approximate beginning of a period of intense Old Testament scholarship in Germany, which was synthesized most famously in a series of writings produced by Julius Wellhausen during the final third of the nineteenth century. Wellhausen's work demonstrates the most well-known proposal of a strand-oriented process of development, known as the "Documentary Hypothesis," a set of ideas that dominated Old Testament study for the next century.

The four "documents" proposed by Wellhausen were given the labels J, E, P, and D. These letters correspond to the names assigned to the four major sources: the Yahwist, the Elohist, the Priestly source, and the Deuteronomist. While these sources and their characteristics are less a matter of consensus now than in the past, and mastery of their comparative contents may no longer be as important a task for students of the Pentateuch, they function as an ideal illustration of how source-critical approaches to the Pentateuch operate. As they are most often understood and used in Old Testaement scholarship, these four sources can be described as follows.

The Yahwist (J—after the German for YHWH, *Jahveh*) is primarily a narrative source, characterized by vivid storytelling. From its initial passages, the creation narrative in Genesis 2–3, this source uses the divine name, YHWH, either alone or along with *Elohim* to name the deity. J tends to describe God as a rather human character who has a body and exhibits a variety of emotions. This source includes accounts of creation, the flood, the patriarchs, Moses and the Exodus, and the wilderness journey. Some readers find this source continuing into the book of Joshua and the story of

[15]These early works did not use the existence of sources to deny that Moses wrote the Pentateuch, but rather to posit more complex modes of Mosaic authorship. See Blenkinsopp, *The Pentateuch*, 3.

the conquest of Canaan. This hypothetical source has often been dated as the earliest of the sources, perhaps originating in the royal court of the early monarchic period in Israel.

The Elohist (E) source is the most nebulous and controversial of the four. It is typically understood to be a narrative source, similar in style to J, but which reserves the use of the divine name, YHWH, until after the revelation to Moses.[16] A much smaller amount of material is usually attributed to this source, such that it is never construed as a lengthy, continuous account of Israel's past on the scope of J or P. Often, stray passages seem to be assigned to E merely because they do not fit the dominant J or P scheme,[17] but more thorough attempts to delineate E have identified texts related to all of the major traditions of Israel—ancestors, Moses, Sinai covenant, wilderness, and Promised Land.[18] As source criticism progressed through the twentieth century, it became common to revise the proposed dates of these documents, so that J and E were roughly contemporary sources, produced in the early to mid-monarchic period, in the southern and northern regions of Israel respectively, while D was primarily the product of the Josianic reform in the late seventh century. More significant was the tendency to view P as the latest source, and the one which brought all of the others together during the exilic or early postexilic period.

As its name implies, the Deuteronomic (D) source was primarily identified with the book of Deuteronomy in the Pentateuch, but many source critics also identified Deuteronomic interpolations earlier in the Pentateuch, such as the fragment of Passover legislation in Exodus 12:24-27, whose language sounds very much like Deuteronomy. Therefore, D has often been characterized as a stage in the process of development of the Pentateuch,

[16]E is often considered to be a Northern Israel counterpart to the Southern J. See Allen W. Jenks, "Elohist," in *The Anchor Bible Dictionary*, 6 vols., ed. David Noel Freedman et al. (New York: Doubleday, 1992) 2:478. The preference for *Elohim* here corresponds to the similar preference in the Elohistic Psalter (Psalms 42–88), which is also associated with the traditions of Northern Israel.

[17]A number of duplicate stories, which parallel J narratives in Genesis, are often assigned to E (20:1-18; 21:8-21; 21:22-34), along with some very important texts in the Pentateuch, such as the binding of Isaac (Genesis 22:1-14), the story of Pharaoh and the Hebrew midwives (Exodus 1:15-21), and the death of Moses (Deuteronomy 34:1-12).

[18]Jenks, "Elohist," 480.

which added a fifth book and lightly edited the earlier materials.[19] One unique feature of this source is its insistence upon centralization of worship in one place, which causes it to be associated with the reforms of king Josiah in the late seventh century. The common Deuteronomic phrase, "the place where I shall cause my name to dwell," is typically understood as a veiled reference to Jerusalem and the eventual centralization of Israelite worship in the temple.

The Priestly (P) source receives much of its attention because it is widely considered to have provided much of the nonnarrative material, such as legal texts and genealogies, which give the Pentateuch its framework. The key text for understanding P as a cohesive strand running throughout the first four books of the Pentateuch, is the revelation of the divine name to Moses in Exodus 6. P names the divine character differently on either side of this watershed event, using *Elohiym* before and YHWH afterward.[20] The name of this source stems from such "priestly" concerns as the establishment of Sabbath in Genesis 1–2, resistance to speaking about sacrificial ritual until the establishment of the priesthood in Leviticus,[21] and careful attention to the role of priests in texts such as Leviticus 1–16. Most source critics consider P to be an exilic or postexilic source, one which provided much of the shaping of the final form of the Pentateuch. A smaller group, most notably Jacob Milgrom, has argued for an earlier, eighth-century date for P.[22]

This kind of source criticism brilliantly resolves some difficult issues in the Pentateuch. It explains, for example, why the divine name, YHWH, appears frequently in the book of Genesis while Exodus 6:2-3 insists that

---

[19]Historical-critical study of the Bible also led to the identification of Deuteronomy as an introduction to the next four books of the Hebrew canon—Joshua, Judges, Samuel, and Kings—which Judaism traditionally refers to as the "Former Prophets." The name most commonly used for these four books among biblical scholars is the "Deuteronomistic History," an indication of the close connection between the perspective of these books and that of Deuteronomy.

[20]Of the 284 uses of *Elohim* in the Pentateuch, more than 200 appear before this passage.

[21]Note below in the proposed source division of the flood story that all references to clean animals and Noah offering sacrifices are assigned to the J portion of the story.

[22]For a sample of this argument, see Jacob Milgrom, "Priestly ('P') Source," in *The Anchor Bible Dictionary* 5:454-61.

this name was unknown before its revelation to Moses. This passage is typically assigned to the P source, which does not use the name until this point, while the J source uses YHWH from the beginning. These kinds of sources explain the two very different creation accounts at the beginning of Genesis. Genesis 1:1–2:4a comes from the Priestly source and presents a grand, orderly account of creation by a transcendent deity called *Elohim*, and it places great importance on the establishment of sabbath. Genesis 2:4b–3:24 presents an account of creation in a more colorful narrative, in which the deity is often anthropomorphic and is called YHWH *Elohim*.

If readers continue to move into the Pentateuch with source-critical assumptions, they find that the Documentary Hypothesis performs even more amazing feats in the flood narratives of Genesis 6–8. Anyone who has ever attempted to read these three chapters straight through is typically surprised by the many conflicting details present in the text. How many animals did Noah take on the ark, one pair of each, or seven pairs of some and one pair of others? How long did the flood last, forty days and forty nights, 150 days, or one year and eight days? How did Noah discover that the flood was over, by opening a window and releasing birds, or by removing the cover of the ark and looking for himself. With some careful attention and practice, it is not too difficult to separate a long, complex text like Genesis 6–8 into separate strands, using a feature such as variations of the divine name. Like the creation stories in Genesis 1–3, the flood narrative uses two different divine designations, *'Elohim* and YHWH. Table 1.7 illustrates the division of this text according to this criterion.

Table 1.7
The J and P Flood Accounts

The J Flood Story	The P Flood Story
6:5-8	6:9-22
7:1-5	7:6-16a
7:16b-17	7:18-21
7:22-23	7:24–8:1
8:2b-3a	8:3b-5
8:6-12	8:13-19
8:20-22	

Finer, more detailed attempts at source delineation sometimes extract individual verses (e.g., 7:7, 10, 12; 8:7) from the larger blocks above and put them into the other column.

> J produces a flood story in which YHWH determines to "blot out" all life, except for Noah, who is sent onto the ark with seven pairs of all clean animals and one pair of all unclean animals. After a forty-day flood, Noah determines the flood has ended by releasing a sequence of birds and emerges from the ark to offer sacrifices from among the clean animals. See the verbal connections between 7:22 in this account and 2:7 in the supposed J creation story. A notable omission of this flood story is the building of the ark.
>
> P produces a flood story in which *'Elohim* determines to "make an end of all flesh," instructs Noah to build an ark, and commands him to take two of each animal on the ark with him and his family. This is followed by a flood in which rain falls for forty days, the waters continue to swell for 150 days, and eventually dry up in just over a year. Noah removes the cover of the ark and sees that the ground is dry and he emerges with his family and all of the animals. Note the verbal similarities between this account at 8:17 and the P creation story at 1:22 and 1:28.

One of the failures of source criticism, however, has always been its inability to explain why the sources would have been used in such widely varying ways at different points in the Pentateuch. Many of the stylistic factors upon which source theory was based, such as the use of different divine designations and the duplicate units with conflicting details, seem to imply that the compiler or editor was seriously constrained in the use of sources and was not able to change them so that they fit together more naturally. On the other hand, the identification of source materials also implied a tremendous freedom in the way that they were edited or combined.[23] The coexistence of such freedom and constraint is difficult to explain.

The Documentary Hypothesis has also been attacked either because it cannot fully explain all of the details of the present form of the Pentateuch, or because scholars have not come to full agreement about the division and identification of sources. These are valid critiques only to a point. This kind of attack would demand that those making it also offer a better explanation for the problems posed by the present state of the Pentateuch. Too often the denigration of critical approaches simply assumes that if they are not com-

[23]For example, the side-by-side juxtaposition of the creation stories in Genesis 1 and 2 is nothing like the weaving together of the two apparent flood narratives in Genesis 6–8.

plete and unanimous in their results, then Mosaic authorship has been proved, or at least should be reclaimed as the default position.

Much of contemporary scholarship still operates with the basic assumptions of the Documentary Hypothesis intact, while additional layers of complexity are often added, including the use of multiple versions of the four basic documents or additional documents in attempts to explain problematic texts which do not fit easily into the four-document framework. Source-critical proposals that make use of an ever-increasing number of proposed documents are sometimes described as "fragmentary" hypotheses. The term "supplementary" hypothesis is sometimes used to describe ideas that describe a process in which an initial document was added to and revised by one or more later writers.

Continuing developments in source criticism might be described in three ways. First, as mentioned above, there are minor modifications that still accept the basic framework of the four-source Documentary Hypothesis. Second, there are major revisions that still use the idea of source documents, but draw conclusions that are in direct conflict in some ways with the basic outline of the Documentary Hypothesis. Third, there are approaches that use source-critical methods, but move in an entirely different direction from the Documentary Hypothesis. There have been too many proposals of all of these types to describe here, but a review of a few of the more influential ones may be instructive.

The work of John Van Seters has had a significant impact on the study of the Pentateuch, because it offers such a distinct alternative from the standard Documentary Hypothesis. Beginning with the publication of *Abraham in History and Tradition* in 1975, Van Seters has focused most of his attention on the personality and work of the Yahwist.[24] While retaining the name of this source, and agreeing in large part with the identification of the texts that are assigned to it, he has made a dramatic turn by moving J's work to the end of the process of the development of the Pentateuch, placing him in the postexilic period and making him primarily responsible for the final shape of the Pentateuch. This view essentially assigns J the date and function assumed for P by most adherents to the Documentary

---

[24]John Van Seters, *Abraham in History and Tradition* (New Haven CT: Yale University Press, 1975). Van Seters has further developed his "late J" view in studies such as *Prologue to History: The Yahwist as Historian in Genesis* (Louisville: Westminster/John Knox, 1992) and *The Life of Moses: The Yahwist as Historian in Exodus-Numbers* (Louisville: Westminster/John Knox, 1994).

Hypothesis. In addition, Van Seters has portrayed the Yahwist as primarily a historian, as opposed to the theologian characterized by the most-significant expressions of the Documentary Hypothesis.[25]

Like Van Seters, Hans Heinrich Schmid has also argued that the material assigned to J appears to be dependent upon the other sources, especially D, and, therefore, later than them. In a further development, in his 1976 work whose German title is translated as *The So-called Yahwist*, Schmid characterized J not as an independent writer, but as a vague stage late in the development of the Pentateuch.[26] Schmid envisioned this editing stage operating entirely under the influence of the Dueteronomistic understanding of Israel's past and present, also in the postexilic era.[27]

Something closer to a clean break from the Documentary Hypothesis has been achieved by Rolff Rendtorff. Abandoning the notion of continous source documents, Rendtorff suggests a model of independent traditions which grew and developed into the component parts of the Pentateuch, such as the story of the ancestors, the story of the Exodus, and the wilderness narrative. These blocks of tradition were later put together to form the Pentateuch as we know it.[28] In such a scheme, the notion of large, continuous source documents, like P and J, can be dismissed, a move which distinguishes Rendtorff's work significantly from most other scholars concerned with the compostion of the Pentateuch.

Ultimately, the dominance of source criticism in the Pentateuch came to an end for three significant reasons. Most important was that it began to approach the limits of what it could accomplish. The discussion began to focus on ever smaller portions of the text, and the results became increasingly speculative. As in all fields of study, when a dominant paradigm begins to lose energy in its capacity to generate research, its influence begins to wane. Second, historical-critical study in general was an

---

[25]See the excellent summary of this development by Rolf Rendtorff in his "What Happened to the 'Yahwist'?: Reflections after Thirty Years," SBL Forum, <http://sblonline.org/publications/article.aspx?articleId=553>, accessed 14 Nov 2007.

[26]Hand Heinrich Schmid, *Der sogennante Jahwist: Beobachtungen und Fragen zur Pentateuchforschung* (Zurich: Theologischer Verlag, 1976).

[27]See further discussion of this proposal in Belnkinsopp, *The Pentateuch*, 23.

[28]Rolf Rendtorff, *The Problem of the Process of Transmission in the Pentateuch*, trans. John J. Scullion, JSOT Supplement series 89 (Sheffield UK: JSOT Press, 1990; German original, 1977).

approach to the text that fit a biblical scholarship dominated by European and American males.[29] As the field became more diverse in terms of ethnicity and gender, a broader spectrum of approaches began to flourish. Third, the historical-critical set of methods was very closely tied to the Modernist agenda that emerged from the Enlightenment. Its emphasis on origins, its commitment to authority, and its illusions of scientific objectivity all began to crumble as the postmodern era emerged at the end of the twentieth century.

Left out of this discussion thus far is the importance of oral tradition in the development of the Pentateuch. This provides an additional layer of complexity to the historical-critical approach described above. Those who developed the Documentary Hypothesis were highly literate people who lived and worked in literacy-based cultures. Therefore, it is not difficult to see why the discussion of sources from its beginning tended to assume that these sources were *written* documents. Alongside the development and use of the Documentary Hypothesis, however, there has always been some acknowledgment of the role of oral tradition and oral transmission. In the study of the Pentateuch, this interest is usually traced back to the work of Hermann Gunkel in the late nineteenth and early twentieth centuries. Gunkel believed that scholarship could move back behind written sources to a preliterary stage. This search for a preliterary stage included the attempt to discover the early settings in which units of oral tradition were used.[30] Gunkel's understanding of the diverse worship life of ancient Israel as the setting for the development and use of oral tradition was carried on by one of his students, Sigmund Mowinckel, and found an important place in the tradition-historical work of Gerhard von Rad and Martin Noth.[31] Nonetheless, historical-critical scholarship never developed precise ways

---

[29]Readers may have noticed that the scholars mentioned and surveyed within this section are all males and of European descent. This is not a matter of bias in selection. It is virtually impossible to find sustained scholarship within these categories which has had any noticeable influence that has been produced by anyone not fitting this profile.

[30]Hermann Gunkel, *Genesis Translated and Interpreted by Hermann Gunkel*, trans. Mark A. Biddle (Macon GA: Mercer University Press, 1997) viii-xxvi.

[31]For an extended discussion of these issues and a more detailed description of the form-critical approach which developed out of Gunkel's work, see John Barton, "Form-criticism (Old Testament)," *The Anchor Bible Dictionary* 2:838-41.

of defining and distinguishing the interplay between oral and written sources in the development of texts in the Pentateuch.

In the last three decades, historical-critical approaches which give attention to oral tradition, but operate with a framework of assumptions from a modern, literate culture have been the target of significant criticism. One example of this criticism can be found in the work of Susan Niditch, most significantly in her 1996 book, *Oral World and Written Word.* Niditch identified within much historical-critical study of the Bible an overly simplistic understanding of the movement from orality to literacy in ancient Israel and the impact of this movement on the text of the Bible.[32] In her words,

> This diachronic approach to orality and literacy is, however, misguided, devaluing the power of oral cultures and misconstruing the characteristics of orally composed and oral-style works. Such an approach ignores the possibility that written works in a traditional culture will often share the characteristics of orally composed works.[33]

Through an examination of numerous texts, Niditch arrived at four models of how oral tradition and writing processes interacted. In all of these cases she assumes that the culture of Israel, throughout the time during which the written text of the Bible developed, remained largely oral in nature.

Niditch's first model, the idea that oral performances were simply "dictated and copied" at some point, is probably far too simplistic for our understanding of the development of the Pentateuch.[34] A second model, which allows for the movement of material in both directions, from oral to written and written to oral, seems more appropriate.[35]

Much of the discussion of orality and oral tradition within biblical studies takes place within the context of a consensus among interpreters that many texts of the Bible, especially in the Pentateuch, retain significant features of orally composed and transmitted material. A third model proposed by Niditch imagines that ancient writers would have been so

---

[32]Susan Niditch, *Oral World and Written Word: Ancient Israelite Literature*, Library of Ancient Israel (Louisville: Westminster/John Knox Press, 1996) 110-17.

[33]Niditch, *Oral World and Written Word*, 3. Niditch appropriately acknowledges that a smaller movement in the field of biblical studies, commonly called the Scandinavian School, took a more serious and nuanced approach to issues of orality.

[34]Niditch, *Oral World and Written Word*, 117-20.

[35]Niditch, *Oral World and Written Word*, 120-25.

immersed in the oral worlds of worship and storytelling that the characteristics of oral material would have been "imitated" even in their writings.[36] It is generally accepted that reconstructing the process and results of oral composition in ancient Israel is beyond our reach. Neither can we make definitive claims about how this oral material made its way into the written compositions of the Pentateuch. What is essential for modern readers to remember is that the cultures that produced these materials operated very differently from ours, and that our understandings of the biblical text are made even more provisional by these differences.

A brief review of oral tradition and its relationship to the Pentateuch serves as a reminder of how the basic questions in Pentateuch research have been shifting in recent years. Questions about the origins of texts, fueled by assumptions that their "original use" is the key to their meaning, are being replaced by questions about the final form of the text, which assume that the meaning of a text is determined by its current shape, its literary context, and the way it affects modern readers. Within this interpretive context, issues of orality and literacy are important not so much as a means of reconstructing the origins of a text, but for understanding how oral characteristics might operate within the text that we have.

Contemporary Approaches to the Interpretation of Pentateuch

The demise of the historical-critical approach to the Pentateuch (and to the rest of the Bible) is often overstated, but there have been significant developments in the critical study of the Pentateuch that bypass many of the concerns of the historical-critical method, especially in favor of more literary concerns. Other approaches are at least inadvertently a response to the fact that the historical-critical method has been formulated and dominated by European and American male scholars, primarily from Protestant Christian backgrounds. These developing approaches attempt to highlight the questions and concerns of other ethnic, gender, or religious perspectives. The following discussion is not intended to be a thorough review of alternative scholarship of the past three decades, but rather a sampling of studies that move in directions that differ from the dominant patterns of historical-critical study of the Pentateuch. The majority of works surveyed in this section could be classified as "synchronic" in approach,

---

[36]Niditch, *Oral World and Written Word*, 125-27.

that is, their concern is with the final form of the biblical text, not with earlier stages of development. The emergence of such approaches over the last few decades has given rise to this term, synchronic, and the accompanying use of the term "diachronic" to describe approaches that attempt to move back behind the final form of the text and describe earlier stages in its development.

One of the primary criticisms of historical-critical approaches concerns their tendency to fragment and atomize the text. The use of ever smaller pieces of the text to examine more detailed questions has often left the larger questions unasked, a task which was taken up by David J. A. Clines when he first published *The Theme of the Pentateuch* in 1978, and produced a slightly revised second edition in 2000. This work was a deliberate response to what Clines identified as two tendencies highly detrimental to biblical studies—atomism and geneticism.[37] Both of these tendencies were largely the result of the dominant historical-critical approach. "Atomism" is the tendency toward working with ever smaller pieces of text. Form criticism, especially, often moved in this direction. "Geneticism" is the assumption that the meaning of the text lies in finding and understanding its origins. Instead of approaching smaller and smaller texts, asking smaller and smaller questions, and working with hypothetical origins, Clines asked the biggest of questions about the final form of the text, as we now have it, essentially, What is the Pentateuch about? Clines delineated several definitions of "theme" including "conceptualization of plot," "central ideas," and " a rationale of the content, structure, and development of the work."[38] Using these overlapping notions, Clines produced his own statement of the theme of the Pentateuch: "The theme of the Pentateuch is the partial fulfillment—which implies also the partial nonfulfillment—of the promise to or blessing of the patriarchs."[39]

Later in the same work, Clines proposed a theme for Genesis 1–11, which he called a "prefatory theme." Here he reviewed three themes for the primeval story which had been proposed by other scholars: (1) "Sin—Speech—Mitigation—Punishment"; (2) "Spread–of- Sin, Spread-of-Grace"; and (3) "Creation—Uncreation—Re-creation."[40] This discussion reveals

---

[37]David J. A. Clines, *The Theme of the Pentateuch*, 2nd ed., JSOT Supplement series 10 (Sheffield UK: Sheffield Academic Press, 1997) 9-12.

[38]Clines, *The Theme of the Pentateuch*, 19-20.

[39]Clines, *The Theme of the Pentateuch*, 30.

[40]Clines, *The Theme of the Pentateuch*, 66-82.

that many others, even during the historical-critical era, had thought in terms of theme, but usually dealt with themes for major portions of the Pentateuch rather than the whole. Clines expressed favor for the second and third proposals and used the second in particular to link his own work to that of Gerhard von Rad. Clines's understanding of "partial fulfillment" resembles the uneasiness that pushed von Rad toward including the book of Joshua with the Torah to produce a Hexateuch, at the end of which the promise of land has been largely fulfilled.[41]

Finally, in his afterword, which was added to the second edition, Clines recognized that his earlier work had been primarily a work of biblical theology, and that it had much in common with rhetorical criticism as this method had developed over the intervening two decades.[42] The period between Clines's two editions of *The Theme of the Pentateuch* witnessed an explosion in the application of literary methods to the Pentateuch.

The work of Robert Alter has been formative in contemporary literary study of the Bible. His groundbreaking 1981 work, *The Art of Biblical Narrative*, gave significant attention to some texts in the Pentateuch. Alter's approach to these texts often utilized some of the same observations common to source criticism and applied them to a discussion of the literary artistry of the biblical text in its final form. The artistic development of a narrative includes attention to its primary elements—settings, characters, events, and plot. The concern for character development, particularly the divine character, was raised to a higher register by Jack Miles in his Pulitzer-Prize-winning work, *God: A Biography*, which addresses the whole of the Hebrew scriptures, but deals with the Pentateuch in about 120 tautly written pages. The central purpose of Miles's work is seemingly simple. The intent is to approach God as a literary figure, to attempt to dismiss preconceptions, and to read the Bible sequentially, asking how this character is developed.[43] This proves to be no simple endeavor. Western tradition has loaded up modern readers with so many preconceived ideas about what we should find when we read the Bible that it is very difficult to read the text on its own terms. Miles has proved more adept at reading the text on its own terms than any other reader to date and the result of his effort is a fresh, and often startling reading of the character, "God," whom Miles considers to be the "protagonist" of the text.

---

[41]Clines, *The Theme of the Pentateuch*, 87-90.

[42]Clines, *The Theme of the Pentateuch*, 128-30.

[43]Jack Miles, *God: A Biography* (New York: Vintage Books, 1996) 12-13.

Literary approaches to the Pentateuch like Miles's may find great assistance in a more recent work by Alter, who has produced a full English translation of the Pentateuch that pays careful attention to the literary features of the text in the Hebrew language and attempts to produce an English rendering that reveals, rather than obscures, these features, as many English translations do. Alter's translation includes a running commentary on the meaning of difficult words and phrases.[44] One of the most prominent features of texts in the Pentateuch, and elsewhere in the Bible, is verbal repetition. The biblical writers have a tendency to use the same word or various forms of the same root word within a limited text, a habit that might be considered poor writing in contemporary English. Alter's translation is careful to preserve this sense of repetition.[45]

The work of Alter, Miles, and other narrative critics addresses the standard narrative portions of the Pentateuch more effectively than the legal parts, but often leaves unanswered the connection between the two types of literature. This deficiency has been addressed in part by James W. Watts in *Reading Law: The Rhetorical Shaping of the Pentateuch*, in which Watts argues that the public reading of legal documents was the primary force behind the formulation of the Pentateuch. Watts pointed to Moses' reading of the "book of the covenant" in Exodus 24, Joshua's reading of "the law" in Joshua 8, Josiah's reading of "the book of the covenant" in 2 Kings 23, and Ezra's reading of "the law (of Moses)" in Nehemiah 8 as indications that public reading played a major role in the development of the Torah in ancient Israel.[46] In contrast, Watts states that the Hebrew Bible lacks "any reference to judicial use of written laws."[47]

If this contrast indicates that the purpose of the Pentateuch was rhetorical rather than judicial, then the criteria by which it should be evaluated are those of ancient rhetoric. The primary rhetorical pattern Watts identified for this purpose is the "story, list, divine sanction" sequence, a pattern which is intended to persuade its audience.[48] Watts moves on to

[44]See Robert Alter's own explanation of the nature and purpose of his translation in his *The Five Books of Moses: A Translation with Commentary* (New York: W. W. Norton, 2004) xvi-xlv.

[45]Alter, *The Five Books of Moses*, xxxii-xxxiii.

[46]James Watts, *Reading Law: The Rhetorical Shaping of the Pentateuch* (Sheffield: Sheffield Academic Press, 1999) 15-20.

[47]Watts, *Reading Law*, 21.

[48]Watts, *Reading Law*, 36-48.

apply this model to texts in the Pentateuch, such as the Sinai covenant account in Exodus 19–24. This passage uses all three components: a framing story in 19:1-25 and 20:18-26; the delivery of two separate law codes in 20:1-17 (the Decalogue) and 21:1–23:19; and divine sanction of these laws, including rewards for keeping them and punishments for breaking them, in 23:20-33. Watts goes on to identify this and similar patterns in blocks of material such as Exodus 25–Numbers 9, which he labels "the Levitical Law," and the entire book of Deuteronomy. Watts does not deny the presence of diverse source material in the Pentateuch. In fact, he assumes the composite nature of the work and makes use of many of the observations about the text from source critics, such as the existence of independent legal codes. What distinguishes Watts's work is his interest in identifying the forces that brought the Pentateuch together, rather than identifying and reconstructing earlier sources.

While Watts's work is primarily rhetorical in nature, it has a sociological dimension, in terms of its concern for how written laws function in a society. This social concern is addressed more extensively in the work of Frank Crüsemann, who, at the same time, displays a more intense interest in the contexts out of which legal traditions and texts arose.[49] Broader sociological concerns and their connections to the texts of the Pentateuch are treated in the 1996 work of E. Theodore Mullen, *Ethnic Myths and Pentateuchal Foundations; A New Approach to the Formation of the Pentateuch*, which arose in large part from the apparent impasse between diachronic and synchronic approaches to biblical texts. Mullen's primary concern is with the final form of the Pentateuch, like synchronic approaches, but his central questions concern the purpose served by this text within the social context in which it was formed. In this respect, Mullen's work connects with some aspects of diachronic approaches and is most accurately described as sociological in nature.

Attention to both the literary and sociological features of the Pentateuch reveals its patriarchal foundations, a force so pervasive that only great acts of interpretive imagination can make headway against it. A thorough and creative attempt to give adequate attention to the female characters in the Pentateuch and the issues that arise out of women's experiences with the text is found in Ellen Frankel's *The Five Books of Miriam*. This study is

---

[49]See, e.g., the list of central questions posed at the beginning of this work, in Frank Crüsemann, *The Torah: Theology and Social History of Old Testamtent Law* (Edinburgh: T. & T. Clark, 1996) 13.

presented as a dramatic dialogue organized around each of the major portions of the Torah within Jewish tradition. The speakers in the dialogue include the Torah itself, which initiates each conversation by identifying the issues, the "Daughters" who are contemporary Jewish women who ask questions, and female characters from the Bible who act as mothers to answer the questions. The premise of the book is that much of the tradition developed and maintained by women of the past has been lost. The fragments that remain in the Torah have been suppressed by interpreters who have given most of their attention to the parts of the tradition that surround and relate to the male characters. The dialogues in *The Five Books of Miriam* are an attempt to direct our attention to these remaining fragments and give some sense of what might have been lost.[50]

While literary approaches to texts avoid attempts to move back behind the final form of the text, they often ignore the fact that the texts of the Bible have had a long "afterlife," which is often ignored in contemporary readings. James Kugel has offered a valuable remedy to some of this neglect in his work on the Torah which has focused upon Jewish interpretation during the formative period of biblical interpretation from the third century BCE to the first century CE. Kugel's work in his massive *Traditions of the Bible* and a somewhat abbreviated version called *The Bible as It Was* focuses on what he calls "exegetical motifs." Kugel defines a motif as "an explanation of a biblical verse (or phrase or word therein) that becomes the basis for some ancient writer's expansion or other alteration of what scripture actually says."[51] This kind of interpretation is based upon a number of assumptions, which Kugel outlines, perhaps the most significant of which is that the Bible is a "cryptic" text, which is not always necessarily saying what it seems to be saying.[52] Kugel moves through the Pentateuch, identifying the most important of these exegetical motifs and presenting material from ancient sources, ranging from translations like the Septuagint to

---

[50]Ellen Frankel, *The Five Books of Miriam* (New York: Putnam, 1996) viii. A broader theological discussion of the lack of attention to women in the Pentateuch and in its reception can be found in Judith Plaskow's *Standing Again at Sinai* (San Francisco: HarperSanFracisco, 1991). A very different and highly creative attempt to restore attention to the female characters in Genesis is Anita Diamant's novel, *The Red Tent* (New York: Picador, 1998).

[51]James L. Kugel, *The Bible as It Was* (Cambridge MA and London: Belknap Press of Harvard University Press, 1997) 33.

[52]Kugel, *The Bible as It Was*, 18.

pseudepigraphical, Jewish literature like 1 Enoch to early Christian literature, including the New Testament, to Jewish historical literature like the works of Philo and Josephus to Rabbinic literature, including the Mishnah and the Talmud. The result is a portrayal of the Pentateuch as the most significant readers of that period understood it. A good example of an exegetical motif treated by Kugel is the bronze serpent fashioned by Moses, at God's instruction, as a response to the plague of poisonous serpents that attacked the Israelites in the wilderness. Ancient interpreters faced various problems when reading this text, the most serious of which was that it appeared to be a violation of the commandment against making images.

Approaches to the Pentateuch which are primarily literary or sociological in nature, and which work with the final form of the text, have often been able to steer their way around the historical-critical method by addressing an entirely different set of questions largely unrelated to the production of the text. While some historical-critical treatments of the Pentateuch have challenged major points of agreement that have developed around the Documentary Hypothesis (e.g., that of Noth, Rendtorff, Van Seters), these studies are still operating within the same essential framework. The newest challenge, and one which may escape this framework, is found in the recent work of Anthony F. Campbell and Mark A. O'Brien: *Rethinking the Pentateuch: Prolegomena to the Theology of Ancient Israel.* What is stated directly in the title to this book is presented in a subtle, but perhaps more ambitious, manner in the subtitle. The goal of Campbell and O'Brien is to get back to a pre-Wellhausen starting point and move in a different direction from the outset. It is too early to tell, at the time of this writing, whether they will succeed, but their work to this point merits examination.

The basic argument of Campbell and O'Brien can be stated in fairly brief and simple terms. The literary units found within the Pentateuch were compiled to provide many options as starting points for other storytellers.[53] This hypothesis explains two of the most striking features of the materials in the Pentateuch, their brevity and the presence of variant forms of the same stories.[54] Two important conclusions can be drawn from their argu-

[53]Anthony F. Campbell and Mark A. O'Brien, *Rethinking the Pentateuch: Prolegomena to the Theology of Ancient Israel* (Louisville: Westminster/John Knox Press, 2005) 15-19. Campbell and O'Brien refer to this as a "Text-as-Base-for-User" approach.

[54]Campbell and O'Brien, *Rethinking the Pentateuch*, 15-16.

ment, one which moves backwards to describe the production of the Pentateuch, and one which moves forward to describe its final form.

First, the Pentateuch was not constructed by weaving together lengthy, continuous sources, such as those designated J and P by the Documentary Hypothesis. Through a careful analysis of vocabulary and other details of texts, Campbell and O'Brien argue that there is no connection between Genesis 1 and the portions of Genesis 6–8 that are typically identified as the P version of the flood story.[55] They proceed along these lines to dismantle the notion of P as a continuous source,[56] arguing instead for the presence in the Pentateuch of "priestly writing . . . by a variety of priestly thinkers."[57] This dismantling of P results in the crumbling of J as a continuous source as well, since the existence of J has so often been supported by the need for "an exegetical counterweight to P." Second, the final form of the Pentateuch is not a carefully constructed literary work, in the modern sense, intended to be experienced through continuous reading. Its purpose is to be "expanded" not "expounded." The Pentateuch is, therefore, not a final form at all, but a starting point.

The first conclusion above destroys one of the primary assumptions and goals of prior historical-critical work on the Pentateuch. Campbell and O'Brien do not deny the existence of sources, but they reject the notion that there is evidence of the use of large sources which can be reconstructed, even tentatively. The second conclusion strikes at the heart of most contemporary literary studies of the Pentateuch. The basic assumption of such work has always been that the Pentateuch is a delicately crafted work of art, the precise final form of which has intended effects on its recipient. In the scenario developed by Campbell and O'Brien, the intended recipient did not experience the final form of the text at all, but an expanded form of storytelling that used bits and pieces of the text as starting points. What modern literary critics experience as a "dense text" requiring careful analysis, is actually a "condensed base text" requiring selection and expansion.[58] Thus, this work moves in a different direction than most studies of the Pentateuch, but is probably still too new to be evaluated fully at this point.

---

[55]Campbell and O'Brien, *Rethinking the Pentateuch*, 12-15. This argument is presented near the beginning of the book and supported in detail in an appendix (107-15).

[56]Campbell and O'Brien, *Rethinking the Pentateuch*, 19.

[57]Campbell and O'Brien, *Rethinking the Pentateuch*, 15.

[58]Campbell and O'Brien, *Rethinking the Pentateuch*, 17.

Similar Literature from Other Cultures in the Ancient Near East

In the middle of the nineteenth century, Europeans began extensive, aggressive campaigns to excavate archaeological sites in the Middle East. Much of this archaeological effort was religiously motivated, intended either to prove the historical reliability of the Bible or, more generally, to provide a better understanding of the background of the biblical literature and the religion of ancient Israel.[59] Archaeological discoveries have led to reconstructions of the history of the Ancient Near East that allow the placement of Israel and its literature into a general context, though these reconstructions are always hypothetical. Of greater significance for our understanding of the Pentateuch has been the discovery, translation, and interpretation of a vast number of ancient texts. Most of these texts come from other cultures, but nonbiblical Israelite texts have also been discovered. Large collections of these texts, along with background information and interpretations are available in a number of places,[60] but only a brief review of some of the most significant texts which parallel texts in the Pentateuch is possible here. (A list of these texts and brief descriptions of each is provided in table 1.8.)

Table 1.8
Major Parallel Texts from the Ancient Near East

Enuma Elish. This Babylonian text from the late second millennium BCE gives an account of the creation of the world in seven tablets. Creation is the result of conflict between the gods in this text, the primary purpose of which is to explain the emergence of Marduk as the most powerful god in the Babylonian pantheon.[61]

[59]There have been nonreligious motivations as well. Many prominent archaeologists have been historians interested in the ancient cultures of Sumer, Egypt, Assyria, Babylon, etc. for their own sakes and their importance in understanding world history.

[60]A good place to begin examining this literature in more detail is with Walter Beyerlin, ed., *Near Eastern Religious Texts Relating to the Old Testament* (Philadelphia: Westminster Press, 1978).

[61]W. G. Lambert, "Enuma Elish," *The Anchor Bible Dictionary* 2:526-28.

The Atrahasis Epic. An ancient, Babylonian account of the Mesopotamian flood story, written in Akkadian. In this story, which likely goes back to the third millennium BCE, the gods choose to flood the earth in order to reduce the human population, which has become too noisy. Atrahasis receives a warning from one of the gods and is able to build a boat and survive the flood. The flood story portion of the Gilgamesh Epic appears to be an adaptation of this flood story.

The Gilgamesh Epic. The most complete version of this highly developed literary work was found in the library of the Assyrian king Ashurbanipal, who reigned in the seventh century BCE. The story is much older, and some partial, extant versions were likely written in the early second millennium. The early tablets tell of the adventures of Gilgamesh, the king of Uruk during the third millennium, and his companion Enkidu, who dies in tablet 7 after the great battle with the Bull of Heaven. The famous flood story appears on the eleventh of twelve tablets, and appears to be a revision of the Atrahasis story with a different hero named Utnapishtim.

The Code of Hammurabi. Hammurabi ruled Babylon in the eighteenth century BCE. A large monument has been found that contains an extensive set of laws ascribed to this king. These laws are most often compared to the covenant code in Exodus 21–23.

The Legend of Sargon. Sargon was the King of Akkad during the late third millennium BCE. The written version of a poem that tells the story of his birth is generally dated to the seventh century BCE, but probably reflects a much older tradition. The poem, in first-person voice, tells the story of Sargon being placed in a basket by his mother and sent off on the Euphrates River. Naturally, this story invites comparison to the story of Moses.

The Battle of Ba'al and Yam. This Ugaritic poem from the thirteenth century BCE, contains many indications about the relationships among the gods which may shed some light on the poem known as the Song of Moses in Deuteronomy 32.

Hittite Treaties. The ancient Hittite Empire covered much of what is modern Turkey in Asia Minor. In the middle of the second millennium BCE they extended their influence down along the eastern coast of the Mediterranean. Numerous treaty texts from this era have been found, and they are often compared to covenant passages in the Pentateuch.

In 1876 George Smith (1840–1876), a British Assyriologist, published a book with the explosive title, *The Chaldean Account of Genesis*.[62] This

[62]George Smith, *The Chaldean Account of Genesis. Containing the Description of the Creation, the Fall of Man, the Deluge, the Tower of Babel, the Times of the*

book had a large impact in England and, subsequently, in Europe and the United States, as the general population was provided with awareness of and access to an ancient piece of literature that dealt with a story of a great flood from the perspective of a culture other than Israel, and which was apparently much older than the book of Genesis. The literary work most commonly known today as the *Epic of Gilgamesh* is an extensive collection of ancient stories, about the size of the book of Genesis. Many copies of this work have been found, ranging from small fragments to nearly complete, twelve-tablet collections. Gilgamesh was a legendary king of the ancient Mesopotamian empire of Sumer, who likely lived during the middle of the third millennium BCE. Texts of the epic have been found ranging in age from the late third millennium down to the early to mid-first millennium BCE.

During the last century and a quarter, as archaeological sites have become more accessible, a large number of ancient texts have been found, along with many other kinds of artifacts, in the Middle East. These discoveries have sometimes generated the kind of popular attention caused by Smith's discovery of the Gilgamesh Epic, but far more important has been the careful study of these texts over many subsequent decades, and the application of the information they provide to our understanding of the Old Testament. We have learned, for example, from texts like Gilgamesh and the Atrahasis Epic that stories of a great flood, survived by a heroic human being with divine assistance, were common in the Ancient Near East. This provides the opportunity to examine the story of Noah and the flood in Genesis by asking how it is like these other stories and how it is different.

A Babylonian creation text called *Enuma Elish* is widely considered to have significant connections with Genesis 1. The two texts have very similar assumptions about the structure of the universe and its components. On the other hand, they contain strikingly different descriptions of how the world came into being. The Babylonian text describes a battle between two gods, Marduk and Tiamat, in which Tiamat is killed by Marduk, who makes the heavens, the earth, and human beings from the parts of her body. This account could hardly be more different from the serene, commanding story of *'Elohim* speaking creation into being in Genesis 1. In some ways, these two texts are so oppositional that many interpreters have argued that

---

Patriarchs, and Nimrod. Babylonian Fables, and Legends of the Gods; from the Cuneiform Inscriptions (London: Sampson Low, Marston, Searle, and Rivington, 1876).

Genesis 1 is a direct refutation of *Enuma Elish*, produced by an Israelite writer who encountered Babylonian ideas about creation during the Exile. Other texts from the Ancient Near East will be discussed at later points as they relate to specific passages in the Pentateuch.[63]

History and the Pentateuch

Speaking with precision about the "historical context" of the Pentateuch requires acknowledgement of at least three different historical contexts. In reverse chronological order, these are the context in which the final forms of the books were produced, the context that produced the individual components of each book, and the context in which the events recorded may have taken place. The relative importance of these different historical contexts is a matter of intense debate. The first two have been addressed significantly in previous sections, but the notion of historical context demands some attention at this point.

Placing the stories of the Pentateuch into a historical context is a difficult process which always yields rather disappointing results. The typical starting point is the attempt to attach an approximate date to either the exodus from Egypt or the entry into Canaan. Only one piece of hard data is available for this effort. A large stone with inscribed writing, called the Merneptah Stele, was produced by or for Pharaoh Merneptah of Egypt and can be reliably dated to about 1200 BCE. The inscription on the stone contains a list of battles fought against rebellious groups in Canaan and surrounding areas, which Egypt was attempting to control, and one line says "I defeated Israel." While it is uncertain whether this "Israel" represents a group of people or an area of land, or both, this inscription confirms that at the end of the thirteenth century something Egypt knew as "Israel" existed in Canaan. Unfortunately, this is as far as hard evidence can take us, and simply determining that the events that led up to the existence of Israel must have taken place before 1200 BCE is not very helpful.

Using biblical chronology to establish dates is problematic for at least three reasons. First, the Old Testament provides only relative dates. For

[63]"Parallels" to the Old Testament in documents from other ancient Near Eastern cultures are available in various printed collections. English translations of most are available in electronic collections. An excellent place to start is <http://www.iTanakh.org>, a website that contains links to many of the most useful texts related to the Pentateuch.

example, Person A lived for 120 years or King B ruled for twenty-five years. It does not tell us which years those were, and biblical chronologies are not extensive and continuous enough to attach them to events for which we know absolute dates. Therefore, matching biblical chronology to our scheme of absolute dates is difficult.

Second, when sequences and numbers of years are given in different places in the Bible we cannot be certain how they relate to one another. Are they strictly consecutive, do they overlap, or are there gaps between them. The chronological problems in the book of Judges, which are related to attempts to date events in the Pentateuch as we shall see later, provide an example of this difficulty. In the book of Judges a length of rule is given for most of the characters identified as judges. If we place those periods end-to-end they produce an era of more than 400 years, but the judges appear to be regional leaders, so the periods of their rule could overlap considerably. Thus, the time period represented by the book of Judges could be considerably shorter than four centuries.

Third, the Old Testament has a fondness for stylized numbers, particularly forty and its multiples. The wilderness period, the rule of judges like Othniel and Deborah, and the reigns of kings like David and Solomon are all assigned forty-year durations. It seems unlikely that such a number always represents a precise, arithmetic value. It also seems to be a means of evaluating the importance of an event or period of time. A king who reigns for "forty years" is one who has an appropriately long and healthy reign.

The first problem above may be partially overcome by the use of more extensive chronological records from other cultures around Israel. For example, the Assyrian King Lists and their references to Israelite kings have been used, along with chronological information in the Bible, to establish a possible date of about 1000 BCE for the beginning of the Israelite monarchy, but where can we go from there? If the period of the judges was about 400 years, which was preceded by Joshua's leadership and forty years in the wilderness, then the exodus can be placed in the middle of the fifteenth century. The Pentateuch provides two different lengths of time for the period of bondage, 400 years in Genesis 15:13 and 430 years in Exodus 12:41. Either of these numbers, along with genealogical information in Genesis would place the period of the Israelite ancestors in the nineteenth and twentieth centuries BCE. The second and third problems indicated above, however, make all of these dates rather tenuous.

Other dating schemes have based their conclusions on different assumptions. The two pharaohs with whom Moses interacts in the book of

Exodus are not identified by name. One of the "store-cities" built by the Hebrew slaves (Exodus 1:11) is called "Ramses," a name that matches that of more than one pharaoh mentioned in Egyptian sources. The pharaoh with whom Moses is in conflict in the plague narratives is often assumed to be Ramses II, who ruled Egypt during the thirteenth century. A mid-thirteenth century date for the exodus and a forty-year period in the wilderness would allow for the emergence of Israel at about the time of the Merneptah Stele in 1200 BCE. Assuming some overlap among the judges in order to reduce the total time period to about two centuries would then place the beginning of the monarchy at about 1000 BCE.

The discussion in the previous paragraph reveals that attempts to establish dates for events in the Pentateuch requires the combination of information from various sources which may not always be compatible. Historical schemes also operate with unproven assumptions and make use of circular reasoning. In the end we can only conclude that fixing such dates cannot be accomplished with reasonable certainty. Fortunately, this may not matter a great deal. What difference does it make to our understanding of Genesis whether Abraham lived in the sixteenth, eighteenth, or twentieth century BCE? Does the meaning of the exodus event depend upon whether we place it in the thirteenth or fifteenth century?

A significantly different question concerning the Pentateuch and history has often been the focus of attention, particularly over the last century. The previous paragraphs have been concerned with the placement of events in the Bible in historical contexts. This question is largely separate from questions about the historicity of the events themselves. The shape of the issue can be illustrated by examining positions at two extremes. At one extreme are those readers who assume that every event in the Pentateuch, as well as in the rest of the Bible, happened exactly as recorded in every detail. Typically, these readers believe that the truth of the Bible actually depends upon its correspondence to our modern sense of history.[64] The other

[64]This view, of course, is reflected in a lot of devotional literature about the Bible. From a more academic perspective, it can be observed in works like Walter C. Kaiser, *A History of Israel: From the Bronze Age through the Jewish Wars* (Nashville: Broadman & Holman, 1998). A significantly different approach that also places tremendous emphasis on historicity is the so-called "American School" of Old Testament studies which was centered in the works of William F. Albright, G. Ernest Wright, and John Bright, throughout the middle of the twentieth century. The most influential work from this perspective is John Bright, *The History of*

extreme, which is sometimes labeled "minimalism," contends that very little of what is in the Pentateuch qualifies as what we would think of as history in the modern sense. Even central characters like Abraham and Moses are legendary accretions who bear little, if any, resemblance to actual persons in the ancient world.[65]

These two extreme positions tend to be determined by their placement of the burden of proof in the debates over history. Using the figure of Abraham as an example, one side would argue that unless definitive proof can be offered that Abraham did not exist as a historical figure or that any particular story about him did not happen as told in Genesis, then the text must be accepted as historically accurate. This is a very powerful method of argument, because proving a negative is extremely difficult. One need only ask the question, "What would proof that Abraham did not exist historically, precisely as described in Genesis, look like?"

Suppose you were asked if you had ever been to China. Assume that you have not, and you were asked to prove beyond question that you have not been to China. What evidence could you produce that would satisfy your accuser? Proving a negative proposition, such as "the Abraham character in Genesis did not really exist, historically" or "I have never been to China" is nearly impossible, if the burden of proof is placed on the one making it.

The other extreme would place the burden of proof on anyone wishing to prove that Abraham existed as a historical figure. Proving the existence of a contemporary figure is relatively easy, but proving the existence of someone who supposedly lived about 4,000 years ago is nearly impossible, especially if the person was rather ordinary, like Abraham. There is no archaeological evidence supporting the existence of Abraham, and, outside the Bible, there is no historical record of Abraham. One could easily respond to this by asking exactly what kind of evidence there could possibly be. Abraham was a seminomadic herdsman, living in a remote part of the world, perhaps 4,000 years ago. Other than recollections, passed from generation to generation by his descendants, there is little else that such a character might leave behind.

Israel, 3rd ed. (Philadelphia: Westminster, 1980/1981; 4th ed., 2000; 2nd ed., 1972; 1st ed., 1960).

[65]This "minimalist" view has become centered around the works of Philip Davies, for example, *In Search of Ancient Israel* (Sheffield UK: Sheffield Academic Press, 1995).

"Literal" Reading of the Bible

The dichotomy between literal and nonliteral reading is perhaps the most common way that people talk about approaches to and assumptions about the Bible, and the issues raised by these terms are crucial to any discussion of the Pentateuch. Rarely does anybody ask what these terms mean. Confusion is increased because these terms are used to talk about two different issues at the same time. First, beliefs about the inspiration of the biblical text are expressed using the literal/nonliteral dichotomy. Those who express belief that the Bible is the "literal word of God" are accepting a view of inspiration that claims that God provided the actual words of the biblical text to the writers, who functioned simply as stenographers. Another view of inspiration assumes that God stirred up the spirit of the writers, but that the human authors chose the words, using their own talent as writers and the cultural conventions of language to produce the text. There are variations of each of these views, and there may be better terminology, but for the sake of simplicity, they might be labeled "literal" and "nonliteral" views of the production of the biblical text. Both accept that that the Bible is divinely inspired in some way.

A second, entirely different, issue, which is often discussed using similar terminology, is the reception or interpretation of scripture. In this case, the word "literal" is typically used in opposition to a figurative or metaphorical interpretation. This issue applies to various kinds of texts in such widely divergent ways that it is difficult to describe with only one or two examples, so several are in order, some fairly simple and some quite complex.

(1) When 1 Kings 2:11 says that David reigned for forty years, is this a precise arithmetic value, or is it a way of saying he ruled for about two generations, an appropriately long and healthy reign.

(2) Exodus 17:1-7 and Numbers 20:1-13 each report an incident involving the miraculous production of water from a rock by Moses at a place called Meribah. A "literal" reading might insist that these are two entirely different episodes that differ in some details. A "nonliteral" interpretation might allow that the same event is described in different ways in two different places to serve different purposes in the ongoing narrative.

(3) Judges 13–16 reports a series of events about a character named Samson. He had long hair that made him strong, he killed and dismembered a lion with his bare hands, he caught 300 foxes and tied

torches to their tails in order to set fire to the fields and produce of the Philistines, and he killed 1,000 men with a donkey's jawbone. Some would understand these as legendary folktales of an ancient super-hero, while others would insist that they are historically accurate in every detail.

(4) Mark 7:26-30, along with many other gospel texts, reports that Jesus cast a demon out of a girl. Literal readings may insist that in all of these cases a supernatural entity was living inside the person, while nonliteral readings might allow that in at least some of these instances the language of demon possession in ancient cultures referred to what we would consider mental illness in the modern world.

(5) Perhaps the most visible and controversial case is the use of the word "day" in the creation story of Genesis 1. Does "day" mean a twenty-four-hour period or could it refer to an indeterminate period of time, even a period of millions of years?

(6) Another creation text in Isaiah 40:12 says that God "weighed mountains in the scale and hills in balances." Is this a poetic image concerning the creation of mountains and hills, or does it mean that God "literally" used a giant set of scales to get the hills and mountains just the right size?

This mixture of examples reveals that literal versus nonliteral interpretation of the Bible refers to very different kinds of questions. Does what the text describes relate precisely to people, places, and events outside of the text with a modern sense of historical and scientific precision? Should the meaning of a word or phrase be understood in the most basic sense? It is unlikely that anyone would answer these questions in a consistently "literal" manner. It would be difficult, for example, to find anyone who insists on a literal reading of the text in example 6.

In the context of Genesis 1, the discussion above has established that there are at least three questions related to literality that can be asked of this text. It is quite possible that most people, myself included, would give a mixed set of answers to this set of three questions. First, concerning inspiration, did God dictate the text word-for-word to the human writer? An affirmative answer to this question can only be based upon faith. It cannot be proven, and to those who accept this kind of inspiration, empirical evidence simply does not apply. My own answer to this question is negative. The wide variety of genres and writing styles in the Bible and the way in which they conform to parallel writings from other ancient cultures argues convincingly that the Bible is the literary work of human authors. God's role in the production of the text is more subtle than word-for-word dictation.

A second question about the literality of this text concerns its correspondence to matters outside the text. Does this provide a description of the origins of the earth and life on it that precisely matches our historical and scientific understandings. This question is actually independent of the first. One could believe that God dictated the exact text of Genesis 1, but that its intent is to talk about creation metaphorically. On the other hand, it is possible to believe that humans wrote the words of the Bible, guided by God in a subtle manner, and produced in Genesis 1 an accurate description of the origins of the universe. While the first question concerns the author's identity, the second is primarily about the author's intent. Again, my own answer to this question is the nonliteral option. The knowledge of history and science that human culture has accumulated cannot be matched precisely with this text.

A third question concerns the meaning of individual words and phrases such as "day" within the text of Genesis 1. Does "day" mean a literal twenty-four hour period? Again, the answer to this question is largely independent of the answer to the previous two questions. I have encountered people who answer the literal inspiration question positively, and who insist on a literal correspondence between science and history and Genesis 1, who will allow for a nonliteral answer here. In their view, God wrote the actual words of the Bible, Genesis 1 provides a scientifically accurate description of the creation of the universe, and "day" does not necessarily mean twenty-four hours but could mean a million years or a billion years. In fact, the affirmative answers to the first two questions almost require a negative answer to the third, unless, like those who insist on a "young earth," one denies overwhelming geological evidence about the age of the universe.

My own answer concerning the literality of "day" in Genesis 1 is affirmative. It means a twenty-four-hour period. "Evening came and morning came a first day." Some may be surprised at this, given my negative answers to the first two questions of literality, so it requires some explanation. Decisions about the intent of a text are crucial in this case. One important purpose of Genesis 1 is to establish the seven-day weekly cycle as a basis for understanding and living a faithful life. Another purpose is either to provide or respond to a program for a week-long festival celebrating the creative acts of God. In both cases, the organization of life into a pattern of seven 24-hour days, ending in Sabbath rest, is vital. Dispensing with the literal meaning of day and week in Genesis 1 risks losing, or at least obscuring, its central purposes.

Some further examination of reactions to Isaiah 40:12 is also instructive. It is likely that everyone would answer a question about the literal meaning of the word "scale" positively. The text says "scale" and means "scale." It does not intend for the reader to think of something other than a scale. It is also likely that all readers would answer a question about the literal correspondence of the text to historical events and scientific processes negatively. The text does not mean that at some point in time God actually used a giant scale to get each mountain on earth just the right weight.

Common questions and debates about reading the Bible "literally" typically take the three individual issues discussed above and mangle them into one question that is meaningless. To have any real meaning, the question of literality needs to be divided into at least three separate questions, something like the following.

(1) Did God dictate the actual words of the Bible to the humans who wrote them down, or did God use the skills and creativity of human authors to produce the Bible, or was there no divine involvement in the production of the Bible?

(2) When reading a particular text, is it essential that the people, places, and events described correspond precisely to our scientific and historical knowledge of people, places, and events?

(3) When examining a particular word or phrase in the Bible, should it be understood in terms of its most basic meaning or can a word or phrase be used to communicate something quite different from its basic meaning?

The foregoing discussion demonstrates two important things. The answers to these questions are, to a large extent, independent of one another, and the second and third questions can only be answered one text at a time.

Key Terms

Deuteronomist
inspiration
diachronic methods
form criticism
historical minimalism
Leningrad Codex
Priestly Source
rhetorical criticism
Septuagint (LXX)
source criticism
synchronic methods
TaNaK
Vatican Codex
Yahwist
YHWH (tetragrammaton)

Sources for Further Study

Alter, Robert. *The Five Books of Moses: A Translation with Commentary*. New York and London: W. W. Norton & Co., 2004.

Blenkinsopp, Joseph. *The Pentateuch: An Introduction to the First Five Books of the Bible*. The Anchor Bible Reference Library. New York: Doubleday, 1992.

Campbell, Anthony F., and Mark A. O'Brien, *Rethinking the Pentateuch: Prolegomena to the Theology of Ancient Israel*. Louisville: Westminster/John Knox Press, 2005.

Clines, David J. A. *The Theme of the Pentateuch*. Second edition. JSOT Supplement series 10. Sheffield UK: Sheffield Academic Press, 1997; Sheffield UK: JSOT Press, 2001.

Frankel, Ellen. *The Five Books of Miriam: A Woman's Commentary on the Torah*. New York: Putnam, 1996.

Gunkel, Hermann. *Genesis: Translated and Interpreted by Hermann Gunkel*. Translated by Mark A. Biddle. Macon GA: Mercer University Press, 1997.

Niditch, Susan. *Oral World and Written Word: Ancient Israelite Literature*. Library of Ancient Israel. Louisville: Westminster/John Knox, 1996; London: SPCK, 1997.

Noth, Martin. *A History of Pentateuchal Traditions*. Translated by Bernard W. Anderson. Chico CA: Scholars Press, 1981.

von Rad, Gerhard. *The Problem of the Hexateuch and Other Essays*. Translated by E. W. Trueman Dicken. Introduction by Norman W. Porteous. Edinburgh: Oliver & Boyd, 1965; London: SCM, 1984, 1965; New York: McGraw-Hill, 1966.

Rofé, Alexander. *Introduction to the Composition of the Pentateuch*. Translated by Harvey N. Bock. Biblical Seminar 58. Sheffield UK: Sheffield Academic Press, 1999.

Watts, James W. *Reading Law: The Rhetorical Shaping of the Pentateuch*. Biblical Seminar 59. Sheffield UK: Sheffield Academic Press, 1999.

Chapter 2

The Book of Genesis

The Literary Landscape of Genesis

The first book of the Bible has two narrative tasks that it must perform. These tasks are revealed in the middle and end of the book, so it might not be clear to a first-time reader of Genesis exactly what the book is doing. The most important task of the book is to identify the particular group of people called "Israel." Genesis begins with stories about humanity that have a universal scope, but in the center of the book (32:28) one man, Jacob, is renamed "Israel" and his descendents are identified as "the children of Israel" or "the Israelites."[1] Likewise, the geographical scope of Genesis is universal at the beginning, but by the end of the book the small group of people called Israelites is in a particular place, Egypt, the place where they need to be at the beginning of the next book in the Bible, Exodus.

While these two narrative tasks seem relatively simple, the way they are accomplished is anything but simple. The book of Genesis is a complex literary work of art and theology that follows a long and treacherous path to accomplish its purposes. Along the way, it introduces hundreds of people, takes us to many mysterious places, and reports dozens of events. At times it may seem that Genesis is a chaotic collage of characters and stories, but it uses a rich and varied set of literary tools to provide a sense of cohesion. Paying careful attention to how the story is told will help to illuminate what is being told along the way. With any attempt to describe the structure of a literary work, it is impossible to distinguish with certainty what was intended by the writer from what is perceived by the reader. Patterns perceived by the reader may have been deliberately constructed or

---

[1]This purpose of Genesis has received extensive, recent attention in E. Theodore Mullen Jr., *Ethnic Myths and Pentateuchal Foundations: A New Approach to the Formation of the Pentateuch* (Atlanta: Scholars Press, 1997). As the title indicates, Mullen has extended this purpose to the entire Pentateuch. His interests are more sociological than literary, as he posits a deliberate redaction of the Pentateuch during the Persian period for the primary purpose of establishing an ethnic identity for Israel (328-32).

accidental, or they may be the result of techniques of writing in the ancient world which were so natural that writers were not always aware when they were using them.

The first literary feature of Genesis that demands attention is its division into two distinct parts, the Primeval Complex and the Ancestral Complex. As a matter of convenience, the boundaries of these sections are usually designated by whole chapter numbers, with the Primeval Complex in 1–11 and the Ancestral Complex in 12–50. The actual division is better understood as lying between 11:26 and 11:27.[2] A number of factors serve to separate the book of Genesis into these two distinct sections. A major point of distinction between them is the stark set of differences between the narrative worlds portrayed in them. The Primeval Complex portrays a strange world in the distant past, perhaps as much for the first readers of Genesis as for modern readers.

Many elements of this literary work contribute to this strangeness. First, God moves back and forth between heaven and earth, sometimes interacting with the human characters in very direct ways that require a human body. Second, other heavenly beings are also able to move back and forth between heaven and earth. For example, the "Sons of God" in Genesis 6:1-4 are able to procreate with human women, spawning a race of giants called *Nephilim*. Third, the human characters in this world have life spans of enormous length, some more than 900 years. Fourth, the human characters are flat, indistinct, and devoid of personality, and readers are completely unaware of their internal lives. Fifth, and perhaps most significant, the world of the Primeval Complex lacks a distinguishable geography. The creation story in Genesis 1 provides no location at all, while the Garden of Eden in Genesis 2–3 is a geographical impossibility, lying at the place where the Tigris, Euphrates, and Gihon (Blue Nile) rivers emerge from a common source. Readers are not told where Cain kills Abel, where Noah builds the ark, or where Noah plants his troublesome vineyard. Even the place names that are provided, such as the land of Nod to which Cain is banished, the city of Enoch which Cain builds, and the Mountain of Ararat where the ark comes to rest, are vague and indistinct. The Valley of Shinar, where the Tower of

---

[2]It is important to remember that the book of Genesis, along with the rest of the Old Testament, existed for more than 1,000 years before the chapter-and-verse divisions and numbers were inserted. In light of modern literary study of Genesis, the division between chapters 11 and 12 would have been better placed six verses earlier.

Babel is built, may be somewhat identifiable as a place in Mesopotamia, and might serve as the beginning of a more distinguishable geography in Genesis.

All of the points above stand in clear contrast to the characteristics of the world found in the Ancestral Complex of Genesis 12–50. First, characters early in this section, such as Abraham, Sarah, Hagar, Rebekah, and Isaac, have direct divine encounters, but they are distinct conversations that occur at particular events. God and other heavenly beings do not simply go down to earth and observe the lives of these character. Jacob's divine encounters are sometimes direct, sometimes ambiguous, and sometimes clearly in dreams. Joseph, the final central character in the book of Genesis, receives divine guidance only through dreams. Second, divine beings make occasional visits to earth in the first half of this section, but these appearances diminish entirely by the end of the section. Third, the lifespans of the characters in the Ancestral Complex shrink rapidly to recognizable periods of just more than 100 years. Fourth, unlike the flat characters early in Genesis, the characters in the Ancestral Complex are highly developed. Readers are able to experience their emotions, their successes and failures, their inner motivations, and their hopes and dreams. Finally, beginning in Genesis 12, every event happens in a recognizable place that can be located on a map. Geography becomes almost obsessively precise in the Ancestral Complex.

While too much speculation about the "implied readers" of Genesis, the audience for whom the book was initially written, can be misguided, it seems safe to say that the seminomadic sheepherders of Genesis 12–50 would have been recognizable characters to them, and that these characters inhabited a familiar world. In contrast, the world of Genesis 1–11 would have been part of the distant, foggy past, its contours unfamiliar and mysterious. The book of Genesis begins with a slightly out-of-focus view of this mysterious, distant past, but the story would have come into clearer focus for these readers, just as the identity of Israel comes into focus in the book of Genesis, through the emerging characters who turn out to be their ancestors. For modern readers, both worlds may be blurry, though the difference is still distinguishable, but the first readers of the book of Genesis were carried from a strange world into a world similar to their own.

Another layer of literary development in Genesis involves the relatively large quantity of genealogical material in the book. Careful attention to this material reveals a distinct pattern (see table 2.1).

Table 2.1
"Genealogies" in Genesis

The Hebrew word *toledot* ("generations," lit. "birthings") occurs thirteen times in Genesis. Ten of those uses occur in introductory phrases that are something like, "These are the generations of. . . . " English versions translate this word in a variety of ways, so the pattern illustrated in this table is not always visible to English readers of the Bible.

2:4	These are the *generations* of the heavens and the earth. . . .
5:1	This is the book of the *generations* of Adam. . . .
6:9	These are the *generations* of Noah. . . .
10:1	These are the *generations* of the sons of Noah, Shem, Ham, and Japheth. . . .
11:10	These are the *generations* of Shem. . . .
11:27	These are the *generations* of Terah. . . .
25:12	These are the *generations* of Ishmael. . . .
25:19	These are the *generations* of Isaac. . . .
36:1	These are the *generations* of Esau. . . .
37:2	These are the *generations* of Jacob. . . .

Except for the first and last of these ten cases, this phrase introduces a genealogy in the familiar form of a list. In what sense the material following 2:4 and 37:2 might be considered a genealogy is more difficult to say. The word *toledot* also appears in 10:32 and 36:9 at the conclusion of genealogical lists, and at 25:13 (a parallel to the introductory formula of 25:12): "These are the names . . . in the order of their *births*."

This genealogical framework has been commonly used to portray the structure of the book of Genesis.[3] Beyond providing a shape for a book that

[3]For example, see Ralph Elliott, *The Message of Genesis: A Theological Interpretation* (Nashville: Broadman Press, 1961) 12; and Joseph Blenkinsopp, *The Pentateuch: An Introduction to the First Five Books of the Bible* (New York: Doubleday, 1992) 58-59. Norman Whybray has argued against understanding the *toledot* series as "a basic structural marker of chs. 1–11 or the whole book of Genesis." Whybray's primary reason for rejecting this scheme is that the word *toledot* is used "in more than one distinct sense, and with more than one distinct function." Contrary to Whybray's argument, this observation would actually seem to support

sometimes seems to lack it, the genealogies also play a role in the development of the identity of Israel. The list in table 2.1 contains not only the names of most of Israel's significant male ancestors, but also their non-Israelite counterparts. As each generation arrives, one individual is chosen to continue the central line, and one or more others are sent away.[4] By the end of the book, this process of elimination leads to the definition of Israel as the descendents of Jacob, a definition that is further emphasized by the renaming of Jacob as "Israel" in 32:28. Once he receives this name, all of his descendents are "children of Israel" or Israelites.

Another major source of narrative continuity in the book of Genesis is the appearance of many sets of stories that are similar in appearance. Perhaps most striking is the series of stories in which ancestral figures who are married claim to be brother and sister while traveling in a foreign land. This occurs for the first time when Abram and Sarai travel to Egypt (12:10-20). It happens again when Abraham and Sarah travel to Gerar (20:1-18), and again when Isaac and Rebekah travel to Gerar (26:1-12).

Source criticism might explain the multiple appearances of such a story as the result of an ancient tradition being remembered and preserved in different sources in somewhat different forms. The final author of the book of Genesis then inherited various forms of the story that had been partially transformed in their details. A more contemporary, literary approach to the book of Genesis might acknowledge the observations and conclusions of a source-critical explanation, while pressing further to ask why all three versions have been included, why they have been placed as they are in Genesis, and what role the various versions of the story might play together in the final form of the book.

The first and second renditions of the "wife/sister" story involve the same set of spouses, though their names have been slightly changed in the

---

the idea of the *toledot* series as a deliberate framework for the book. The author of Genesis appears to go to some lengths to make repeated use of this particular word, when a different word might be more precise in some of the passages. See R. Norman Whybray, *Introduction to the Pentateuch* (Grand Rapids MI: Eerdmans, 1995) 31.

[4]The most thorough discussions of this issue are found in Devorah Steinmetz, *From Father to Son: Kinship and Conflict, and Continuity in Genesis* (Louisville: Westminster/John Knox Press, 1991) and R. Christopher Heard, *The Dynamics of Diselection: Ambiguity in Genesis 12–36 and Ethnic Boundaries in Postexilic Judah*, SBL Semeia studies (Atlanta: Society of Biblical Literature, 2001).

intervening chapters. The second and third occurrences happen in the same place and involve a foreign king with the same name. These observations might indicate a deliberate linking of this series of stories. Further, the story in 12:10-20 raises a number of important questions that remain unresolved at the end. Among these questions might be the following.

> How far does the marital relationship between Pharaoh and Sarai progress?
>
> How does Pharaoh know that his marriage to Sarai is the cause of the plague?
>
> Why are Abram and Sarai never admonished for being dishonest?
>
> Why do innocent Egyptians suffer because of the deceptive behavior of Abram and Sarai and what might be construed as greediness or lust on the part of their king?
>
> Why is Abram rewarded at the end of the story?

These questions, which lie unresolved at the end of the first wife/sister story, seem to be resolved by the second story in 20:1-18, where Abimelech is informed by God in a dream that Abraham and Sarah are married—and this happens before Abimelech has "touched" her. Abimelech berates Abraham rather severely for his deceptive behavior, and Abraham's response is that he has merely told a half-truth, since he and Sarah are half-brother and sister. The second story, however, raises at least one additional question. The reader might wonder why God would resolve this situation by appearing to the foreign king in a dream instead of to the great patriarch involved. This question would seem to be resolved in the third story in 26:1-12, in which Abimelech discovers the deception when he looks out a window and sees Isaac and Rebekah acting romantically toward one another.[5]

Not all of the sets of stories in Genesis seem to operate in this way, but each group provides an opportunity to practice one of the most important aspects of a literary approach to biblical texts: careful observation of both repetition and variation. A list of some of these sets of "linked stories" in Genesis appears in table 2.2.

---

[5]I have discussed this function of this series of stories and identified other such series as "linked stories" elsewhere. See John H. Tullock and Mark McEntire, *The Old Testament Srory*, 7th ed. (Upper Saddle River NJ: Prentice-Hall, 2005) 39-48.

Table 2.2
Linked Story Sets in Genesis

Wife/Sister	Birth of Twins
12:10-20	25:19-28
20:1-18	38:27-30
26:1-12	
Drunken Father	Finding a Wife at a Well
9:18-28	24:1-33
19:30-38	29:1-14
Endangering the Son	Confusion of Siblings
21:8-21	27:1-29
22:1-19	29:15-30
	48:1-22

The appearance of these sets of stories plays a number of important roles in the book of Genesis. For the reader they provide connecting threads within what might otherwise seem to be a disparate collection of literary units in Genesis. Multiple appearances of similar stories might provide a sense of familiarity, and a further reminder that these people are related to one another. Reading through the book of Genesis and paying attention to these features might then be something like looking through a photograph album containing pictures from several generations of a family and noticing the resemblances. Perhaps most important, the primary themes of Genesis, such as God's protection of the ancestors, the preference for the younger brother, the promise of offspring, the barrenness of the female ancestors and the continuation of the covenant are all highlighted in these stories, many of which will receive more attention later in this chapter.

One final, large narrative trend in the book of Genesis has to do with the development of the character of God. As mentioned briefly above, many readers have noticed a distinct progression in the way God interacts with human beings in Genesis. In the early parts of Genesis, God seems to have regular conversation with the human characters in the book, such as Adam, Eve, Cain, and Noah. God speaks directly with ancestral characters like Abraham, Sarah, Hagar, Isaac, and Rebekah, but this happens on special occasions or in ritualized ceremonies like the making of covenants. Jacob is a transitional figure in Genesis, when it comes to divine visitation. While he receives some visits which involve direct conversation, Jacob also has dreams that reveal something about God to him. The transition is completed with Joseph, who only receives divine guidence through dreams. This feature plays a role in the distinction between the primeval world and the ancestral world, but the trend seems larger and more significant.[6] The hiddenness of God is a major theological issue in the Old Testament that will continue to appear as our study of the Pentateuch progresses. Readers will also notice significant variation in the way the divine character is designated in Genesis.

Table 1.6 in chapter 1 provides data on the divine names in the Pentateuch as a whole. Three of the nine designations listed appear exclusively in Genesis, and a fourth appears only one time outside of Genesis. Further breakdown of these data in table 2.3 below reveals patterns among the separate books of the Pentateuch.

Table 2.3
Divine Designations in the Books of the Pentateuch

Book	*Elohim*	YHWH
Pentateuch	284	1,820
Genesis	188	165
Exodus	65	398
Leviticus	5	311
Numbers	11	396
Deuteronomy	15	550

In terms of frequency—based on quantity of appearances and the relative sizes of the two books—*Elohim* appears nine times as often in Genesis as in Deuteronomy, and YHWH appears more than five times as often in Deuteronomy as in Genesis. Genesis is the only book in the Pentateuch that uses *Elohim* frequently throughout. Source criticism would explain this phenomenon primarily in terms of the change in the way the P material

[6]This change in the way God interacts with humans in the entire Hebrew Bible is the subject of Richard Elliott Friedman, *The Disappearance of God: A Divine Mystery* (Boston: Little, Brown, and Co., 1995). Larger questions of the development of God as a narrative character in the Hebrew Bible have been addressed most effectively and influentially in Jack Miles, *God: A Biography* (New York, Vintage, 1995). Miles evaluates the development of God's character in Genesis (25-84), and deals with this issue of withdrawal specifically (78-79). The most extensive discussion of God as a narrative character in Genesis is in W. Lee Humphreys, *The Character of God in Genesis: A Narrative Appraisal* (Louisville: Westminster/John Knox Press, 2001).

names the divine character after Exodus 3. From a literary perspective, the shift is from the more universal, impersonal title (*Elohim*) to the more specific divine name that is exclusive to Israel's deity (YHWH).

The Primeval Complex

The familiarity of the opening chapters of Genesis, particularly the first chapter, presents some problems for many readers who are so certain they already know what is in these texts that they have trouble looking at them carefully. The idea that there are two distinct creation stories at the beginning of Genesis goes back many centuries.[7] The only seriously debated question concerning the division of the two stories is whether 2:4a goes with the account that is found primarily in Genesis 1 or with the account found primarily in Genesis 2. It is possible to split the difference and call it a transitional element, but the language of this half-verse links it more closely to Genesis 1. Note the switch from "the heavens and the earth" in 1:1 and 2:4a to "the earth and the heavens" in 2:4b. The first account of creation has clear boundaries and is a majestic piece of literature, almost poetic in its patterns and rhythms. Understanding the major emphases of this text and how it functions as the introduction of all introductions, leading us into the book of Genesis, the Pentateuch, the Old Testament, and the whole Bible, requires careful attention to its form and content. The most striking feature is its use of repetition, but the overwhelming nature of this repetition should not hide the significance of variation in the text. Many of the repeated phrases are identified and listed in table 2:4.

Table 2.4

Repeated Phrases in Genesis 1:1–2:4a

And God said, "Let . . . be"	1:3, 6, 9, 11, 14, 20, 24, 26 (8 times)
God saw that it was good	1:4, 10, 12, 18, 21, 25, 31 (7 times)
And it was so	1:7, 9, 11, 24, 30 (5 times)
Evening came and morning came	1:5, 8, 13, 19, 23, 31 (6 times)
And God called . . .	1:5, 8, 10 (3 times)

[7]The Leningrad Codex, which is 1,000 or more years old, has a large gap between 2:4a and 2:4b.

And God separated between . . .	1:4, 7, 18 (3 times)
And God blessed . . .	1:22, 28, 2:3 (3 times)
And God made . . .	1:7, 16, 18, 25 (4 times)
God created . . .	1:1, 21, 27 (3 times)

Among the important variations in Genesis 1 is the use of the word translated "create" in the opening verse and in the descriptions of the fifth and sixth days, while the word translated "make" is used on the occasions in between these. Also, the evaluation, "it was good," is heightened in its final use by the addition of "very" in v. 31. In so carefully crafted a literary unit it is difficult to imagine that such variations are simply incidental, though interpretations of their meanings vary.

The stories in Genesis 2–3 require some special consideration for many reasons, not least is the enormous impact these texts have had on Western culture. Images of Adam's rib, forbidden fruit, and crafty serpents dance through our consciences and subconsciouses, influencing our thought and behavior on more levels than we could ever count. Source criticism has revealed the heavy cost of placing chapters 2 and 3 beside chapter 1, in terms of creating incoherencies and destabilizing the text of Genesis, a cost which the author of Genesis must have judged as outweighed by what the stories of Adam and Eve accomplish.

A closer look at Genesis 2:4b-25 reveals five distinct components:

vv. 4b-9	The forming of the man and the planting of the garden.
vv. 10-14	The geography of Eden.
vv. 15-17	The placement of the man in the garden and the prohibition.
vv. 18-23	The search for a partner and the naming of the animals.
vv. 24-25	Conclusion with a proverb about marriage.

Certain elements serve to hold these parts together, such as the "forming" of the man in v. 7 and the "forming" of the animals in v. 19; the use of the name "Eden" in vv. 8, 10, and 15; the description of the "tree of knowledge" in v. 9 and v. 17. At the same time there are tensions which strain against the cohesiveness of this text. Verse 6 says that a "mist rose up from the earth" to water the ground, while v. 10 says that a "river flows from Eden to water the garden." Verse 9 mentions the "tree of life" along with the "tree of knowledge," but v. 17 describes the latter with no mention of the former. Verse 9 describes all the trees as "pleasant to see and good for food," while v. 17 prohibits eating from the tree of knowledge. Why plant a tree with fruit that is pleasing and which yields edible fruit, but forbid the eating of it?

In every case but one in this passage, when the Hebrew word *'adam* is used it occurs with a definite article (*ha'adam*), indicating that it functions as a definite noun, "the man," and not yet as a proper name (Adam) for this particular man. The exception is v. 20b, where *'adam* could be functioning either as an indefinite noun, or a proper name.[8]

Finally, 2:18-23 must be acknowledged as an altogether strange passage. Are we to understand the making of each animal species as a failed attempt to make a partner for the man? Enormous theological issues are raised by this text. When a part of the first "living being" (v. 7) which God formed is taken and "built" (v. 22) into a woman, are the two subsequent beings both distinctly different from the original? How should we understand the relationship between these two individuals who are designated *'ishah* (woman) and *'ish* (man) in v. 23?[9] Further, how do we understand the sequential creation of a man and a woman in Genesis 2 in comparison to the simultaneous creation of men and women in Genesis 1?[10]

A narrative approach to Genesis demands some explanation of how these two texts, Genesis 1 and Genesis 2–3, operate together, rather than just how they are distinct. Many of the observations and interpretive conclusions drawn by source critics are valid and helpful. The assumption that the writer or compiler of the book of Genesis was unaware of the tensions and contradictions inherent in these stories, however, seems dubious. Why these two stories were placed together and what role they play in the early development of the Genesis narrative is a subject that demands further

---

[8]Verse 20b might be read either as an intrusion from later texts, such as 4:25 and 5:1, where Adam is clearly used as a proper name, or as a more general statement that for men in general—not just this one—there was no appropriate partner found. English readers should be aware that when the word "man" appears in vv. 23 and 24, it is a translation of the more common word *'ish*, rather than *'adam*.

[9]The most common English rendering of the woman's purpose in v. 18 is "helper," and this is an appropriate understanding of the Hebrew word *'azer*, as long as one remembers that this is not a term of subservience. The character in the Bible most often described as a "helper" using this word is God.

[10]For a thorough, groundbreaking discussion of issues of language and gender in the creation narratives, see Phyllis Trible, *God and the Rhetoric of Sexuality* (Philadelphia: Fortress Press, 1978) 1-30, 72-143.

attention. One way to begin to answer these questions is to observe the limitations present in each of the stories. The seven-day creation story in Genesis 1:1–2:4a is majestic in scope and vision. It has a poetic quality that lends itself to the attitude and act of worship. Thus, it appropriately leads the reader to Sabbath as its endpoint. The problem with this story is that it has no characters with which its readers can identify, or whom its readers can follow in a next scene. The people created in 1:26-27 are as vague and generalized as the fish and the plants created earlier in the story. By comparison, the story in Genesis 2:4b-25 is very appealing on a human level. The "man" God creates in 2:7 searches for companionship and intimacy, and he rejoices when he finds it at the end of this story. This personal human struggle continues powerfully in the next scene in Genesis 3 as Adam and Eve experience failure, freedom, knowledge, and rejection. What this story lacks is scope. A single-family creation story runs up against the incest taboo and seems to have no way forward.

Remarkably, what each of these stories lacks, the other has in abundance. Genesis 1 provides a large world, teeming with plants, animals, and people. It is the world that Adam and Eve walk into when they are banished from the Garden of Eden at the end of chapter 3. Genesis 2 provides the book of Genesis with real characters who have names and faces. The first two, Adam and Eve, quickly produce two more, Cain and Abel (Genesis 4:1-2). The combination of these two stories provides the book of Genesis with a way forward.

Oddly, the way these two stories assist each other in initiating the larger Genesis narrative has typically been missed. This is revealed by the common sense of puzzlement over 4:17, which often produces the question, "Where did Cain's wife come from?" The most common answer, that she is an unnamed sister, only delays the problem. It might have been fine for the ancient Israelites to tell a story in which all of Cain's descendents were products of incest, but the problem recurs in 4:26 when Seth has a child. The Israelites themselves are included among Seth's descendants, so an incestuous solution will not do. It is possible that the most obvious answer, that Cain and Seth find wives among the people created in Genesis 1:26-27, is missed because of a misreading of these verses. Because most readers know the Genesis 2 story, in which exactly two people are created, they misread the making of *two kinds of people*, male and female, in Genesis 1 for the making of just two people. Therefore, they read Genesis 2 back onto

Genesis 1 and mistakenly assume that Adam and Eve are being created in 1:26-27, when the text says nothing like this.[11]

So, when Adam and Eve are cast out of the garden in Genesis 3, they walk into an inhabited world. The placement of Genesis 1 and Genesis 2 next to each other doubtless creates some difficulties and tensions, but the composer of the book of Genesis seems quite willing to let these be, in order to achieve the tremendous sense of narrative productivity created by the juxtaposition of the stories.

The Cain and Abel story performs a number of functions in Genesis and requires careful consideration. The first murder story is carefully constructed and woven into the Primeval Complex. The threefold repetition, "X knew his wife and . . . ," in 4:1, 17, and 25 reveals the internal structure of the chapter and blends it into the genealogical framework of Genesis. There are striking similarities in narrative pattern between Genesis 3 and 4. The most significant of these are the conversation with God after the act of disobedience (3:9-19 and 4:9-15), the curses involving the ground (3:17 and 4:11), and eastward movement as the result of human action (3:23-24 and 4:16).

The preference for younger sons appears immediately with the first generation of offspring in Genesis 4 and pervades the remainder of the book. The story of Cain and Abel, though brief, is critically important because it initiates this pattern and, thus, lies in the background of all the stories of Isaac and Ishmael, Jacob and Esau, and Joseph and his older brothers. The book of Genesis introduces these brothers to us very carefully. In a series of four parallel statements, the brothers are born (4:1-2a), take on occupations (4:2b), bring offerings to God (4:3-4b), and have their offerings accepted or rejected (4:4b-5). The order of their names in each statement is carefully alternated so that each appears first twice. Cain precedes Abel in the first statement, of course, because he is born first, but Abel is first in the fourth, because his offering is "looked upon." The text seems to take great care to treat the brothers equally until Cain commits murder and is

[11]An additional barrier to this reading of the text is theological in nature. Since the time of St. Augustine in the fifth century CE, the notion that "original sin" was genetically transmitted from Adam and Eve to all of the human race has often been assumed. In order for this idea to work, there have to be only two original people, from whom all other humans are descended. Unfortunately, this nonbiblical idea has been taken back and transposed onto the biblical text, obscuring the most natural narrative reading of the book of Genesis.

banished.[12] His crime justifies the preference for younger brothers throughout the rest of the book of Genesis.

Many attempts have been made to justify God's failure to "look upon" Cain's offering. Is it because his offering consists of grain rather than animals? This answer is difficult to accept, since the Torah will go on to authorize many types of grain offerings in subsequent texts. Is it because the text indicates that Abel's offering was specifically from the "firstborn of his sheep," while no equivalent indication is given for Cain's offering? This solution is problematic for several reasons. Among them is that sacrificing firstborn animals seems to have been customary, while there is no real equivalent notion of birth order for grain. Further, God's response to Cain gives no indication that there was a specific problem with his sacrifice.[13] Claus Westermann's suggestion provides the best sense of resolution for this difficult text. In considering what "looked upon" actually means, Westermann proposed that the story is simply telling us that Abel prospered and Cain did not. The characters would have interpreted their success or failure as the result of God's favor, or lack thereof, and differential success leads to conflict in the story.[14]

The differences between the two brothers are further magnified by Abel's resemblance to Israel, in comparison to the great empires that often surrounded it. Abel is a shepherd, assumedly a seminomadic one like the ancestral figures described later in the book of Genesis. Cain, on the other hand, is an agriculturalist and a settler. These aspects of Cain's identity are magnified further in the genealogy in 4:17-22, which links him to city building, the development of culture, and metal working. This genealogy of Cain is often ignored because of the problems it presents for the Primeval Complex. The notion that the flood wiped out all humans except those who descended from Noah is undermined by the winking acknowledgment that Cain's line is responsible for the continuing development of many elements

---

[12]See my discussion of the alternating priority of the brothers' names in *The Blood of Abel: The Violent Plot in the Hebrew Bible* (Macon GA: Mercer University Press, 1999) 19-20.

[13]The depth of this exegetical difficulty is demonstrated by James L. Kugel's discussion of the many ancient attempts to resolve it in *The Bible as It Was* (Cambridge MA and London: Belknap Press of Harvard University Press, 1997) 92-98.

[14]See Claus Westermann, *Genesis: A Practical Commentary*, trans. David Green, Text and Interpretation (Grand Rapids MI: Eerdmans, 1987) 32-33.

of human culture. The conflicts contained within the Cain and Abel story—agriculture vs. herding, settled life vs. nomadic life, development of technology vs. suspicion of technology, urban vs. rural—do not disappear with the first brothers.

The work of Modupẹ Oduyọye has presented to the Western world a striking set of parallels between the Primeval Complex and the cultural reservoir of Africa. These attitudes toward technological development and the conflicts between ways of life are present in African folklore and continue to exist in some African settings today. One result of the conflict in Genesis 4 is the absorption of Abel's genealogy into Cain's, with the inclusion of Jabal and Jubal, both names linked to Abel, in 4:20-21.[15]

On the surface, the lengthy genealogy in Genesis 5 functions primarily to move the story along quickly through ten generations from Adam to Noah, connecting the stories of the first family to the stories of the flood. This relatively simple function is complicated by the observation of several similarities between this Adam/Seth genealogy and the genealogy of Cain in 4:17-26. Table 2.5 lists the names in the two genealogies and demonstrates the striking similarities between them.

Table 2.5
Comparison of Genealogies in Genesis 4 and 5

Genesis 4:17-26	Genesis 5:1-31
[Adam]	Adam
Cain	Seth
Enoch	Enosh
Irad	Kenan
Mehujael	Mahalel
Methushael	Jared
Lamech	Enoch
Jabal, Jubal, Tubal-Cain, Naamah	Methuselah
	Lamech
	Noah
	Shem, Ham, Japheth

[15]Modupẹ Oduyọye, *The Sons of God and the Daughters of Men: An Afro-Asiatic Interpretation of Genesis 1-11* (Maryknoll NY: Orbis Books, 1984) 63-74.

In addition, the two genealogies resemble one another in form, with a narrative or poetic expansion of the seventh generation after creation, Lamech (4:23-24) and Enoch (5:22-24), and the division into three lines, represented by three sons, in the final generation.

Source criticism has typically identified these as two versions of the same genealogy, which diverged within the development of two different sources, J (4:17-26) and P (5:1-31), before they were brought back together in the composition of the book of Genesis. This argument raises two questions: (1) How and why did both of the genealogies get included in Genesis? and (2) Why did the final form tolerate the tensions and questions created by the presence of both? The genealogy of Cain would seem to be an unnecessary dead end, but the economy of the Primeval Complex implies that all of its components play a vital role.

In light of this, Cain's genealogy performs two important functions. The first involves its etiological components, which give credit to the line of Cain for several important developments in human culture. One of the oddities of this aspect of the genealogy is that these cultural developments (e.g., city building, music, and metal working) survive the flood, which supposedly destroys Cain's line of descendants. Questions about the flood story and the ways it does and does not fit easily into the larger narrative will be discussed later.[16] A second function of the genealogy of Cain is to initiate an important theme within the Primeval Complex, its view of civilization and technology, but this issue must await further evaluation until near the end of the Primeval Complex, where it reaches some sense of resolution.

The genealogical framework of Genesis, presented in table 2.1, marks out Genesis 6–9 as the middle and longest section of the Primeval Complex. The genealogy itself, in 6:9-10, is not placed at the beginning of this section, but appears just after the narrative introduces Noah in 6:8. All of the material in these four chapters may be related to the flood as the central event, but the components do not fit together easily.

Our introductory chapter presented some of the difficulties in the flood story, such as conflicts about the number of animals on the ark and the length of the flood, and demonstrated how source criticism can resolve

---

[16]It is possible that this genealogy comes from a source that is unaware of the flood tradition, but, in the final form of Genesis, perhaps this is one subtle acknowledgement that the flood is not to be understood as such a universal event as other texts imply.

some of these difficulties by unweaving two different flood stories. Rather than resolving the meaning of the flood story, however, these source-critical observations lead to larger, more persistent questions:

> Why would the author of Genesis weave together disparate elements, creating a conflicted story?
>
> What is the role of a literary unit like 6:1-4, which not only does not fit into the standard source scheme, but stands out as one of the oddest texts in all of the Bible?
>
> What role does this awkward story of the flood and its aftermath play in its present condition and position?

The opening section of this chapter demonstrated on a broad scale how the book of Genesis is in the process of bringing the portrait of Israel into sharper focus. It is this task which holds together all of the parts of the flood narrative. Genesis 6:1-4 has puzzled interpreters for almost as long as the book of Genesis has been in existence, and it is not possible to unravel all of its mysteries.[17] What these few verses accomplish in the book of Genesis is to take a very different kind of world, one where earthly beings and heavenly beings interact and legendary giants roam the earth, and move it aside, so that the more familiar, and ordinary, world of the Israelite ancestors can be brought to the center of the reader's view.

The reason for the flood is given twice, once on either side of the Noah genealogy in 6:9-10 and, though the two explanations differ, they are not incompatible. Genesis 6:5-8 says that "the evil of humanity was great on the earth" and that "every inclination of the thoughts of their heart is only evil all day long." On the other hand, 6:11-14 says that "the earth was full of violence" and "was corrupt." Developed and situated as they are, these two passages that explain the flood form a significant progression, with 6:5-8 presented as the internal consideration of YHWH, which leads to merciful regard for Noah, while in 6:11-14 God explains the reason for the coming destruction to Noah, after the intervening genealogy has introduced him more fully. The two explanations are fittingly internal ("inclinations" and

---

[17]This small fragment of text is related in some way to a greatly expanded story in the first portion of the book of First Enoch (1–36), commonly called "The Book of the Watchers." It is possible that the Book of the Watchers is similar to a larger, ancient story from which Genesis 6:1-4 was taken. It is also possible that this mysterious little text in Genesis inspired the production of the Book of the Watchers.

"thoughts" in 6:5-8) and external ("violence" and "corruption" in 6:11-14).[18] Table 1.7 delineated the major issues in the flood story in the remainder of chapters 6–8.

It is not possible to read a smooth, fully coherent story in the present form of these chapters, but the major contours of the narrative should not be obscured by the recognition that multiple stories have been blended. However long the flood lasted, it is portrayed as an undoing of creation in which the waters that were divided vertically and horizontally in Genesis 1 come crashing in on humanity until creation is reduced to the tiny box that holds Noah and his party, but the ark floats "on the face of the waters" in 7:18, just like the creative spirit of God did in 1:2. The turning point in the story comes at 8:1 when God "remembers" Noah, and once again the spirit-wind from God moves over the earth.

The retraction of the waters reestablishes livable space so that the living beings on the ark can emerge and begin to "fill the earth" again (8:17). At the time of this emergence, Noah offers sacrifices to God and God makes a number of agreements with Noah and his family. In the midst of these agreements, in 8:15–9:17, the word "covenant" appears for the second time in Genesis (9:9), as an extension of the promise of covenant God initially makes to Noah in 6:18.[19] The war that God had declared on the world in chapter 6 is over, and God signals this end with the laying down of a weapon, the bow, in 9:16.

With an examination of the components of the flood story complete, it is now possible to consider a larger sense of structure in the narrative of Genesis 6–9. Building on the work of Bernard Anderson,[20] Laurence Turner has proposed a chiastic model for this portion of the book which begins with the closely related statements about Noah and his sons in 5:28-29 and 9:28–10:1. This structure moves from these boundaries at each end, through

---

[18]The purpose of the flood here is both like and unlike the divine rationale in the Atrahasis/Gilgamesh tradition, where the gods flood the earth because there are too many humans and they are too loud. Perhaps the starkest contrast is between the apparent annoyance of the Babylonian gods and the agonized grief of YHWH in 6:6.

[19]See the more extensive treatment of this concept below in the discussion of Genesis 12.

[20]Bernard Word Anderson, "From Analysis to Synthesis: The Interpretation of Genesis," *Journal of Biblical Literature* 97 (1997): 23-39.

matching units, to its center at 8:1, "And God remembered Noah." The full chiasm is presented in table 2.6.[21]

Table 2.6

The Structure of Genesis 6-9

Offence: Judgment on Offenders; "Grace" to Noah (6:1-8)

A Noah and his three sons (6:9-10)

B Violence in God's creation (6:11-12)

C First Divine Address: Resolution to destroy (6:13-22)

D Second divine address: command to enter the ark (7:1-10)

E Beginning of the flood (7:11-16)

F Rising flood waters (7:17-24)

God's remembrance of Noah (8:1a)

F' Receding flood waters (8:1b-5)

E' Drying of the earth (8:6-14)

D' Third divine address: Command to leave the ark (8:15-19)

C' God's resolution to preserve order (8:20-22)

B' Fourth divine address: Covenant of blessing and peace (9:1-17)

A' Noah and his three sons (9:18-19)

Offence: Judgment on Canaan:
Blessing on Shem and Japheth (9:20-27)

Unfortunately, the story of humanity soon continues as if the flood never happened. The sons of Noah come into conflict outside the ark just as the sons of Adam and Eve did outside of the garden, and the initial difficulties of this new first family will also involve fruit, nakedness, and shame. Genesis 9:20 reports that Noah became a man of the soil, and he planted a vineyard. This description links Noah to Cain (4:2) and the image of Noah as the developer of wine making causes him to resemble the inventors of culture in Cain's genealogy.[22]

[21]See Laurence A. Turner, *Genesis*, Readings, a New Biblical Commentary (Sheffield UK: Sheffield Academic Press, 2000) 55.

[22]Israel Knoll has suggested that the genealogies in the Primeval Complex have been slightly rearranged. He proposed that Genesis 5:29, which presents Noah as a son of Lamech, was originally between 4:25 and the final line of 4:26, where Noah would also have been a son of Lamech in a continuation of Cain's genealogy, rather than a reiteration of Adam's. Here, Noah would have brought the line of Cain rest from its wandering. See Knoll, "Cain the Forefather of Humanity," in *Sefer*

The conflict between the sons of this new first family is again obscure in its origins. The youngest son, Ham, has caused some offense related to "the nakedness of his father" (9:21-22).[23] The curse and blessings that result from the behavior of Noah and his sons present enormous problems, but the primary narrative function of the story in 9:18-27 is easy to identify. This is the only case in Genesis where the younger brother (Ham) is not favored over the older brother(s) and is not the one who continues the genealogical line. Such a deviation from the standard pattern requires some explanation, which this story provides, but it also raises issues about ethnicity and power which have painful results. Aside from the obscure nature of the offense, the other major question generated by the story is why the curse falls on Canaan when it is apparently caused by his father's behavior.

The categories "Hamitic" and "S[h]emetic" are still used by modern anthropologists to classify people groups and languages. If the cursed Canaan is linked to the Canaanites—and the connection is fairly obvious—then it is also apparent that this person, and the group that later bears his name, is out of place here and in the genealogy that follows in chapter 10. The Canaanites are clearly Semitic, not Hamitic, people and are closely related to the Hebrews, who are descendants of Shem through Eber in Genesis 11:10-26. Nevertheless, Canaan is deliberately misplaced in order to put as much ethnic distance as possible between him and the family of Shem. The ideology behind future animosity between the Israelites and the Canaanites, and the displacement and subjugation of the latter by the former, is established early in the biblical tradition.[24] One final issue within the text itself is the surprising harshness of the punishment in the curse. Whatever Ham's offense was, it does not justify his descendants be sub-

---

Moshe: The Moshe Weinfeld Jubilee Volume: Studies in the Bible and the Ancient Near East, Qumran, and Postbiblical Judaism (Winona Lake IN: Eisenbrauns, 2004) 64-66.

[23]See the proposed explanations of the offense and the ambiguity of the text in Nahum Sarna, *Genesis*, JPS Torah Commentary (Philadelphia: Jewish Publication Society, 1989) 63-65.

[24]The legacy of this text is long and painful, extending into our own era. During the days of slavery in the United States, Genesis 9:18-28 was the most common text used by preachers who proclaimed that the enslavement of Africans by those of European descent was a part of God's plan. For more on this subject, see Stephen R. Haynes, *Noah's Curse: The Biblical Justification of American Slavery*, Religion in America series (New York: Oxford University Press, 2002, 2007).

jected to slavery forever, but this text serves as an anchor for Israel's understanding of its place in the world.[25]

The story of Noah's sons establishes the foundation for the huge genealogy in Genesis 10, often called the "Table of the Nations." This genealogy is divided into three parts under the headings of Noah's sons, with a diversion into the family of Canaan, one of his grandsons. Two generations are provided for Japheth and three for Ham. As an aside, vv. 15-20 presents Canaan and one more generation of his lineage, specifically identifying the Canaanites and their territory in vv. 18-19. The final section gives five generations of Shem's family, emphasizing his line as the one of greatest importance.[26] Even readers unfamiliar with ancient Near Eastern geography will recognize enough place names to realize that this genealogy is more about people groups and nations than it is about persons. One of the reasons the genealogical lines stop so abruptly is that they are drawing maps more than they are tracing lineages, and the maps get full at some point. In areas closer to Israel, those listed under Canaan and Shem, there is greater detail, demonstrating greater awareness and/or interest in the geography of these nearby places.

Some confusion is often created by the assumption that Genesis 11:1-9, the story of the Tower of Babel, follows chronologically upon chapter 10. It seems more likely that two elements of chapter 10 elicit questions that a recollection of the Babel story addresses. The conclusion of the Shem genealogy in 10:31 echoes 10:5 and 20 in reporting that the groups of people have their own languages. The conclusion to the Table of Nations, 10:32, says that the nations "spread out on the earth." Why did they have different languages and why did they spread out? The Babel story in 11:1-9 uses different vocabulary for "language" (vv. 7 and 9) and its "scattered" is different from the "spread out" of the Table of Nations, so it is doubtful that it was composed in response to concerns raised in chapter 10.[27] It is

[25]For more on this text and the ethnic issue it raises, see Modupẹ Oduyọye, *The Sons of God and the Daughters of Men*, 60-62.

[26]The unevenness of the genealogies in Genesis 10 has been explained as the result of inserting two J passages, 10:8-19 and 24-30, into an overall P framework. See Clauss Westermann, *Genesis 1-11*, vol. 1 of *Genesis: A Commentary* (Minneapolis: Augsburg Publishing House, 1984) 498-501.

[27]See the discussion of these issues in Terrence Fretheim, "The Book of Genesis: Introduction, Commentary, and Reflections," *The New Interpreter's Bible*, vol. 1 (Nashville: Abingdon Press, 1994) 410-11.

more likely that Babel is an independent story which is inserted here and which may not have originally had this etiological function. Nevertheless, the theological issues raised and addressed by the Babel story fit well into the Primeval Complex. The theme of human action that threatens God in some way, followed by an act of banishment or destruction, follows a line from Eden to Flood to Babel.

The nonchronological, reflective nature of 11:1-9 is further confirmed by the reversion to the beginning of Shem's genealogy at 11:10. This time the genealogy is concerned only with the one family line, and its components seem to be more persons than nations, though some of the names match place names, and 11:10-26 looks much more like Genesis 5. Both genealogies have a very regular pattern, present ten generations, name only one son in each generation, and end by diverging into three sons in the final generation. The succeeding story in 11:27-32 concerns the final father of the genealogy, Terah, and his three sons (Abram, Nahor, and Haran), just as the flood story concerns the father and three sons named in 5:32.

Two members from the middle of Shem's genealogy merit further recognition. Eber is the fourth individual in the list, and has already aroused some curiosity by the way he is described in 10:21, before his natural position in the earlier Shem genealogy, at 10:25. In some way, this particular person embodies the image of those who will be Israelites, and his name is the source of their other designation, the "Hebrews" (Heb. *hebraios*, "belonging to Eber"). The derivation of this name from the root meaning "pass over" or "pass by" (*abar*) provides a tantalizing possibility that these seminomadic people understood themselves as the "passers-by."[28] Eber's son is Peleg, whose name is connected to the word for "divide" in the previous genealogy in 10:25, "because in his day the earth was divided." The earlier genealogy continues with his brother, Joktan, however, even though Peleg's name seems to fit so well with the Babel story which follows.

When these texts are all put together, one effect seems to be that the first Shem genealogy (10:21-31) takes a wrong turn at the fifth generation, but the Tower of Babel story restarts it and keeps it on the right track, so that it ends where it needs to end, with Abram, son of Terah. One distinct feature in this final genealogy of the Primeval Complex that serves to bring the story forward into the clearer setting of a recognizable world is the

---

[28]This notion receives extensive attention, along with striking analogies to contemporary African tribal relations in Oduyọye, *The Sons of God and the Daughters of Men*, 63-64.

steady reduction in lifespans in 11:10-26, from the 600 years of Shem to the 148 years of Nahor. Even the slight increase for Terah, to 205 years, is reduced again with Abraham in 25:7 to 175 years.

At several earlier points in the exploration of the Primeval Complex, connections among some of the more enigmatic texts have been mentioned. At this point, it is possible to look at Cain's genealogy (4:17-26), the story of the "sons of God" (*benay 'Elohiym*, 6:1-4), the legend of Nimrod (10:8-12), and the story of the Tower of Babel (11:1-9) together in terms of a trajectory that is formed within Genesis 1–11. The three ideas that connect these four strange passages are building, the development of skills or technology, and the establishment of a name. Table 2.7 illustrates where each of these three elements is found in these four texts.

Table 2.7

Fame and the Development of Human Culture in Genesis 1-11

Text	Building	Development of skills	Establishment of fame
4:17-26	4:17	4:20, 21, 22	4:17
6:1-4			6:4
10:8-12	10:10-11	10:8-9	10:9
11:1-9	11:3-4	11:3	11:4

As table 2.6 indicates, the genealogy of Cain introduces all three of these issues and the Tower of Babel story pronounces God's judgment upon them. In light of the pending emergence of Abraham as a wandering herder of livestock, it is fitting that the Primeval Complex has resolved this ideological conflict. The nomadic ways of the Israelite ancestors will continue to come into contact and conflict with civilization and its great empires, but the cultural identity of the Pentateuch's protagonists has been settled. They are the *unsettled*.[29] The construction of a distant, unfamiliar world within the Primeval Complex provides an adequate arena for such a struggle between two very different cultural paths. In the familiar world which the Israelites knew, their nomadic way of life always lost to empires and technology. Perhaps a few small victories in this other, imagined world assured them of their chosen status, even as they were forced to accommodate and become more settled, urban, and technological.

[29]On the conflict between settled and wandering ways of life, see the brilliant insights of Oduyọye in *The Sons of God and the Daughters of Men*, 63-82.

The Ancestral Complex I: The Abraham and Sarah Cycle

The opening of the Ancestral Complex provides occasion to address more thoroughly the concept of covenant. The covenant idea has arisen previously in Genesis but, beginning with Abraham, becomes a major feature. There is common agreement among contemporary interpreters that the second half of Genesis properly begins at 11:27 with the *Toledot* of Terah, but the booming voice of covenant in 12:1-3, both in the text and in Jewish and Christian tradition, steals the show and is likely the reason that the chapter division was placed there instead. Table 2.8 lists covenant texts in Genesis.

Table 2.8
Covenant Passages in Genesis

Text	Recipient*	Contents of the Promise
1:28-30[30]	Humankind	Plants for food
9:1-7	Noah and his sons	Protection and animals for food
12:1-3	Abram	Blessing, greatness in number and name
13:14-17	Abram	Land and numerous offspring
15:4-6	Abram	Many descendants
15:13-16	Abram	Deliverance of descendants and long life
16:10-12	Hagar	Many offspring
17:1-22	Abram and Sarai	Numerous offspring, land, power, new names
21:22-34	Abraham (from Abimelech)	A well and peace
22:15-18	Abraham	Blessing, offspring, power
26:2-5	Isaac	Blessing, offspring, land
26:23-25	Isaac	Offspring, Blessing
26:26-31	Isaac (from Abimelech)	Peace
28:13-15	Jacob	Blessing, offspring, land
31:43-50	Jacob (from Laban)	Loyalty?
32:27-29	Jacob	Blessing, a new name
35:9-13	Jacob	Blessing, offspring, land, power, a new name

*Unless otherwise noted, the one making the covenant promise is God. There are important questions to ask of any covenant. Among them are (1) Who is the

[30]This passage is not always classified as a covenant, but it contains some of the characteristics of one. It raises the question of definition which will be addressed below.

initiator of the covenant?; (2) What is being promised and what is expected in return?; and (3) What are the power relations between the two parties?

In 12:4-10 Abram fulfills his part of the arrangement by traveling south from Haran into Canaan. But after visiting some of the important places in Canaan, such as Shechem, the Oaks of Moreh, and Bethel, Abram moves on out of the southern end of the Promised Land. Very quickly, he and Sarai find themselves in Egypt, because the land of Canaan will not support them during a period of drought. Most of the details of their sojourn in Egypt in 12:10-20 were treated in the first section of this chapter because this story's connections to 20:1-18 and 26:1-12 make it an ideal example of a "linked story." Another important aspect, however, is this story's resemblance to the exodus narrative. The captivity of Sarai in Egypt, the resulting plague, and the confrontation with Pharoah are readily apparent similarities. In addition, the statement by Abram in 12:12 that "they will kill me and they will let you live," is an echo of Exodus 1:22 and helps establish Genesis 12:10-20 as the exodus story in miniature. This first example of the "wife/sister" motif, therefore, is a literary foreshadowing of the exodus and much of the remainder of Genesis, in which the ancestors face repeated threats which they overcome with God's guidance, sometimes in spite of their own questionable behavior.

The tension between covenant promises and threats to existence in Genesis 12 establishes a pattern that will repeat itself throughout the Ancestral Complex and holds together a collection of stories that are otherwise only loosely connected. The Abraham and Sarah cycle (Genesis 12–25) forms the sixth of ten *toledot* sections in Genesis. The individual literary units are listed in table 2.9.

Table 2.9

Literary Units in the Abraham and Sarah Cycle

12:1-3	Initial Covenant Statement
12:4-10	Journey from Haran to Canaan
12:10-20	Famine and Danger in Egypt
13:1-18	Separation of Abram and Lot
14:1-16	Abduction and Rescue of Lot
14:17-24	Abram's Encounter with Melchizedeck
15:1-21	Renewal and Expansion of the Covenant
16:1-16	Marriage of Abram and Hagar, Birth of Ishmael
17:1-27	Covenant Renewal, Renaming of Abraham and Sarah,

	Circumcision of Abraham's Household
18:1-15	Visit of Three Strangers and Promise of a Son for Sarah
18:16-33	Discussion of the Fate of Sodom
19:1-29	Angels Visit Lot, Destruction of Sodom
19:30-38	Lot and His Daughters Produce Offspring, Ammon and Moab
20:1-18	Abraham and Sarah in Danger in Gerar
21:1-7	Birth of Isaac
21:8-20	Expulsion of Hagar and Ishmael
21:22-34	Covenant between Abraham and Abimelech
22:1-19	Binding of Isaac
23:1-20	Death and Burial of Sarah
24:1-67	Marriage of Isaac and Rebekah

Most of these stories function quite independently, but they are tied together by some important ideas and literary features, some of which have already been described. After the initial statement of the covenant between God and Abraham, it is restated or renewed at least five times. (See table 2.7.)

Terrence Fretheim has observed that most of the stories in the Abraham and Sarah cycle have a double. The first doublet one might notice is the pair of genealogical notices on either side of the Abraham stories in 11:10-32 and 25:1-18. Within the Abraham and Sarah cycle there are two stories about endangering Sarah (12:10-20 and 20:1-18), two stories involving the rescue of Lot (13–14 and 18:16–19:38), two stories centered around extensive statements of the covenant (15:1-21 and 17:1-27), two stories about Hagar and Ishmael (16:1-16 and 21:8-21), two accounts related to the birth of Isaac (18:1-15 and 21:1-7), two stories involving Abimelech (20:1-18 and 21:22-34), two stories in which Abraham is tested and goes on a journey (11:27–12:9 and 22:1-19), and two stories pertaining to the gift of land (13:1-18 and 23:1-20).[31]

Notice that some texts appear twice in this list and some are paired with other texts in the "linked stories" listed in table 2.2. It should become apparent from these observations that the literary layers and connections in Genesis are complex and multifaceted. Perhaps the best image for this phenomenon comes from Janice Capel Anderson's study of the Gospel of Matthew in the New Testament, a book that undoubtedly uses both Genesis and Exodus as literary models. Anderson described the complex network

[31]Fretheim, "The Book of Genesis," *NIB* 1:420.

of repetitions and connections in Matthew as a "narrative web."[32] The repetitions of stories, motifs, and language in Genesis likewise serves to provide cohesion both to the book as a whole and to units within it.

In the list of linked stories in Genesis presented earlier (table 2.2), the only one of these sets that extends across the boundary between the Primeval Complex and the Ancestral Complex is the one consisting of Genesis 9:18-28 and 19:30-38. The significant connections between the Flood and the destruction of Sodom and Gomorrah extend beyond these two stories of their immediate survivors. In both cases, God decides to bring destruction because of human evil and informs a chosen human of the plan. In each story of destruction the disaster is survived by one man and his family. Both sets of stories conclude when inappropriate behavior toward a drunken father leads to the identification of offspring who represent enemies of Israel.

The climax of the Abraham and Sarah cycle is the story of the "binding" of Isaac in 22:1-19. The Hebrew word for binding, *akedah*, is often used as something of a title for this story. Before examining this story itself, it is important to notice that a similar one about Ishmael appears shortly before it in 21:8-21. Aside from the same general narrative framework in which a father endangers the life of his son who is miraculously saved by an angelic visit, there are numerous points of contact between these two stories. Recognition of these similarities causes the differences between the two stories to become more pronounced. Perhaps most significant is that the prominent role of Hagar in 21:8-21 highlights the absence of Sarah in 22:1-19. Another important factor is the chronological anomaly present in the first of these stories. In 16:16, the age of Abraham at the time of Ishmael's birth is given as eighty-six. Apparently, the year before Isaac was born (17:21), Abraham was ninety-nine and Ishmael was thirteen years old (17:24-25).

The story of the banishment of Hagar and Ishmael is linked to the weaning of Isaac, which would seem to have taken place when Ishmael was in his mid-teens. In this context, the story in 21:8-21, in which Ismael appears to be an infant who is placed on his mother's shoulders (21:14) and tossed under a bush (21:15), seems to be out of place. This may be an indicator that chronology is not the only factor the writer of Genesis used to place these stories in their present order. It seems likely in this case that

---

[32]Janice Capel Anderson, *Matthew's Narrative Web: Over, and Over, and Over Again*, JSOT Supplement series 91 (Sheffield: Sheffield Academic Press, 1994).

the author wanted the stories about the endangering of Ishmael and Isaac to appear in closer proximity than chronology would have dictated.

One final difference between the two stories is that the divine rescue of Ishmael does not bring him back to his father and to the covenant promises received by Abraham's descendants.

The *Akedah* story itself has something of a double ending. Before the covenant statement in 22:15-18, the story seems to conclude with a place-name etiology in v. 14. The naming of the place *YHWH Yireh*—traditionally, *Jehovah-jireh*, "The Lord Will Provide"—is explained as an acknowledgement of YHWH's "provision" of the lamb to sacrifice in Isaac's place. Traditionally, this place is linked to Jerusalem and, thus, the binding of Isaac and the sacrifice of the ram by Abraham becomes the inaugural act of worship on what will be the temple mount.

Within the narrative flow of Genesis, the most important aspect of this story may be the impact it seems to have on the characters involved. The absent Sarah dies immediately afterwards (Genesis 23) and is replaced by Abraham's third wife, Keturah (25:1), who bears him at least six children. Abraham lives on and becomes the father of this new family before dying himself (25:7-8). But Abraham's only significant acts recorded after the Moriah incident are the burial of Sarah and the procuring of a wife for Isaac. Isaac himself marries Rebekah in chapter 24, but the only other story in which he is the lead character is the one in which he travels to Gerar and claims Rebekah is his sister in order to protect himself, a story that repeats events that happened twice in his father's life. The climactic episode in Genesis 22 diminishes the vibrant characters who enter into it, and they quickly fade away, allowing the emergence of a new generation.

A small event of lasting importance occurs in Genesis 23, when Abraham acquires a burial place for Sarah. The text is very explicit about the location of this "cave of the field of Machpelah east of Mamre in the land of Canaan" (23:19). It was also to become the burial place of Abraham himself (25:9-10), Isaac (35:27-29) and Rebekah (49:31), and Jacob (50:13) and Leah (49:31). Genesis does not mention the death or burial of Hagar, Bilhah, or Zilpah. Of the ancestors whose deaths and burials are mentioned, this leaves only Rachel who was not buried in the cave of Machpelah, an issue that will arise later in chapters 35 and 48. The book of Genesis will end with the Israelites living outside the Promised Land, unable to keep hold of it, but most of their ancestors are buried in the cave in Canaan, where the Promised Land holds them.

The lengthy Abraham and Sarah cycle is followed by the very brief family record of Ishmael in 25:12-18. This genealogy extends only to the next generation, but lists all twelve of the sons of Ishmael, designating them "princes," in fulfillment of God's promise to Abraham in 17:20. Thus, this section about an "unchosen" son provides an interesting sense of foreshadowing to the story about a chosen son in the next generation, who will also have twelve sons.

The Ancestral Complex II: The Jacob Cycle

In the *toledoth* structure presented in table 1.1, the Jacob cycle of stories is the third panel in the second set of five, beginning with the statement, "These are the generations of Isaac" (25:19). Jacob is, without doubt, the most complex and intriguing character in the book of Genesis, and the changing of his name to Israel in Genesis 32 identifies him as the most important character.[33] He is the embodiment of the entire group of people that the rest of the Old Testament will be about.

The story of Jacob may be understood in three segments. His early life in Canaan, characterized by his conflicts with Esau, is recorded in 25:19–28:9. In 28:10 Jacob leaves Beer-sheba, the home of his father, Isaac, and travels north to Haran, and this northern sojourn period is described in 28:10–33:17, featuring Jacob's dealing with his uncle, Laban. Jacob eventually travels back south and resettles in Canaan, in the city of Shechem, and 33:18–35:29 reports this third segment of his life. Jacob does not die at this point, but remains a significant figure in the background as Joseph takes over as the main character in Genesis, until the deaths of both father and son are reported near the end of the book.

Each of these three segments of Jacob's life is characterized by conflict, and important transitions are often marked by divine encounters. This kind of movement within a narrative, away from home and back, is an important pattern. It is followed by important characters outside the Bible, like Odysseus, and characters inside the Bible, like Moses and David. It also fits the larger pattern of the movement of Israel, from Canaan to Egypt and back in the Exodus, and from Jerusalem to Babylon and back in the Exile and Restoration. Jacob will earn the name Israel as the incarnation of many of

---

[33]On the link between the person, Israel, and the people of Israel, see Fretheim, "The Book of Genesis," *NIB* 1:516.

the forces which shape the nation that will descend from him. The major events in the life of Jacob are listed in table 2.10.

Table 2.10
The Jacob Cycle of Stories

25:19-26	The Birth of Jacob and Esau
25:27-34	Jacob's Acquisition of Esau's Birthright
26:1-16	Isaac and Rebekah in Gerar
26:17-33	Continuing Negotiations between Isaac and Abimelech
26:34-35	Esau's Marriage to Hittite Wives
27:1-40	Jacob's Acquisition of Esau's Blessing
27:41–28:5	Jacob Flees to Padan-aram
28:6-9	Esau Marries Ishmael's Daughter
28:10-22	Jacob's Divine Encounter at Bethel
29:1-14	Jacob and Rachel Meet
29:15-30	Jacob Marries Leah and Rachel
29:31–30:24	The Birth of Jacob's Eleven Sons and One Daughter
30:25-43	Jacob Becomes Wealthy by Tricking Laban
31:1-55	Jacob Departs from the Household of Laban
32:1-21	Jacob Travels Back to Canaan
32:22-32	Jacob's Divine Encounter at Peniel
33:1-17	Jacob's Reconciliation with Esau
33:18-20	Jacob Settles in Shechem
34:1-31	The Story of Dinah
35:1-15	Jacob Returns to Bethel and Encounters God Again
35:16-20	Rachel dies Giving Birth to Benjamin
35:22-26	Summary of Jacob's Sons
35:27-29	The Death of Isaac
36:1-43	The Genealogy of Esau

There have been some attempts, as with other large sections of Genesis, to develop a large chiastic scheme for the Jacob Cycle. Michael Fishbane, for example, proposed a structure bound by Rebekah's labor in 25:19-26 and Rachel's labor in 35:16-20, with Rachel's struggle for fertility in 30:1-22 at the center.[34] Whether or not the chiastic structures are part of an intentional design, they can be proposed because, like the Abraham and

[34]See Michael Fishbane, *Text and Texture: Close Readings of Selected Biblical Texts* (New York: Schocken Books, 1979) 42. See the evaluation of such proposals in Fretheim, "The Book of Genesis," *NIB* 1:518-19.

Sarah cycle, the Jacob Cycle contains many literary units that seem closely matched to each other in pairs. The units of the Jacob Cycle also have important connections to units outside of it. The opening story of the birth of Jacob and Esau is an important example. The barrenness of Rebekah (25:21) connects her backward to Sarah (11:30) and forward to Rachel (30:1). Rebekah's struggles during pregnancy and the resulting divine reassurance delivered to her in a dramatic oracle (25:22-23) link her to Hagar (16:6-13) and the story of the birth of Rebekah's twins (25:24-26) reembles the birth of Tamar's twins (38:27-30). There are still more elements of the intricate "narrative web" in Genesis, described earlier, which is more complex than a string of chiastic structures.

Jacob's reputation as a deceiver is established immediately in the first two episodes recorded about him, his birth and his acquisition of Esau's birthright. We have seen the importance of names and their meanings already in the book of Genesis, both with regard to people and places, but have not given the issue close attention yet. The names associated with Jacob and Esau provide a good occasion for a cumulative examination of this feature.

The first human character, Adam, receives as a name the Hebrew word for "humanity." It is not always easy to tell in Genesis 2–3 when this character is being called by a name and when he is simply being designated as a human. The first distinct giving of a name within the text, in Genesis 3:20, begins the common practice of using a play on words by making reference to a Hebrew word that is connected to the character or story in some way and also resembles the name, though this match is seldom precise.[35] Adam calls his wife "Eve," a name that resembles the Hebrew word for "life." Eve then gives Cain a name similar to the word "acquire," because she had "acquired a man with YHWH" (4:1). Abel's name is neither given nor explained, but it is the Hebrew word for "fleeting" or "breath," a name that certainly fits the part he plays in the story. Noah's name resembles the word for "comfort," and is explained by the statement in 5:29, while Shem is, oddly, the word for "name" itself, though no explanation for it is given.

The original names of Abram and Sarai are not explained in the text. The former means something like "exalted father," and the latter seems to be a variation on her later name, Sarah, which means "princess." The new names of Sarah and Abraham ("father of many") are given in 17:1-15,

---

[35]In literary form, these name explanations are etiologies, but their lack of precision has also led to the use of the term "folk etiology" to describe them.

though it is unclear to what "Sarah" refers. God tells Abraham to name his son "Isaac" (17:19), a name resembling the word for "laughter," because Abraham laughs at the suggestion that he and Sarah will have a son at an advanced age. Jacob's name is associated with his grasping of Esau's heel during their birth (25:26).[36] Esau is quickly connected to the Edomite people (25:30), which explains, in part, the strange description of his physical appearance at birth, where he is said to be "red and hairy" (25:25). The word for "red" (*'adhmoni*) resembles the territorial name "Edom" (*'edhom*); the word for "hairy" (*se'ar*) resembles the name of Mount Seir, a prominent place in that territory and the region of the Edomites (32:3).

This last point deserves special attention. Physical description of characters is rare in Genesis, as it is in the entire Bible. Imagine a modern writer producing stories like this and providing no physical description of Adam, Eve, Noah, Abraham, Moses, Solomon, Isaiah, Ezra, Jesus, or Paul. Prior to Esau, the only physical description is of Sarai, whom Abram describes in 12:11 as "beautiful." After the description of Esau, Rebekah will be described as "good-looking" (24:16 and 26:7) and Joseph as "beautiful of form and beautiful in appearance" (39:6). In all three of these cases (Sarai, Rebekah, and Joseph) the beauty of the Israelite ancestor relates to their desirability in the eyes of foreigners and plays an important role in the story. This points to an important aspect of these rare physical descriptions. They appear only when they are integral elements of the story, such as the description in 29:15-20 of Rachel as "beautiful of form and beautiful in appearance" (the same description used of her son Joseph) and Leah as having "weak eyes," which explains Jacob's preference for the younger daughter of Laban.

The redness of Esau not only links him to the Edomites, but also points to his craving for the "red stuff" Jacob was cooking (25:30). And Esau's hairiness becomes a key element in the story of the stolen blessing when Jacob uses animal hair to disguise himself (27:16).

After Jacob has taken one step to replace Esau as the designated heir, by extracting his birthright, a diversion appears in Genesis 26. This small collection of stories is the only place where Isaac acts as the main character. Still, the stories of Isaac traveling to Gerar, passing Rebekah off as his

---

[36]Some translators understand Jacob's name to mean something like "replace" or "supplant," rather than "heel," which is what he was trying to do to Esau by grabbing his heel. See the discussion of Jacob's name and its possibilities in Sarna, *Genesis*, 180.

sister, and squabbling with the Philistines over land and wells serve little purpose other than to make him look like his father, Abraham. The most significant elements of this chapter are the brief divine encounters in vv. 2-5 and vv. 23-25. Until this point, Isaac has had no divine encounter of his own and, while God promises Abraham more than once that Isaac would inherit the covenant after him, no direct promise has been made to Isaac. If Isaac is to confer to Jacob the blessing of the covenant with YHWH, then Isaac must receive it first. So, while this set of stories is ostensibly about Isaac, it really serves as an essential part of the story of Jacob.[37]

With Isaac holding the blessing, Jacob's reputation as a deceiver established, and the preference of Genesis for younger brothers well developed, the basic idea of Genesis 27 may be rather predictable. Its details, however, are anything but. Parents showing favoritism for children is a detestable idea to modern readers, but it is an element that lends great drama to this story. Jacob manages, with Rebekah's assistance, to acquire the blessing from Isaac intended for the older son.[38] Traditional readings of this story tend to perceive Isaac as an old man, fooled by his crafty wife and son, but 27:4 casts doubt on such readings. With so much plotting and deception going on, wise readers will wonder whether they are being deceived as well. To be sure, chronology in this part of Genesis is not precise and orderly. Isaac is sixty years old when the twins are born (25:26) and 26:34 reports that Esau is forty when he marries Hittite wives. If chronology is in order then we might suppose Isaac is about 100 when the story of the blessing of Jacob follows this statement. It is also quite possible, however, to read the story as if Jacob and Esau are still young men, and that Isaac is closer to eighty years old. Either way, Isaac still has 80 to 100 years to live, according to his death notice in 35:28-29, so it seems reasonable to doubt Isaac's own claim of being near death in 27:2 and the narrator's claim of blindness in 27:1, and to think that Isaac may be fully aware of what is happening.

Of course, historical-critical methods have ways of explaining these difficulties. For example, the blessing story may have come near the end of Isaac's life in one source, but was moved forward to explain Jacob's sojourn in Haran, which comes from a different source.[39] At the point of

---

[37]For additional discussion of Isaac's odd identity, see Sarna, *Genesis*, 177.

[38]See the description of the rights of the firstborn in ancient Near Eastern cultures in Sarna, *Genesis*, 180-81.

[39]See the additional discussion of possible source assignments in Fretheim,

Jacob's departure, it is difficult to deny that two or more originally separate stories have been combined. Indeed 27:46ff. would seem to follow 26:35 quite naturally, and there seem to be two reasons why Jacob leaves home. A combination of 26:34-35 and 27:46–28:9 would provide a smooth story in which Esau's Hittite wives cause difficulty for Isaac and Rebekah, so they send Jacob to Padan-aram to find a wife among Rebekah's kin, and Esau responds by taking additional wives from among the Ishmaelites. Another cohesive story could be formed by 27:1-45 and 28:10-22, in which Jacob acquires Esau's blessing by deception and must flee to escape Esau, so he is sent by his mother to Haran.[40]

On his way out of Canaan, Jacob has the first of four dramatic, divine encounters that will serve to reshape his life. The first encounter in 28:10-22 and the last one in 35:1-15 both take place in Bethel (lit. "house of God," 28:17), a name Jacob gives to the place after the first encounter (28:19). A major shift begins with this experience at Bethel, as YHWH appears to one of the ancestors for the first time in what is clearly identified as a dream.[41] Jacob responds to the dream of the heavenly ladder, by building and anointing an alter, naming the place Bethel, and vowing one-tenth of his belongings in exchange for divine protection and blessing.

Haran is the site of Jacob's next set of conflicts. This time his opponent is his uncle, Laban. In the well-known story of Jacob's marriages, not only is there a personal reversal, with Jacob becoming the victim of deception, but there is also a reversal on a larger scale, as the older sister (Leah) benefits from the deception. The fourteen years in Haran allow time for God's promises to be fulfilled for Jacob, who acquires significant wealth

---

"The Book of Genesis," *NIB* 1:534. Sarna has argued that the two elements in the narrative as it stands function well together, as the story of Esau's Hittite wives "lends intelligibility to Rebekah's stratagem for saving Jacob from Esau's anger." See Sarna, *Genesis*, 189-95.

[40]The alternation of "Haran" and "Padan-aram" is another sign that may indicate alternation of sources in the story, though they are not completely incompatible locations. Padan-aram may be understood as a designation of the region in Northwest Mesopotamia where the city of Haran was located.

[41]Abraham's encounter in Genesis 15 may be read as a dream in part, but it is unclear whether he is still asleep when God speaks to him (15:12, 13). The word "dream" is not used there, and there is no report of Abraham waking. The word for "dream" occurs in Genesis for the first time in 20:3, 6, when God speaks to the foreign king, Abimelech, in a "dream" (20:3-7).

and offspring during this period. The cohesive nature of the set of stories in Genesis 29–31 has prompted Terrence Fretheim to describe this section as a "unified 'novella' or short story," and to compare these stories to the collection of stories about Joseph in Egypt.[42]

The initial meeting of Jacob and Rachel is of great importance because it is the most significant example of what Robert Alter has called a major "type-scene" in the Bible.[43] An encounter of a future wife at a well has already occurred in Genesis 24 when Abraham sent his servant to Haran to find a wife for Isaac from among Sarah's kin. A certain element of romance may have been lacking in that earlier story because it was not the husband-to-be who encountered his future wife in the dramatic scene at the well, but this version of the story fits the passive Isaac well, and the other major elements of the type-scene are present. In 29:1-14, Jacob's presence along with the obstacle he must help Rachel overcome (the stone), Rachel's hurried trip to report the meeting to her father, and Jacob's subsequent arrival at Laban's house complete the type-scene.

In chapter 3 ("Exodus") we will demonstrate how a nearly identical version of this type-scene—involving Moses in Exodus 2—is used as part of a block of material that serves to remake Moses in the image of Jacob.[44]

To this point everything has gone Jacob's way, so the emergence of Laban as a malevolent force, and an even more accomplished deceiver than Jacob, comes as a surprise. The deceptive wedding of Jacob and Leah offers the first departure from the preference for young siblings in Genesis since the cursing of Ham/Canaan in 9:20-28. In this case, Jacob must work hard to overcome the disruption of the pattern. Along with the seven extra years he must work in order to acquire Rachel as a wife, Jacob carries out an intricate and deceptive livestock breeding plan in order to secure his own prosperity apart from Laban (30:25-43),[45] and he escapes from Haran by subterfuge in order to take his fortune back to Canaan (31:1–32:2).

---

[42]Fretheim, "The Book of Genesis," *NIB* 1:552, 560.

[43]See the discussion in Robert Alter, *The Art of Biblical Narrative* (New York: Basic Books, 1981) 47-62.

[44]Alter also calls attention to a disrupted and incomplete version of this type-scene involving Saul, in 1 Samuel 9:11-12. Alter, *The Art of Biblical Narrative*, 60-61.

[45]The details of this plot are seemingly impenetrable for modern readers. Likely it involves elements of superstition about animal breeding that are no longer recoverable.

In the middle of Jacob's adventures in Haran and his conflicts with Laban is the crucial passage reporting the birth of his daughter and his first eleven sons. The accumulated birth announcements in Genesis 29:31–30:22 continue to develop themes of barrenness, sibling rivalry, and preference for the younger son, which themes have become central to the plot of the book. In addition, this is the first place that the names of the Israelite tribes appear, except for Benjamin, though at this point they are the names of children presented in birth announcements. Table 3.1 in the next chapter will compare the list produced here to lists of the tribes in several other places, demonstrating that negotiation of identity and status of the tribes is a major purpose of such lists. Several factors seem to be at play in the fifteen such lists that appear throughout the Pentateuch. Two of these factors are birth order and the identity of each son's mother. This first list is the only one that explicitly provides the birth order and identifies each son with one of the four mothers—Leah, Bilhah, Zilpah, and Rachel.

The Ancestral Complex III: The Joseph Cycle

The story of Joseph in Genesis 37–50 is literature of a different quality than the components of the Ancestral Complex in 12–36, and this has already been acknowledged at a number of places. Among the many ideas concerning the process of composition of the Pentateuch has been the proposal that the material about each of the great ancestors developed independently, with all of the pieces being constructed into a family lineage by the "author" of the book of Genesis. The unique character of the Joseph cycle, which is often labeled a "novella," may provide support for this idea. Many interpreters have observed the affinity of the Joseph story with other "diaspora literature" in the Old Testament—stories like those of Daniel, Esther, and Nehemiah, which seem to provide models of faithful living for young Israelites who are captive in foreign lands. However chapters 37–50 made their way into the book of Genesis, they serve vital purposes in the final form of the book.

In the introduction to this chapter, we described many of the changes in the book of Genesis concerning the ways in which God interacts with human beings. Joseph, who experiences only indirect dreams about the divine purpose in his life, serves as the final stage in the distancing of God in Genesis. The Joseph story also has a very different setting, since the most of it takes place in Egypt. One of the primary narrative tasks of the book of Genesis is to get the Israelites to Egypt, so it is important to pay attention to this setting of the story. One way to understand the very different "feel" of the Joseph cycle is to see how it matches this setting. The relative smoothness of Genesis 37–50 fits the calm regularity of Egypt as much as the frequently uneven and startling nature of 12–36 matches the tenuous nature of life in Canaan. Simon Schama has brilliantly observed how closely Egyptian religion resembles the reliable ebb and flow of the Nile throughout the year, while the rash unpredictability of Israelite religion matches the sudden, rushing torrents of the Jordan river and the smaller, flash-flooding wadis of the central hill country of Canaan.[46] In both form and content, Genesis 37–50 locates readers in Egypt, with the Israelites as welcome visitors, for now.

The preference for younger brothers is so powerful a theme in Genesis that it cannot simply fade away, even now that Jacob has been named Israel, making all of his children Israelites. So, while all of the sons of Jacob and their descendants are "chosen people," Joseph is more chosen than the rest, and, as if to counteract the more subtle nature of his preferential status, he is the most precocious of the younger brothers in Genesis. The well-worn story of the special coat has made Joseph a popular favorite of Bible readers, but in the larger story of Genesis 37, it is not difficult to see why his brothers would have grown weary of him. This conflict gives rise to his departure from Canaan, just as sibling conflict had driven his father, Jacob, away from home.

The story of Tamar and Judah in Genesis 38 has long been considered an interruption in the Joseph saga, albeit an interesting one. More recent study of this passage, however, has given significant attention to the role it plays within 37–50. Judah will become the most important tribe in Israel, and will produce its greatest royal dynasty, an eventuality of which Genesis demonstrates an awareness in the Judah portion of the Song of Jacob (49:8-12), but this Tamar-Judah story hardly flatters David's ancestor. If there is a faithful hero in the story it is Tamar, who endures many trials and humiliations in order to perpetuate the family into which she has married. That she is a Canaanite serves to balance a number of other passages in Genesis, such as 27:46, which take a dim view of marriage outside the family.[47] This is one of many points of contact between Genesis 38 and the book of Ruth, both of which demonstrate the importance of a custom sometimes called

---

[46]Simon Schama, *Landscape and Memory* (New York: Vintage, 1996; New York: Knopf and Random House, 1995) 263-67.

[47]Genesis 38—along with the book of Ruth—serves to debate the case for foreign wives against texts like Ezra 10 and Nehemiah 13.

"levirate marriage" in a culture in which early death is common. This custom is codified in Deuteronomy 25:5-10, but the only two stories that refer to it demonstrate that actual situations often do not fit a law in the abstract, and both Tamar and Ruth must operate well beyond the basic instructions in order to fulfill the spirit of the law.

The birth of Tamar's twins (38:27-30) provides a vital connection to earlier parts of the Ancestral Complex, most notably to the other story of the birth of twins in Genesis 25:19-26. The twins struggle in the womb in both stories and, in both cases, *redness* (Esau's skin and the thread around Zerah's finger) marks the firstborn twin. The preference for the younger brother is maintained and is emphasized when the book of Ruth begins its Davidic genealogy in 4:18 with Perez. So, the apparent interruption of the Tamar episode serves to help diminish the character of Judah, the oldest brother, and clears the way for Joseph's exemplary character to emerge, while making the case for Israelite men to marry foreign women, which Joseph will do when he takes the Egyptian Asenath as his wife (Genesis 41:45). In this particular place, the Tamar-Judah story also fills some narrative time while the slave caravan makes its way with Joseph to Egypt.

The events that make up the long saga of Joseph in Egypt are outlined in table 2.11.

Table 2.11
Joseph's Life in Egypt

39:1-18	Joseph in the house of Potiphar
39:19–40:19	Joseph in prison, interpreting dreams
40:20–41:57	Joseph interprets Pharaoh's dream and rises to power
42:1-38	First journey of Joseph's brothers to Egypt
43:1–44:34	The second journey and the detention of Benjamin
45:1-28	Joseph's reconciliation with his brothers
46:1–47:12	Jacob's entire family moves and settles in Egypt
47:13-26	Joseph acquires land for Pharaoh during the famine
47:27–48:22	Jacob prepares for death and blesses his grandsons.
49:1-27	The Song of Jacob
49:28–50:14	Death and burial of Jacob
50:15-26	Death of Joseph

This story is characterized by more than one fall and rise. The precociousness of Joseph, introduced as a theme in Genesis 37, is demonstrated further as even in Egypt he is always the smartest person in the room. His rapid rise in influence in the house of Potiphar[48] foreshadows the subsequent events in Pharaoh's palace, where, with divine guidance, he is able to help an entire nation survive the effects of a famine, in contrast to the other ancestors who were unable to cope with the famines of Canaan. This contrast leads to the reunification of Jacob's family, when he travels to Egypt to survive the famine under Joseph's care. When the family is gathered together textually in the Song of Jacob in Genesis 49, the addition of Benjamin makes their total twelve for the first time.

This is the first ending of a book in the Bible, so no precedent has been set for how to finish. The most prominent features of this ending are the deaths of two major characters, Jacob and Joseph. The two death stories are sharply differentiated by the issue of burial, because much is made of the massive procession, Egyptian representatives included, which takes Jacob's body back to the family cemetery in Canaan, the cave at Machpelah. Joseph, on the other hand, is mummified and left in limbo in Egypt. This model of ending a book with an important death(s) will be followed elsewhere in the Old Testament, as in Deuteronomy (Moses), Joshua (Joshua and Aleazar), and 1 Samuel (Saul), and may also serve to emphasize the lingering of David, beyond his expected death at the end of 2 Samuel. Joseph's bones will also linger for a long time, until they are carried out of Egypt (Exodus 13:19) and finally buried in Canaan (Joshua 24:32). These bones symbolize the condition of Israel itself, left hanging at the end of Genesis with the promises of covenant unfulfilled.[49]

History and Genesis

General issues of history and the Pentateuch were discussed in the introduction in chapter 1. There is no evidence outside the Bible that directly con-

---

[48]The brief story of Joseph and Potiphar is the kind of story that has invited great imaginations to interpret and expand it. Joseph's marriage to Asenath, daughter of Potiphera (Genesis 41:50), which may be considered part of this story as well, generated a separate literary work called "Joseph and Asenath," which was likely written near the beginning of the Common Era. Such expansions form the primary basis for James Kugel's brilliant study of early biblical interpretation, *In Potiphar's House: The Interpretive Life of Biblical Texts* (San Francisco: HarperSanFrancisco, 1990).

[49]For an extensive discussion of this tradition, and its theological implications, see Gareth Lloyd Jones, *The Bones of Joseph: From the Ancient Texts to the Modern Church: Studies in the Scriptures* (Grand Rapids MI: Eerdmans, 1997).

firms the existence of any of the characters in Genesis or the historicity of any of the events. Readers may respond to this set of facts in three basic ways.

First, many readers insist that they are entirely historical anyway and often assume that the truth of the text is dependent upon historical issues.

Second, when some readers see this lack of outside verification and recognize the implausibility of many of the elements of Genesis, they dismiss the book as old and useless. Ironically, these two groups operate with the same assumption that the truth and value of the book of Genesis is dependent upon how it measures up to our modern understanding of history.

A third possibility is to acknowledge that there is no evidence to decide the historical questions one way or the other, but that the truth of Genesis lies in the power of its story and the theological meaning it communicates. (Those who accept this option may still be interested in history in terms of trying to place the characters and stories of Genesis into a general context that may help us better understand the text.)

The story of Joseph is of particular interest in this regard. It has been well established that a group of people, of Semitic origins, gained power over Egypt in the eighteenth to sixteenth centuries BCE. Information regarding these so-called "Hyksos" people offers a tantalizing connection to the biblical story in the book of Genesis of Joseph rising to power to rule over large parts of Egypt. There is, however, no direct evidence linking Joseph or the Israelites to the Hyksos, so the best that can be said is that this information makes the Joseph story plausible. The dates of Hyksos rule in Egypt have subsequently become an issue in attempts to establish a date for the period of bondage in Egypt, the exodus, and the arrival of the Israelites back in Canaan. Possibilities and questions related to this subject will be discussed in the section called "Exodus and History" in the next chapter.[50]

---

[50]For an extensive discussion of this subject, see Donald B. Redford and James M. Weinstein, "Hyksos," in *The Anchor Bible Dictionary* 3:341-48. For a much briefer but astute (and readable) summary discussion of this thorny subject, see Carolyn Higgenbotham, "Hyksos," in *The New Interpreter's Dictionary of the Bible*, vol. 2 (D-H) (Nashville: Abingdon Press, 2007) 921-22.

Key Terms

Akedah	Epic of Gilgamesh
Babel	etiology
Bethel	genealogy
covenant	Hyksos
Deluge	Shechem
Enuma Elish	Song of Jacob

Questions for Reflection

1. How do you understand the idea of covenant? What are its terms and conditions in Genesis? To what extent is the covenant fulfilled by the end of the book.
2. What are the major differences between the literature of the Primeval Complex and the Ancestral Complex, and what are the effects of these differences?
3. In what ways is Jacob the most important character in the book of Genesis? How does he effectively embody the entire Israelite people?
4. How is the divine character developed in the book of Genesis? What changes have taken place by the end of the book in terms of how this character is presented?

Sources for Further Study

Brueggemann, Walter. *Genesis*. Interpretation, a Bible Commentary for Teaching and Preaching. Atlanta: John Knox Press, 1982.

Fokkelmann, Jan P. *Narrative Art in Genesis*. Assen, Netherlands: van Gorcum Press, 1975.

Fretheim, Terrence E. "The Book of Genesis: Introduction, Commentary, and Reflections." In *The New Interpreter's Bible*, edited by Leander E. Keck et al., 1:319-674. Nashville: Abingdon Press, 1994.

Gunkel, Hermann. *Genesis Translated and Interpreted by Hermann Gunkel*. Translated by Mark A. Biddle. Macon GA: Mercer University Press, 1997. German original, 1901.

Humphreys, W. Lee. *The Character of God in the Book of Genesis: A Narrative Appraisal*. Louisville: Westminster/John Knox Press, 2001.

Oduyọye, Modupẹ. *The Sons of God and the Daughters of Men: An Afro-Asiatic Interpretation of Genesis 1–11*. Maryknoll NY: Orbis Books, 1984, 1983; Ibadan, Nigeria: Daystar Press, 1983.

Miles, Jack. *God: A Biography*. New York: Alfred A. Knopf, 1995; New York: Vintage Books, 1996.

Pagels, Elaine H. *Adam, Eve, and the Serpent*. New York: Random House, 1988; New York: Vintage Books, 1989.

von Rad, Gerhard. *Genesis: A Commentary*. Revised edition. Translated by John H. Marks. The Old Testament Library. Philadelphia: Westminster Press, 1972; first edition, 1961.

Steinmetz, Devora. *From Father to Son: Kinship, Conflict, and Continuity in Genesis*. Literary Currents in Biblical Interpretation. Louisville: Westminster/John Knox Press, 1991.

Trible, Phyllis. *God and the Rhetoric of Sexuality*. Overtures to Biblical Theology 2. Philadelphia: Fortress Press, 1978.

Westermann, Clauss. *Genesis. A Commentary*. Three volumes. Translated by John J. Scullion. Minneapolis: Augsburg Publishing House, 1984–1986.

Chapter 3

The Book of Exodus

The Literary Landscape of Exodus

Describing the literary development of the book of Exodus presents some difficulties. Like the other books of the Pentateuch, Exodus is obviously a composite work, but unlike any of the others it is divided into two halves that are distinctly different from one another and which do not fit together easily. Moreover, the first half of Exodus (1–18) has strong affinities to the book of Genesis which comes before it, and the second half (19–40) is closely linked to the book of Leviticus which comes after it. Therefore, when attempting to read the book of Exodus as a unified literary work, one must acknowledge that it is being pulled in opposite directions from both sides, and the unifying factors are significantly strained. One significant alternative to this understanding of the divisions of Exodus is William H. C. Propp's proposal that Exodus is a "diptych" with the Song of the Sea in chapter 15 functioning as its center. This great poem brings closure to the Egyptian period and points forward to the fulfillment of God's promises in the second half of the book.[1] Alternative proposals like this notwithstanding, the seismic shift that occurs when the Israelites reach Sinai (19:1)—both in the flow of the story and the nature of the literature—is impossible to deny as the major point of division within the book.

The first half of the book of Exodus is composed almost entirely of narrative material. Moses quickly appears as the main character, and is developed into a character who resembles the great ancestors of Israel, a literary process that will be demonstrated more fully below. After the establishment of the character of Moses in Exodus 1–6, the Plague Narratives fill chapters 7–12, and a collection of wilderness stories makes up most of chapters 13–18. There are a few notable exceptions to the narrative character of Exodus 1–18: the Passover legislation passages in 12:1-20, 12:43-51, and 13:3-10, and the law concerning the sacrifice of the firstborn in 13:1-2, 11-16. These legal texts are closely related to each other, as the entangled

---

[1]William H. C. Propp, *Exodus 1–18: A New Translation with Introduction and Commentary*, Anchor Bible 2 (New York: Doubleday, 1999) 31.

nature of 13:1-16 indicates, and they are carefully placed at the major turning point in the narrative account in Exodus 1–18, helping to form the transition between the period in Egypt and the period in the wilderness.

Exodus 19–40 is dominated by legal material, much of which is difficult for modern readers to navigate. Exodus 19 introduces the Sinai encounter between God and Israel; chapter 20 contains the Ten Commandments; and chapters 21–23 present another set of laws often called the "Covenant Code." Exodus 24 takes Moses back up on Mount Sinai, accompanied for part of the way by Aaron and seventy elders, and the rest of the book of Exodus is dominated by legal instructions for the production of the tabernacle and its equipment (chapters 25–31) and a corresponding description of this project (chapters 35–40).

In this second half of the book of Exodus there is also an exception to the dominant literary mode. In the midst of this large mass of legal texts sits an extended narrative in chapters 32–34, which includes the story of the golden calf and its aftermath.

These texts will receive more detailed attention later in this chapter. At this point, it is important to recognize that the two halves of the book of Exodus are constructed in inverse fashion. Exodus 1–18 is primarily narrative, with small portions of legal texts in the center, and Exodus 19–40 is primarily legal material, with a narrative interlude at it center. This literary shape performs at least two important functions. First, in each half of the book, the core, which stands out and seems misplaced, provides important interpretive keys for the dominant material that surrounds it. The Egyptian bondage and the flight into the wilderness are interpreted by the practice of Passover, as dictated by the legislation in chapters 12 and 13. The instructions for building the tabernacle and its actual construction are interpreted by the story of the golden calf episode. Second, the texts at the core of each half of the book are carefully connected to one another. The jewelry which is taken from the Egyptians in the aftermath of the Passover event (11:2 and 12:36) is the material from which the golden calf is made (32:3). The self-plundering of jewelry (33:6), which had been plundered from the Egyptians (12:36), is the final stripping away of the lure of Egyptian wealth and religion that prepares the Israelites for appropriate worship of YHWH, the primary concern of the entire book of Exodus. Thus, Exodus, whose halves are pulled in opposite directions because of their literary forms, is intricately bound together by the concern for proper worship.

As was mentioned in the introductory chapter, the division between Exodus and Leviticus is problematic. In some ways, the flow from tabernacle construction in Exodus 35–40 to instructions regarding sacrifice in Leviticus 1–7 is fairly smooth. An important shift in word use concerning these institutions themselves, however, marks a significant divide. Exodus uses the terms typically translated as "tabernacle" and "tent of meeting" somewhat interchangeably, with a preference for the former. "Tabernacle" appears in Exodus about sixty times and "tent of meeting" thirty-four times. On the other hand, "tabernacle" appears only four times in the book of Leviticus—not at all in its first seven chapters—while "tent of meeting" is used in Leviticus forty-three times. This data would support the view that the end of Exodus and the beginning of Leviticus were not originally unified texts, which have now been pulled apart in the five-book scheme of the Pentateuch, but are separate traditions, which speak about the institutions of worship in different ways, but have been pulled into close proximity in the final form of the Pentateuch.

Israel in Egypt

The book of Exodus opens with a list of the twelve sons of Jacob, who are in the process of becoming the twelve tribes of Israel. The Hebrew title for the second book of the Pentateuch, "These are the Names," or simply "Names" (*Shemot*), places even greater emphasis on this list. Beginning a discussion of the book of Exodus provides occasion to take a wider look at such lists in the Pentateuch. There are fifteen such lists of the sons of Jacob and/or tribes of Israel, the first five of which appear in Genesis and Exodus and are presented and described in table 3.1.

Table 3.1
Lists of the Twelve Sons of Jacob or Twelve Tribes of Israel

Genesis 29:31–30:24. Birth accounts of the first eleven sons in assumed chronological order. Reuben, Simeon, Levi, Judah, Dan, Naphtali, Gad, Asher, Issachar, Zebulun, and Joseph. The birth of Benjamin is reported in 35:16-21.

Genesis 35:23-26. A list of the sons of Jacob concluding the Jacob cycle. The sons are presented in order within maternal groups: Leah (Reuben, Simeon, Levi, Judah, Issachar, and Zebulun); Rachel (Joseph and Benjamin); Bilhah (Dan and Naphtali); and Zilpah (Gad, and Asher). They are within birth order within those maternal groups, but the ovrall birth order is disrupted.

Genesis 46:8-27. A genealogy of the sons of Jacob, which names the sons in the next generation. The sons are listed by maternal groups again, but Gad and Asher (the Zilpah group) are moved to seventh and eighth positions, putting Joseph and Benjamin (the Rachel group) ninth and tenth, and Dan and Naphtali (the Bilhah group) last.

Genesis 49:2-27. The Song of Jacob, containing poetic recollections of all twelve sons/tribes. The changes include the reversal in order of Zebulun and Issachar and their movement to fifth and sixth positions, the separation of Naphtali from Dan and movement of Naphtali to a position after Gad and Asher, and the addition of Benjamin to the end of the list.

Exodus 1:2-4. A list of the names of Jacob's (Israel's) sons "who came to Egypt." Changes include the placing of Issachar and Zebulun back in original order, but still in fifth and sixth position, the movement of Benjamin to seventh position, and the omission of Joseph from in the list. Joseph is mentioned separately in the following verses.

The introduction of the tribes in Exodus 1:2-4, along with the separation of Joseph, provides the entry point into the Exodus story. The "narrative of oppression" in Exodus 1:8-22 is a brief, but carefully designed passage. One of the difficulties of this text is its presentation of three separate plans to limit the growth of the Israelite population, which do not fit easily together. In vv. 8-14 the Egyptian king and his people conspire together to enslave the Israelites in a passage filled with burdensome words such as *taskmaster*, *afflict*, *heavy burdens*, *oppress*, *dread*, *bitter*, *hard service*, and *mortar and brick.*[2] It is not clear how this plan is supposed to accomplish the desired effect of limiting the Israelite's population growth, as expressed in v. 10.

The second plan appears in vv. 15-21 and involves an attempted conspiracy between the Egyptian king and the Hebrew midwives. The refusal of the midwives to cooperate by killing all of the baby boys results in a second failure.

This leads to a third plan, the command by Pharaoh to his people to throw the male children of the Hebrews into the Nile River. This plan is limited to v. 22, and it is not made clear who is responsible for carrying it out, nor are any such acts described. The only baby boy put into the Nile will be Moses himself, in an ironic fulfillment of Pharaoh's command by Moses' own mother.

[2]See the discussion of this effect in my *The Blood of Abel: The Violent Plot in the Hebrew Bible* (Macon GA: Mercer University Press, 1999) 40-42.

Source critics have attempted to explain the uneven nature of Exodus 1:8-22, of course, often assigning vv. 8-12 to J, vv. 13-14 to P, and vv. 15-21 to E.[3] The nature of the passage does suggest that it is a composite, though there are also ways in which the components of the final form work together to address important issues. One of these issues is the changing identity of the characters involved. The story begins with the "king of Egypt" and the "Israelites," a positive relationship that was established in Genesis because of the influence of Joseph. By the end of this narrative of oppression, "Pharaoh" has enslaved and abused the "Hebrews." Both of these characters are named in a way that indicates the master-slave relationship, a very different set of identities than those with which the story began.[4]

The Appearance and Development of Moses

As stated above, it is the great irony of the book of Exodus that obedience to the command of Pharaoh in 1:22 ultimately saves the life of the Hebrew child who will lead the Israelites to freedom, but once the baby Moses is saved from death, the book of Exodus faces a distinct problem. Moses has taken on the identity of an Egyptian prince, not a suitable identity for one who will lead the Israelites to freedom from slavery. To address this problem, Exodus must transform Moses from an Egyptian prince into the kind of sheepherding nomad familiar to the ancient Hebrew people. Exodus 2–4 accomplishes this task with a series of stories that relate how Moses begins to resemble Jacob, the father of all the Israelites. By becoming like Jacob, Moses becomes like Israel.

The first story that serves this purpose is the encounter between Moses and his future wife, Zipporah, in 2:15c-22. While dwelling in Midian, Moses happens upon a well where he helps the seven daughters of Reuel water their sheep by fighting off a band of local thugs. The daughters return to their father and tell him the story, and he tells them to go invite the man to come and eat with them. By the next verse, Moses and Zipporah are married. Compare this story to the encounter between Jacob and Rachel at the well in Haran in Genesis 29:1-14. Finding a future wife during an

---

[3]There is significant disagreement about these source assignments. See the extended discussion in Propp, *Exodus 1–18*, 125-45.

[4]See the explanation of this feature in McEntire, *The Blood of Abel*, 37-40.

encounter at a well is also established as a common plot line by the story of Abraham's servant finding Rebekah as a wife for Isaac in Genesis 24.[5]

In Exodus 3 Moses is tending to the sheep of his father-in-law, just as Jacob tended the sheep of Laban. Moses has been transformed from an Egyptian nobleman to a shepherd in just one chapter. The story of the burning bush theophany in Exodus serves to develop further the resemblance between Jacob and Moses. Jacob is explicitly mentioned by God in 3:6, and the divine speech here is reminiscent of that which Jacob hears in his dream at Bethel in Genesis 28. Moses has now talked with God as did the great Israelite ancestors of the past.[6]

Two more events in Exodus 4 continue the reformation of Moses. First, he is mysteriously attacked by God in the night while he is traveling back toward Egypt to rejoin the Israelites. The infamous "bridegroom of blood" passage in 4:24-26 defies interpretation. Why would God attack Moses when the plan seems to be developing just as intended? The bizarre nature of this event invites connections to the wrestling match between Jacob and God in Genesis 32:22-32. Jacob was also traveling back toward home with his family and possessions he had acquired in a foreign land. Both Moses and Jacob become dangerously close to God, and this proximity becomes a threat to their lives. Both survive and move forward in the task that God has given them, but this leaves the reader puzzling over the purpose of these frightening and violent encounters. For Moses this experience points forward to the many struggles he will have with God in the wilderness as he leads the Israelites and, ultimately, to his death at the hands of God in Deuteronomy 34. For Jacob, the wrestling match points back to his struggle with Esau in the womb, where his loss, ironically, insured his status as the preferred, younger brother.

Second, as Moses travels back to his people, he is met on the way by his brother, Aaron, who comes out to meet him in the wilderness (Exodus 4:27), much as Jacob's brother, Esau, had come out to meet him as he journeyed back home (Genesis 33). So, by the time Moses arrives back in Egypt to meet Pharaoh (Exodus 5:1), the preceding stories in Exodus 2–4 have differentiated Moses from this Egyptian leader, whom he would other-

---

[5]Robert Alter has described this phenomenon as a "type-scene." See his discussion in *The Art of Biblical Narrative* (New York: Basic Books, 1981) 47-65.

[6]Notice that this reverses the trend away from direct divine encounters throughout the book of Genesis, which was demonstrated in the previous chapter.

wise have resembled very closely. Instead, Moses now looks like the namesake of the people he will lead to freedom.

This connection between the character development of Jacob and Moses is part of a larger trajectory in the Pentateuch. It is also a pattern of character development found on a much larger scale in the history of literature. An examination of this larger framework will help to shed some light on its expression in the Pentateuch. The story of a charismatic hero, wandering the hills, the jungle, or the ocean is one of the most powerful archetypal stories in the world. Its appeal crosses all boundaries of culture and time. This mythic tale may reach its pinnacle in Homer's *Odyssey*, but its literary use extends powerfully, both backwards and forwards in time, from this classic Greek drama which emerged from the early to mid-first-millennium BCE. There are variations on the theme, of course. In many cases, like the story of Odysseus, the hero who survives in the wild parts of the world is a past and/or future leader. American audiences would seem to prefer to separate political leadership from this myth and are most fascinated with outlaw figures like Billy the Kid, Jesse James, Butch Cassidy and the Sundance Kid, and Bonnie and Clyde, the last of which may have begun this figure's crossing of the gender gap, which was completed in *Thelma and Louise*. The great American adaptation of the *Odyssey*, the Coen brothers' brilliant film, *O Brother, Where Art Thou?* makes the hero an eloquent but ordinary man rather than a king. The enormous popularity of Disney's *Lion King* might raise questions about the American hesitancy to blend the fugitive image with the image of leader, but the setting of the story in the animal kingdom may make the combination less threatening.

The influence of this plot line on the Pentateuch is extensive. It begins small, as Genesis, and most subsequent use of the Bible, shows more interest in Cain, the murderer and fugitive, than in Abel, his victim. It builds with Abraham who, though he would appear most often to be a quiet shepherd, has a wandering warlord side which emerges in stories like Genesis 12:10-20, 14:1-16, and 20:1-18. The theme becomes more prominent in the story of Jacob, who spends two decades or more on the run and living in a foreign land after stealing the birthright and blessing of his brother, Esau. Jacob must flee again, as he heads back toward Canaan, after the dubious acquisition of much of Laban's livestock. This series of bandit stories rescues Israel's most important ancestor from the weak image of his early life, which is hinted at in Genesis 25:27-28. After an interlude, provided by a much different kind of story in the Joseph narratives,[7] the fugitive theme returns full force in the character of Moses. The story of Moses, which might be summarized as (1) fleeing from Pharaoh, (2) traveling in the wilderness, (3) encountering YHWH at Sinai, (4) again traveling in the wilderness, and (5) returning to Egypt, establishes the pattern for Israel as the fugitive nation whose story matches that of Moses in all but the final element. One obvious but often ignored question in the book of Exodus is why Pharaoh did not simply kill Moses when he returned to Egypt, as he had sought to do before Moses fled (2:15). Is Pharaoh as fascinated by the fugitive character as we are, and unable to kill him?[8]

The fugitive character of course finds its final Old Testament expression in David. This portion of David's life is often ignored, though it fills about a dozen chapters of 1 Samuel, and is connected, through the titles, to many of the psalms. The Pentateuch was likely produced while looking back at Israel's distant past through a Davidic lens, and the story of the great king is at least legitimized, if not lionized, by Israel's fugitive past. How can a contemporary reader see verses like Genesis 49:8-12 through any other lens?

The call of Moses encompasses Exodus 3:1–6:13, with well-known divine encounters at the beginning and end of this section. The first episode, most famous for the burning bush image, extends from 3:1 to 4:17. These verses are typically designated by source critics as a mixture of J and E material. This is a crucial juncture for source criticism because the most overt distinction between J and E, and between J and P, fades away here with the revelation of the divine name to Moses (3:14 and 6:2). From this point on, the E source Uses the name YHWH. In addition to revealing this name, YHWH also reveals to Moses the plan to deliver the Israelites from bondage and to punish the Egyptians. In 4:1-17 YHWH counters Moses' objections with the miraculous signs of the staff turning into a serpent and

[7]The story of a powerless person making his or her way up through the ranks of life by charm and wit becomes more important in later biblical tradition, producing figures like Daniel and Esther, who mirror Joseph. These are often understood as "diaspora tales," whose function is to illustrate to young Israelites of the postexilic era how to live a faithful and successful life in a foreign land, under foreign rule. Contemporary American culture seems more comfortable assigning this role to female characters, like Cinderella.

[8]Even God seems torn between the urge to exterminate or to elevate this character-type in Exodus 4:24-26.

Moses' hand turning leprous then being healed. Moses' continued objections lead to the inclusion of Aaron in the plan, as a spokesperson for Moses.

The remainder of chapter 4 moves Moses quickly back to the house of his father-in-law,[9] where he packs up his family and leaves for Egypt. One last set of divine instructions in 4:21-23 seems entirely redundant, but the reader, along with Moses, may need one more dose of divine reassurance to be prepared for the stunning event that follows in 4:24-26. Perhaps all that can be said about the internal meaning of this odd text, in which God attacks and attempts to kill Moses, is that its central concern is circumcision.[10] Its external role within a collection of texts that serves to transform Moses into a proper reflection of Jacob, has already been described. The story accelerates again after this event, and, by the end of Exodus 4, Moses and Aaron are reunited, the elders of Israel are informed of the plan, and they are all prepared to face Pharaoh.

Given the relative speed and ease with which Moses and Aaron have made progress so far, the dismal failure of chapter 5 is surprising.[11] This begins a pattern, however, of trial and error by God and Moses, which seems to match deliberately the multiple efforts of Pharaoh in Exodus 1 to limit the Hebrew population. In terms of narrative effect, these repeated attempts build suspense into the story. The initial failure in chapter 5 also provides occasion for the second great divine encounter of Moses in chapter 6. The presence of this text is mysterious, but it is quite possible that two separate stories of Moses' encounter with YHWH existed in Israelite tradition, one at Sinai and one in Egypt, and the author needed to include both. Nothing very new and different appears in 6:1-13, but the genealogical material in vv. 14-25 comes as a surprise. At first, the lists of the sons of Reuben (v. 14), Simeon (v. 15), and Levi (v. 16) may lead us to believe that this is another list of the sons of Jacob, with the inclusion of the sons in the

---

[9]Notice the name change here from "Reu'el" to "Jethro." This situation would seem to indicate that there were multiple, divergent traditions about Moses' father-in-law, which have been pulled together in the Pentateuch, without an attempt to harmonize them fully.

[10]See the discussion of this text, its many ambiguities, and various interpretive possibilities in Nahum M. Sarna, *Exodus*, JPS Torah Commentary (New York: Jewish Publication Society, 1991) 24-26; and Propp, *Exodus 1–18*, 233-41.

[11]Propp has emphasized Moses' failure to follow YHWH's instructions here. See Propp, *Exodus 1–18*, 259.

next generation, but such a list of the tribes stops at Levi and diverges into a complex list of the "heads of the fathers of the houses of the Levites." The genealogy serves to identify Moses, as v. 26 indicates is its purpose, and it supplies the names of Moses' parents, Amram and Jochabed (6:20), who have not appeared in the text up to this point. At the same time, the genealogy presents enormous difficulties, such as the assumption that Levi was the great-grandfather of Moses, which does not fit with the tradition that the period of Egyptian bondage lasted for four centuries or more. This passage is far more interested in Aaron than in Moses,[12] but this slightly awkward placement of traditions about the two brothers does help to move the story forward toward the plague narratives with a more complete portrait of them in place.

The Plague Narratives

The sequence of stories about the plagues does not arrive in Exodus 7 without significant notice to the reader. We first overhear YHWH telling this plan to Moses in 3:20, where phrases characteristic of the plague narratives, like "I will stretch out my hand," "all of my wonders," and "by a mighty hand," first appear. This theme recurs in 4:21-23 where, for the first time, the killing of the firstborn of Egypt is threatened. Along with the introduction of what will become the final plague, this text also initiates the troubling tradition of the "hardening" of Pharaoh's heart. After the initial failure of Moses' mission, the threat of violence against Egypt and its characteristic language reappear in 6:1.

The plague narrative proper begins with a strange step back by YHWH, who appoints Moses "as a god" and Aaron as his prophet and sends them to do battle with Pharaoh. The prologue in 7:1-7 piles up the formulaic language of the plagues which has appeared in earlier texts and will become common as the cycle begins. The first wonder performed by Moses and Aaron is not the first plague, but the turning of the rod into a snake, which had been performed privately for Moses in 4:1-5. This seemingly gives Pharaoh a chance to let the Israelites go before any of the destructive

[12]This genealogy is almost certainly a polemical text from a later period during which struggles took place within Israel over priestly lineage and authority. It's attachment to the theophany in 6:1-13 provides more evidence that the latter was an independent tradition that did not assume its readers already knew who Moses and Aaron were. See the discussion of this text and related issues in Propp, *Exodus 1–18*, 284-86.

plagues begin, but we have been informed multiple times that God has hardened Pharaoh's heart, so that it will take much more than a parlor trick to convince him to release them. Thus, the plagues begin in earnest at 7:14. Table 3.2 lists the plagues and some of the narrative characteristics found in each.

Table 3.2

The Ten Plague Narratives and Their Components

1. Blood (7:14-24)	A	B	C	D	E	F	G		
2. Frogs (8:1-15)	A	B	C	D	E	F	G	H	I
3. Gnats (8:16-19)	A	B				F	G		
4. Flies (8:20-32)	A	B	C	D	E	F	G	H	I
5. Death of livestock (9:1-7)	A	B	C	D	E	F	G		
6. Boils (9:8-12)	A	B				F	G		
7. Hail (9:13-35)	A	B	C	D	E	F	G	H	I
8. Locusts (10:1-20)	A	B	C	D	E	F	G	H	I
9. Darkness (10:21-29)	A	B				F	G		
10. Firstborn	A	B	C		E	F	G		

A – Divine command to Moses
B – Hardening of Pharaoh's heart
C – Meeting with Pharaoh
D – Request to release the Israelites
E – Warning about the plague with description
F – Execution of the plague
G – Pharaoh's response
H – The plague ended
I – Pharaoh's renewed refusal

Table 3.2 represents only one possible way to compare the contents of the ten plague accounts, but it is enough to reveal some interesting patterns. Four of the accounts (2, 4, 7, and 8) are presented in the fullest form, containing all nine elements listed in the table. This group is matched closely by two additional accounts (1 and 5), which follow the same format for the first seven components, but lack the last two. Three other accounts (3, 6, and 9) contain only four of the elements listed, and match each other very closely. The final plague, which is connected to the commemoration of Passover, is obviously quite different in form from any of these groups. Historical-critical studies of this portion of the book of Exodus have typically proposed the idea that the plague narratives were from different sources, and that two or more shorter lists were combined to make the present list of ten, a nice Pentateuch number.

There are also some logical difficulties presented by the present text of the plague narrative that might be explained by a combining of sources. If the first plague killed all of the life in the Nile (7:18), then where did the frogs of the second plague come from? If the fifth plague killed the Egyptian livestock, then why was there still livestock to be affected by the seventh and tenth plagues? The divisions above would separate the plagues which are in apparent conflict into different groups. While it seems likely that the present arrangement of ten plagues is the result of a combination of varying traditions, the final form of Exodus 7–12 cannot be explained by a simple folding together of multiple lists.

There are some features of the narrative that present problems for these attempts to divide the plague stories into such groups. The magicians of Pharaoh, who initially duplicate the rod and snake trick after Moses, are present in four of the plague accounts (1, 2, 3, and 6). In the first and second plagues, they duplicate the wonder performed by Moses, but they fail to produce gnats after Moses' execution of the third plague. They are not mentioned at all in plagues four and five, but the account of the boils specifically mentions that the magicians were themselves afflicted. Two of the plague accounts (4 and 7) specifically mention protection for the land of Goshen, where the Israelites live. Three other plagues (5, 9, and 10) specifically exempt the Israelites from the effects of the plague, without reference to their segregation in Goshen. These two elements exhibit a clear sense of narrative development, the fading of Egyptian power and the approaching deliverance of Israel, which crosses the boundaries of the groups of plagues demonstrated above. The most comprehensive explanation of the final form of the text involves both the notion that multiple sources were used, and that the present account was carefully crafted by a highly skilled author and/or editor.

One more issue presented in the table above requires more detailed consideration. The hardening of Pharaoh's heart presents theological difficulties that cannot be ignored, but the manner in which this tradition is presented must be carefully examined first. This idea is present in the prediction of the plagues in 4:21, the prologue to the plague narrative in 7:3, and within each of the ten individual plague accounts. The grammar of these appearances, however, takes three very different forms:

(1) An active verb with God as subject—"I [YHWH] hardened Pharaoh's heart"—in 4:21, 7:3, 9:12, 10:1, 10:20, 10:27, 11:10, 14:4, 14:8. In 4:17 YHWH hardens the heart of the Egyptians.
(2) An active verb with Pharaoh as subject—"Pharaoh hardened his heart"—in 8:15, 8:32, 9:34.

(3) A passive verb with Pharaoh's heart as subject and no true agent—"Pharaoh's heart was hardened"—in 7:13, 7:14, 7:22, 8:19, 9:7, 9:35.

These texts use three different verbs, which may have a somewhat different sense. In the cases where Pharaoh hardens his own heart the verb literally means "make heavy." These occurrences appear in plagues 2, 4, and 7, all of which appear in one particular group of plague stories above, but plague number 8, also in the group, uses a different word. This verb meaning "made heavy" also appears in one case when God is the subject (10:1) and in one case with no agent (9:7). In most of the other cases, the verb literally means "make strong."[13]

The Passover narrative, which begins at 11:1, merits some attention apart from the other plagues for a number of reasons. First, this is more than just one of the plagues, or even just the worst one. It is a crystallizing event that is linked to an annual festival that continues to be celebrated even to the present day in Judaism. Second, as mentioned in the introduction to this chapter, the Passover account contains the first example of legal material in the Pentateuch, the Passover legislation in 12:1-20. Finally, while the first nine plagues come to a distinct end, the Passover narrative has no clear ending, but blends into the next event in Exodus, the escape into the wilderness. Certain elements of the Passover account were predicted earlier in Exodus, most notably the killing of the firstborn and the "plundering" of the Egyptians. Indeed, this observation can make the previous nine plagues look like an unnecessary diversion. The killing of the Egyptian firstborn is more than just an affliction designed to bring about the release of the Hebrew slaves. It is repayment in kind, revenge, for Pharaoh's attempts to kill the male children of the Hebrews.

The death of the firstborn, Egyptian males is presented in unusual fashion. In essence, the event is described once in Exodus 11 and three times in 12. First, God gives Moses an advance summary of what will happen on the night of the plague in 11:1-3. This dialogue between YHWH and Moses is followed by Moses' announcement to Pharaoh in vv. 4-8. The stage is set for the final showdown, but 12:1-20 slows the pace of the narrative with a lengthy description of what is about to happen, combined with

---

[13]This literary feature, and those discussed earlier are sometimes used to assign portions of the plague narratives to the standard sources of the Pentateuch, typically, some to J and some to P. See the discussion in Joseph Blenkinsopp, *The Pentateuch: An Introduction to the First Five Books of the Bible* (New York: Doubleday, 1992) 140-41.

a set of instructions given by God to Moses and Aaron. Included are both immediate instructions for the night ahead, entailing how the Israelites are to avoid being victims of the "striking down" of the firstborn themselves (vv. 1-13), and perpetual instructions for future commemoration of the event (vv. 14-20). In vv. 21-27, Moses delivers these instructions to the elders of Israel, again describing the event and telling them what to do, but this version is significantly different from the preceding one. The most striking difference between the two is their lengths. God's speech to Moses (vv.1-20) is about three times longer than Moses' subsequent report to the leaders (vv. 21-27). In addition, Moses uses significantly different language in his speech than YHWH used in the speech to Moses and Aaron. The most noticeable shift is Moses' introduction of the "destroyer" who will enter the houses to kill (v. 23) instead of YHWH doing the killing directly (v. 12).

Source criticism has explained these differences as the result of the combining of two sets of Passover instructions from two different sources in vv. 1-20 (P) and vv. 21-27 (J). This explanation seems very likely, especially in light of the appearance of numerous sets of Passover instructions that we will encounter as the Pentateuch progresses, none of which are exactly alike.

The third and final description of the Passover event comes in the terse report of v. 28. While the existence of multiple sources can explain the differences between such texts, the inclusion of multiple reports appears to be a deliberate narrative choice. The successive decrease in length of these discussions of that fearful night, from twenty verses, to seven, to one, creates in the text the sense of urgency which will characterize the response to this event in the verses that follow.[14]

Israel in the Wilderness

The report of the departure is difficult to follow, primarily because of several interruptions in 12:37–13:16. The hurried departure is described briefly in 12:37-39. A great deal of information is packed into these few verses, including the route of the first leg of the journey (Rameses to Succoth), the number of Israelite men departing Egypt,[15] the inclusion of

---

[14]See the more extension discussion of this text and its literary structure in McEntire, *The Blood of Abel*, 49-60.

[15]Issues surrounding this number, 600,000, will be examined later in this chapter.

non-Israelites ("a mixed multitude") with them, and the hasty baking of unleavened bread for the journey. This last element provides the first link in the Pentateuch between the festivals of Passover and Unleavened Bread, an issue that will be encountered later in the portions of the legal material dealing with ritual calendars.[16] The report of the departure is then interrupted by a somber summation of the period of bondage in 12:40-42. Additional Passover legislation appears in 12:43-49, this time concerned only with future observance of the feast, and chapter 12 ends with another summary statement.

Chapter 13 begins oddly, with legislation regarding the consecration of the firstborn. These legal texts in 13:1-2 and 13:11-16 alternate with additional Passover material in 12:43-50 and 13:3-10. Such perplexing laws likely arose from Israelite traditions which developed over a long period of time. In their current place in Exodus, the laws concerning the firstborn, entangled with Passover and sitting on the boundary between slavery in Egypt and freedom in the wilderness, serve as a reminder of what YHWH has done for Israel and what Israel owes in return. Their descent into bondage took their firstborn, and their liberation cost the firstborn of Egypt. The festivals of Passover and Unleavened Bread will function as ways of remembering the deliverance of the Israelites, but the joy of liberation should never be separated from its enormous price.

Once the Israelites leave Egypt (Exodus 12–13), the remainder of the Pentateuch takes on a distinctive shape in terms of its macrostructure, based on movement and literary style. In Exodus 14–18 the Israelites move through the wilderness. In Exodus 19–Numbers 10, the Israelites sit still at Sinai while they receive the law. In Numbers 10–36, the Israelites move through the wilderness again, this time for forty years. In Deuteronomy the Israelites are again stationary while they receive a "second law" from Moses. This large section of the Pentateuch can be outlined as follows.

Wilderness I	(Exodus 14–18)
Law I	(Exodus 19–Numbers 10)
Wilderness II	(Numbers 10–36)
Law II	(Deuteronomy 1–31)

The primary giving of the Law at Mount Sinai is framed by two sets of wilderness stories, and the primary wilderness experience, the forty-year wandering, is bracketed by two sets of laws. Given this shaping of the text,

---

[16]See the related discussion in Propp, *Exodus 1–18*, 428-29.

it is difficult not to assume that in some way the law is intended to interpret the wilderness experience and, likewise, the wilderness experience helps to interpret the law. If the law represents the ultimate attempt to bring order to Israelite society, what does it mean for the law to be presented in the midst of the disorder of wilderness? The recurrence of the wilderness motif in Numbers means that Sinai does not have the final word. Wilderness surrounds the Sinai legislation. Moses' revision of the law in Deuteronomy serves to close the sequence, so that law surrounds the forty year wilderness experience.

The significance of these general observations is heightened by the realization that texts in one of these sections are sometimes reflected in corresponding sections. One example is the story about receiving water from a rock in the wilderness, which appears in both Exodus 17:1-7 and Numbers 20:1-13. A source-critical approach to the Pentateuch would conclude that these are two stories about water in the wilderness that come from different sources, and have different agendas, and that may be true, but it may be more productive to ask what these stories are doing in their current positions in the Pentateuch, regardless of their origins. On the front side of Mount Sinai, the water-in-the-wilderness story looks like Exodus 17:1-7 and on the back side it looks like Numbers 20:1-13. Both stories are associated with the place name "Meribah," which means "quarreling." The Exodus story also uses the place name "Massah," which means "testing." Both involve the shortage of water and subsequent complaining by the Israelites. Moses is given similar, but not identical, instructions by God in each story. In the Numbers story, which involves Aaron along with Moses, some kind of disobedience is involved for which the brothers will be punished, though it is not entirely clear what wrong they have committed.

Along with the similar stories in Numbers, these wilderness episodes in Exodus 14–17 have been labeled the "Murmuring Tradition," using the translation in the King James Version of the verb in 15:24, 16:2, and subsequent texts ("murmur," KJV; "complain," NRSV). Chapter 5 will include a complete listing of the larger collection of these kinds of stories in Numbers. Here in Exodus 14–17 there are four such stories, the first of which is the result of Pharaoh's belated pursuit of the Israelites. When trapped on the shore of the sea by the Egyptian army, the Israelites complain to Moses in 14:11-12; the result is God's deliverance from this enemy. The second and fourth stories (15:22-25 and 17:1-7) both involve complaints about thirst and the miraculous production of water by Moses. The third complaint story tells about God sending manna and quail in response to the hunger complaints of the Israelites (16:1-36).[17]

Exodus 14–15 provides an example of an interesting phenomenon. Exodus 14 contains a prose narrative account of the miraculous crossing of the "sea,"[18] while 15:1-18 is its poetic counterpoint.[19] This "Song of the Sea" is the second long poem embedded within the Pentateuch, following the Song of Jacob in Genesis 49.[20] The two accounts of the event at the sea tell essentially the same story of YHWH delivering the Israelites by drowning the Egyptian army. The prose account in chapter 14 is much more detailed, though, and it might be difficult to gain a very clear picture of the event from 15:1-18 alone. The poem, for example, does not mention a dry path through the sea with water on both sides. Thus, the preceding prose account is typically allowed to interpret the poem.

It is commonplace to criticize the behavior of the Israelites in these wilderness stories. To most readers it seems difficult to understand how this group of people who had been so profoundly liberated by YHWH could become so easily disheartened during the wilderness experience, and could even consider a seemingly faithless return to the certainty of slavery in Egypt. Closer examination of the text, however, raises some concerns about this common perception.

First, the book of Exodus, along with most of the Old Testament is reported from a heavenly point of view.[21] The reader is led to read the story

---

[17]In the book of Numbers these two items are separated into two distinct complaint stories.

[18]The identity of this body of water is problematic. "Sea of Reeds" is a more accurate English translation of *Yam Suph*. For a list and evaluation of the possibilities, see John R. Huddlestein, "Red Sea," in *The Anchor Bible Dictionary* 5:633-42.

[19]The other most prominent example of this phenomenon is the duplicate presentation of Deborah's battle against a Canaanite army in Judges 4 (prose) and 5 (poetry—the so-called "Song of Deborah").

[20]There have been other, shorter poems, such as Genesis 3:14-19, 4:23-24, 9:25-27, and 16:11-12. Readers should be aware, however, that presenting such passages as poetry by shaping the line structure is often entirely the choice of translators and editors of modern versions. The text itself does not always provide clear signals that a different mode of discourse is present.

[21]See the discussion of this literary effect in Meir Sternberg, *The Poetics of Biblical Narrative: Ideological Literature and the Drama of Reading*, Indiana Studies in Biblical Literature, 1st Midland Book ed. (Bloomington IN: Indiana

through the eyes of God, while the vantage point from earth, where we live our daily lives, is significantly different, and the sense of divine presence and guidance that is obvious when presented from above is not so obvious from below. Second, the things about which Israel complains are matters of life and death: the impending attack of the most powerful army in the world (14:10-12); the deadly thirst of the desert (15:22-25 and 17:1-7); and the painful hunger of their children (16:1-21). Finally, all of these stories, along with their reflections in the larger collection in Numbers, fit a pattern in which YHWH never provides for the Israelites until they complain. Even the initial deliverance of the Israelites from slavery comes only in response to their outcry in 2:23-25.

In light of these observations, we may be forced to ask of the text some more difficult questions, such as, What were the Israelites supposed to eat in the desert if they did not receive the manna in response to their complaints? Had there been another plan for a noncomplaining people that was disrupted by their "lack of faith"? These issues will be deferred for now until the treatment of the much larger and more highly developed set of wilderness stories in the book of Numbers, but these kinds of questions should be allowed to hover over the long and tedious collections of legal material that lie between the two wilderness accounts.

The complaint stories in Exodus 14–17 conclude with the strange story in 17:8-16 of the battle against the Amalekites at Rephidim. This battle story forms an important transition, because, unlike the earlier confrontation with the Egyptian army, this one requires the Israelites to fight the opposing army. Still, the raised arms of Moses, holding the rod of God, which helps lead them to victory, is reminiscent of Moses' hand "stretched out over the sea" (14:21). The Israelites will have to fight many more battles, beginning in the book of Numbers, but the notion that they will have to fight for themselves is initiated here.

While the account in Exodus 18 sits next to the preceding wilderness stories, it is quite different from the rest of the section, and is something of an interruption at this point. The location of Moses' rendezvous with his father-in-law is given as "the mountain of God" in 18:5, but the Israelites arrival at this mountain is not reported until 19:2. So, the story appears to be out of place and, at first glance, plays no significant role in the movement of the narrative. On further inspection, however, two important issues emerge from Exodus 18. First, it provides a sense of closure to the

---

University Press, 1987, ©1985) 12-13, 86-87.

long story of Israel's liberation, which began, in many ways, in Exodus 3 when Moses encountered YHWH while tending the sheep of his father-in-law. Therefore, bringing Jethro back to bless Moses and assist him as he tends to the needs of a different kind of flock brings an appropriate ending to this long episode. Second, the portrait of Moses as a judge points forward in the larger Exodus narrative to Moses' upcoming role as lawgiver. The story in chapter 18 depicts Moses as willing to and capable of fulfilling this role, but overwhelmed by its volume. A need for more careful organization and "statutes" (v. 20) points ahead to the function of the law that is presented in the remainder of the book.

The Beginning of the Sinai Experience

The portion of the Pentateuch that takes place while the Israelites are encamped around Mount Sinai is frequently referred to as the "Sinai Pericope." This scene is typically identified as Exodus 19:1 through Numbers 10:10, thus including all of the book of Leviticus as well. Such a designation has been a convenient means of reference for scholars of the Pentateuch, but is raises some important issues about the shape of the Pentateuch as a whole. This grouping of texts crosses the boundaries between books twice, revealing that the books of Leviticus and Numbers are not clearly separate from what precedes them. In fact, Leviticus begins with a conjunction that could be translated as "and," though modern-day translators typically choose not to include this word.[22]

Exodus 19 returns to the theme of covenant. Reminding the Israelites of their deliverance from Egypt, YHWH initiates an agreement in vv. 4-6. Moses relays the message, the Israelites agree, and preparations are made for the meeting on "the third day" (v. 11). The announcement from YHWH to Moses in 19:9b-15 is significant in what it reveals and the questions it raises. This is still a dangerous God with whom the Israelites are dealing. Proximity to YHWH in the past has crippled Jacob and nearly killed Moses, and getting to close to this God can still be deadly, as v.12 indicates. The words of YHWH also disclose who is included in the covenant ceremony.

---

[22]Older and routinely more literal translations (and their modern "revisions") do include the connective "and" (sometimes translating as "now" or "then")—KJV/NKJV, ERV, ASV/NASV, and Moffatt, as also, notably, the recent "translation" by Robert Alter of *The Five Books of Moses*—thus linking Leviticus sequentially with Exodus.

Moses' command, "do not go near a woman" (v. 15), reveals that not only are women excluded from the process, but they can even indirectly contaminate it. This is a problematic text for interpreters with feminist concerns.[23] The contents of the law will reveal at many points that its intended audience is an exclusive group of free, property-owning males, which continues to raise significant questions about the place of such texts in contemporary Judaism and Christianity. The danger of coming up on the mountain is reiterated in vv. 16-25. This speech of YHWH leads into the Ten Commandments with sufficient ambiguity that we cannot determine who is listening when YHWH speaks them.

Table 3.3

The Numbering of the Ten Commandments

	Jewish	Catholic	Orthodox	Lutheran	Reformed
20:2	1	—	—	—	—
20:3-6	2	1	1,2	1	1,2
20:7	3	2	3	2	3
20:8-11	4	3	4	3	4
20:12	5	4	5	4	5
20:13	6	5	6	5	6
20:14	7	6	7	6	7
20:15	8	7	8	7	8
20:16	9	8	9	8	9
20:17	10	9,10	10	9,10	10

The Ten Commandments, or Decalogue, are not the first laws to appear in Exodus, as the earlier discussion of Exodus 12–13 indicates, but they are the first broad collection of laws and they serve as an introduction to the portion of the book of Exodus which is composed primarily of legal material. The slightly different version of the Decalogue in Deuteronomy 5 serves a similar purpose. This is the briefest of the self-contained law codes in the Pentateuch, but the most influential. Without the overlay of more than 2,000 years of tradition, the notion that Exodus 20:1-17 consists of ten laws is not immediately obvious. The first reference to "ten words"

[23]See the discussion in Drorah O'Donnell Setel, "Exodus," in *The Women's Bible Commentary*, expanded edition, ed. Carol A. Newsom and Sharon H. Ringe (Louisville: Westminster/John Knox, 1998) 33.

written on a tablet by Moses appears in Exodus 34:28, but again it is not obvious that this is a reference to 20:1-17. That ten distinct "commandments" are not readily apparent is revealed by the multiplicity of numbering schemes used by different religious traditions as illustrated in table 3.3.

As the differing number of verses in the list in table 3.3 or a quick glance at the text of the Decalogue reveals, the commandments themselves differ greatly in length and format. The commandment against making images in 20:4 is expanded by a threat of punishment in vv. 5-6. The commandment to remember the Sabbath in 20:8 is provided with a reason in vv. 9-11. Two basic kinds of explanations may be offered for such a situation. The Decalogue may have originated as a more uniform list of brief commands, some of which were expanded over time to create the present, uneven format, or the commandments may have originated independently or in small groups which were brought together, in full or in part, in the current list. Either of these scenarios indicates a history of development of these laws before they were placed in the book of Exodus. The variations in the version of the Decalogue in Deuteronomy 5 likely demonstrate that there was more than one pathway of development for these laws. The notion of the development of law codes will be addressed further as more codes are encountered in the book of Exodus. These observations also raise important narrative questions concerning what role a particular form of the list plays in a particular position in the book of Exodus or Deuteronomy. In Exodus 20:9-11, the references to creation and Sabbath recall Genesis 1 and place the entire story line which brought the Israelites to the foot of Sinai within this framework of the establishment of Sabbath.

The giving of the Ten Commandments and Israel's response is followed immediately by what appears to be another, longer, self-contained collection of laws, referred to as the Covenant Code. Exodus 20:22–23:33 presents a body of legal material expressed in a fairly regular format. These laws govern issues such as the taking and releasing of slaves, murder and assault, property damage, and festival observance. In many cases, very specific examples are provided, along with applications of more general laws to these specific circumstances. As a result, much of what is in the Covenant Code is often defined as "casuistic" law, or case law. In opposition, the short, declarative statements like those found in the Ten Commandments are called "apodictic" law. These two categories were first delineated by Albrecht Alt, who argued that the casuistic legal tradition had Canaanite origins and that its purpose was clearly for use in ordinary legal settings.[24] On the other hand, Alt contended that apodictic laws were probably uniquely Israelite in origin and were tied to the institutions of worship.[25] These terms can be useful, but it is important to remember that they are not categories used by the biblical text itself, and that any notion of using them to establish a hierarchy of importance among the laws of the Pentateuch is entirely foreign to the text.

A careful reading of the Covenant Code immediately raises questions about the origins of the legal material in the Pentateuch. As the discussion in the introductory chapter of this book indicated, the traditional position is that God gave Moses the law intact on Mount Sinai, some in oral form and some in written form, and the written part is what ended up in the Pentateuch. Case law, however, is a legal practice that continues into the modern period, and its development is relatively easy to describe. New situations constantly arise which do not fit existing laws precisely, and judges are asked to rule on such cases by interpreting the law. The written records of these legal interpretations are preserved and become part of the basis for future decisions. In some societies, legislative bodies revise the written law to include some of this case-law material, so that over time the law grows into a very large and complex body of material. The presence of this kind of law in Exodus 21–23 raises some difficult questions about the traditional understanding of the origin of the Pentateuch. These look like the kinds of laws that develop over a long period of time, as new situations arise and must be addressed. Furthermore, the situations described in the Covenant Code sound like those that would arise in a relatively settled society, not among a roving band of fugitive slaves in the wilderness.

Furthermore, it is quite stunning that the casuistic section of the Covenant Code opens with laws concerning the management of slavery, coming so soon after the liberation of the Israelites from this hideous activity. These observations have given rise to a common alternative to the traditional position. Many interpreters now assume that the laws in the Pentateuch may have origins as early as Moses, but that the materials we have in these books were produced over a long period of time, probably many centuries, and were placed back into the mouth of Moses within the Pentateuchal narrative as a dramatic way of presenting and teaching these

---

[24] Albrecht Alt, "The Origins of Israelite Law," in *Essays in Old Testament History and Religion* (Garden City: Doubleday, 1967), 112-25.

[25] Alt, "The Origins of Israelite Law," 133-69.

legal traditions. Still others see no need or evidence to trace this legal tradition all the way back to Moses in any form.

The identification of the Covenant Code as a body of laws distinct from what is around it helped to establish the common view that the legal portions of the Pentateuch in its present form were composed from several originally independent law codes. A list of the most significant of these "law codes," along with the names that have frequently been used for them is in table 3.4.

In the final form of the Pentateuch, these legal texts have been placed within narrative contexts, so detailed discussions of these legal texts will occur at the appropriate places. At this point, however, it is also important to recognize that, as the name of the final code in table 3.4 suggests, the identification of these codes overlaps with the general effort to identify sources in the Pentateuch.

Table 3.4
Law Codes in the Pentateuch

The Decalogue	Exodus 20:2-17, Deuteronomy 5:6-21
The Covenant Code	Exodus 21:1–23:33[26]
The Holiness Code	Leviticus 17–26
The Deuteronomic Code	Deuteronomy 12–26[27]
The Priestly Code	Exodus 25–30, 35–40; Leviticus 1–15; Numbers 3–10, 27–30[28]

Some disagreements about establishing the boundaries of the Covenant Code were mentioned above, but there is a fair amount of agreement about

[26]There is some disagreement about the boundaries of this code. Often, the remaining verses of chap. 20, following the Decalogue, are included, providing boundaries of 20:22–23:33. An example of this division of the text is in R. Norman Whybray, *Introduction to the Pentateuch* (Grand Rapids MI: Eerdmans, 1995) 118-19. Still other interpreters begin the section at 21:1 but include chap. 24 as a "ritual ratification" of the document. See Sarna, *Exodus*, 117-18.

[27]The book of Deuteronomy contains other legal texts closely related to these, but this collection appears to be the core of the book.

[28]As is apparent from this list, the laws identified as priestly are dispersed throughout much of the Pentateuch. This is not an exhaustive list, and some interpreters include the Holiness Code as a subsection of the Priestly Code.

the basic outline of its content. Most of this code is a core of casuistic laws in 21:1–23:8, which follow a regular pattern of introducing a situation with a conditional clause followed by a ruling on the situation. The major areas of life covered by these laws are the management of slaves (21:1-11), infractions that receive the death penalty (21:12-17), bodily injuries (21:18-36), theft and damage of property (22:1-16), and the administration of justice and other social issues (23:1-9). The core collection of casuistic laws is bounded on either side by sets of apodictic laws in 20:23-26 and 23:10-19. The latter section deals mainly with the observance of the ritual calendar, including Sabbath observance and annual feasts. One internal section, 22:18-31, does not fit easily into this scheme. The laws in this section seem miscellaneous in both subject (e.g., sorcery, lending practices, and offerings) and form (both apodictic and casuistic forms).

Moral problems abound for modern readers of a collection of laws like the Covenant Code. Not only is slavery condoned and regulated, but its raw brutality is recognized and accepted, with only the barest of limits. The most egregious example is 21:20-21, which requires only that slaveowners avoid beating their slaves so severely that they die immediately. Passages such as 21:22 and 22:16-17 treat a fetus and an unmarried daughter as mere property of the father. On the other hand, 22:21-24 commands a rigorous defense of the vulnerable of society, including strangers, widows, and orphans. Such texts certainly leave us wondering what to do with them in the modern world. It is common for contemporary readers to choose certain, isolated legal texts which serve their purposes and urge obedience to or even enforcement of them. Careful reading of all of the legal material in the Pentateuch should raise serious questions about the validity of this practice.

The Tabernacle and the Golden Calf

Modern readers often find the second half of the book of Exodus among the most tedious portions of the Bible to read. The density of Exodus 25–40 is due partly to its content and partly to its construction. The intricate instructions for the construction of the tabernacle and its furnishings in 25:1–31:17 are difficult enough, but then they are virtually repeated in the description of the building of the tabernacle in 35–40. The concentric pattern formed by this repetition places great emphasis on what lies in the middle of this section, the series of stories associated with the making of the golden calf by the Israelites. The introduction to this chapter has already described how this construction is the inverse of the situation present in Exodus 1–18 where the predominant narrative of captivity, liberation, and wilderness surrounds the Passover legislation in chapters 12–13. These observations about chapters 25–40 lead to a clear sense that the primary concern of this large section of the book is the proper worship of YHWH.

Table 3.5 lists the primary components of the tabernacle and the parallel passages that treat each component.

Table 3.5
Components of the Tabernacle

Preparations and List of Materials	25:1-10	35:1-29
The Ark of the Covenant	25:10-22	37:1-9
Table of the Bread of Presence	25:23-30	37:10-16
The Lampstand	25:31-40	37:17-24
Framework and Curtains	26:1-37	36:8-38
The Altar of Burnt Offerings	27:1-8	38:1-7
The Court and its Components	27:9-19	38:9-20
The Priestly Vestments	28:1-43	39:1-31
The Incense Altar	30:1-10	37:25-28
The Bronze Basin	30:17-21	38:8
The Anointing Oil and Incense	30:22-38	37:29

The language, structure, and theological framework of Exodus 25–31 and 35–40 have reminded a number of interpreters, most notably Joseph Blenkinsopp, of the creation account in Genesis 1. Along with using these observations to assign this part of Exodus to the P source, Blenkinsopp and others have used them to explicate a creative purpose for a text that might otherwise seem arcane. Blenkinsopp's analysis begins with two kinds of statements, which he calls the "solemn-conclusion formula" and the "execution formula." The solemn-conclusion formula of Genesis 2:1-2, "And the heavens and the earth were finished, and God finished on the seventh day his work which he did," is reflected in similar statements in Exodus 39:32 and 40:33.[29] The execution formula, "X did according to all that YHWH had

[29]Joseph Blenkinsopp, "The Structure of P," *Catholic Biblical Quarterly* 38 (1976): 275-76. Blenkinsopp also found this formula at Joshua 19:51 along with other similarities in the land allotment portion of Joshua, creating a three-part trajectory in P from creation (Genesis 1) to the construction of the tabernacle (Exodus 25–40) to the construction of boundaries in the Promised Land (Joshua 13–22).

commanded him," in its variant forms is found at Genesis 6:22,[30] Exodus 7:6, 12:28, 36:1, and 39:1, among other texts. From these lists of common formulas, Blenkinsopp moved on to find additional parallel structures between Genesis 1:31–2:2 and Exodus 39:32, 43 and 40:33. Walter Brueggemann has taken this idea another step by dividing the instructions for the tabernacle construction in Exodus 25–31 into seven divine speeches, each beginning with the formula, "And YHWH spoke/said unto Moses. . . ." These formulas appear at 25:1, 30:11, 30:17, 30:22, 30:34, 31:1, and 31:12.[31] Most significantly, the final speech of these seven, 31:12-17, deals specifically with observance of the Sabbath, making the connection to Genesis 1 dramatic.[32]

Previous discussion has established that the development of the book of Exodus serves to focus tremendous attention on chapters 32–34, and this astounding text both deserves this attention and withstands the pressure it brings. These three chapters dealing with the golden calf episode are dense and complex and, therefore, issues concerning their composition have been the subject of intense scholarship. The rapid, spatial movement within this text begins in its opening verses. At the end of chapter 31, the reader is on the mountain with Moses while he receives the instructions for the tabernacle from YHWH, then 32:1 brings the reader to the Israelite camp at the foot of the mountain, where Moses' long absence has created concern. After the episode of idolatry in 32:1-6, the reader is quickly transported back up the mountain to hear the conversation between YHWH and Moses, who speak in turn, YHWH in vv. 7-10 and Moses in vv. 11-13. This emotional dialogue is highlighted by each speaker's attempt to disown the

---

[30]This also led to the discovery of connections between the building of the tabernacle and the building of Noah's ark. See Blenkinsopp, "The Structure of P," 283.

[31]See Walter Brueggemann, "The Book of Exodus: Introduction, Commentary, and Reflections," in *The New Interpreter's Bible*, vol. 1 (Nashville: Abingdon Press, 1994) 884ff. One difficulty with this scheme is that the seven formulae are not identical. The fifth and seventh occurrences use the verb most often translated as "said" rather than the verb translated as "spoke," which occurs in the other five. In addition, it is immediately apparent that the seven speeches vary widely in length.

[32]See further discussion in Samuel E. Balentine, *The Torah's Vision of Worship*, Overtures to Biblical Theology (Minneapolis: Augsburg/Fortress Publishers, July 1999) 136-41.

Israelites. In 32:7 YHWH refers to them as "your people," but Moses reverses this in 32:11 by using the same phrase to refer to the Israelites. The conclusion of each character's speech is carefully linked to the other's. YHWH wishes to "consume" the people and "make a great nation" of Moses, but after appealing to YHWH's reputation, Moses recalls the promises made to Abraham, Isaac, and Jacob, who should not now be replaced by Moses himself. When YHWH repents (v. 14), the reader returns with Moses to the camp where Moses witnesses the revelry, shatters the tablets, and confronts Aaron and the Israelites (vv. 15-24).

While there is an unmistakable sense of unity to the entire passage, there are forces that exert considerable internal tension. The report of Israel's initial sin, the forging of the calf (vv. 1-6), is straightforward, but YHWH's response is not. Interpreters have typically identified three different layers in this response.[33] The bulk of the remaining narrative concerns a threat of removal of YHWH's presence from among the Israelites, and Moses' attempt to keep this from happening.[34] This threat is particularly clear in 33:1-6, 7-12. The narrative is complicated, however, by a second kind of response in the story of the Levites in 32:25-34. In this episode, Moses uses the Levites to punish and purge the Israelites, and 3,000 "men" are killed. This story clearly has a purpose other than simply addressing the problem of idolatry in the golden-calf episode, and it succeeds in portraying the Levites as the tribe most loyal to YHWH. A third layer of response to the idolatry is found in the brief report of a plague in 32:35.

Another source of tension within the structure of chapters 32–34 is the passage concerning the "tent of meeting" (33:7-11). One problem with this passage is that it uses the same phrase that is sometimes used for the tabernacle in Exodus 25–31 and 35–40. The tabernacle is not built until chapters 35–40, however, and this tent in 33:7-11 seems to have a different function. The portrayal of Moses meeting with YHWH "face to face like a man speaks to his friend," a tradition affirmed in other places, such as Deuteronomy 34:10, directly contradicts the nearby tradition presented in Exodus 34:1-10, which says that Moses could not look at the face of YHWH. The interruption to the storyline created by this description of the tent, and its strain against the surrounding ideas about the relationship between YHWH and Moses,

[33]See the identification of this problem and an evaluation of various solutions in John I Durham, *Exodus* (Waco TX: Word Books, 1987) 426-27.

[34]As often elsewhere in the Old Testament, "presence" in this passage translates the word that literally means "face" (e.g., 33:14).

raises serious questions about what the passage is doing here. Even a recognition of what could be this passage's most important function, its designation of Joshua as Moses' "servant"[35] who remained permanently in the tent, does not explain its presence.

After the tent passage, Moses pleads one more time in 33:12-16 for YHWH's presence not to be removed, and YHWH agrees. Is the tent passage a diversion, allowing the necessary time to pass for this change of heart to take hold? When YHWH grants Moses' request, Moses makes another one, which leads to the dramatic encounter in 34:1-9, in which Moses seems to sense the need for a new beginning. John Durham has noted the strong connection between 33:18–34:9 and Exodus 3–4.[36] Most notable is the double declaration of the divine name in 34:6, which echoes 3:14. In this tradition, Moses cannot look at the face of YHWH, but only at YHWH's back. The creed in 34:6-7 is central to this entire passage, though it is not clear whether Moses or YHWH speaks these words. All or part of this creed is repeated at eight other places in the Old Testament.[37]

After the reaffirmation of Moses' divine encounter comes a renewal of the covenant with the people, reminiscent of Exodus 20–24. The set of laws in 34:11-26 is sometimes called the "Ritual Decalogue." It is possible, but not easy, to count ten distinct laws, and like the components of the better-known Decalogue in chapter 20 (also called the "Ethical Decalogue"), they are not uniform in length or structure. Two of the laws concern overlapping issues, not making idols and keeping the Sabbath. The remaining eight laws are primarily concerned with festivals and worship, hence the designation, "Ritual Decalogue."

This lengthy section surrounding the golden calf stumble-and-recovery concludes with the strange story of Moses' "shining face" in 34:29-35.[38]

---

[35]This is the fourth appearance of Joshua in the Exodus narrative. In 17:8-13, he is a soldier under Moses' command; in 24:13ff. (see also 32:17), he is Moses' "servant" who goes up and down the mountain with him.

[36]Durham, *Exodus*, 458.

[37]Numbers 14:18-19, Joel 2:13, Nahum 1:2-3, Jonah 4:2, Psalms 86:15, 103:8, 145:8-9, and Nehemiah 9:17. On the massive theological significance of this creedal statement, see Walter Brueggemann, *Theology of the Old Testament: Testimony, Dispute, Advocacy* (Minneapolis: Fortress Press, 1997) 215-28.

[38]The word translated "shone" in this passage has been problematic. This Hebrew verb, *qaran*, occurs in the O.T. only here (34:29, 30, 35). Its resemblance to the word for "horn" (*qeren*) caused Jerome to translate it in this direction in the Vulgate. This resulted in depictions of Moses with horns—e.g., Michelangelo's

John Durham has argued that this story functions to reassert Moses' position as the mediator between YHWH and Israel.[39] In addition, this text seems to emphasize Moses' distinct "otherness," and the foregoing experience has left him even more detached from the Israelites. The veil may serve to cover his shining face, though the reason it needs to be covered is not explained, but it also serves to separate him. Moses has become closer to a divine being, and just as Moses' ability to look at the face of YHWH is in question in 33:11 and 33:20, so is the ability of Israel to look at the face of Moses. Many interpreters have recognized the prominence of the word "face" in Exodus 32–34.[40] It appears fourteen times, though most English translations obscure this slightly by translating the occurrences in 33:14, 15 as "presence." The prominence of YHWH's "face" in 33:14-23 and Moses' "face" in 34:29-35 may now explain why the strange little passage about the tent (33:7-12), which brings Moses and YHWH "face to face," has been inserted into this narrative.

On the way out of the golden calf episode, where the presence of YHWH is under intense negotiation, we should also observe that Exodus 32–34 is framed by references to "the "bread of the presence" (literally, "the bread of the face.") in 25:30 and 35:14. This half of the book of Exodus, and perhaps the whole book, is about the presence of YHWH and how Israel should respond to that presence in worship. The false understanding that an idol made of gold or silver might embody this presence (20:4, 20, 32:1-6, 34:17) is contrasted with the idea that YHWH's presence dwells invisibly within cloud or fire among the Israelites. This is a dangerous presence, which both liberates and threatens to kill them. So, in the end, it must be properly contained within the tabernacle, the equipment for which is made from the gold of which the Israelites "plunder" themselves (33:6), the same gold which they "plundered" from the Egyptians (12:36).[41] The presence of

---

famous sculpture in St. Peter's Basilica in Rome—and the unfortunate medieval superstition that Jewish men have horns. Some modern translations, probably rightly, translate on the order of "Moses' face was *radiant*," that is, his face seemed to send out *rays* of light. Durham's suggestion has merit: "*qaran*, lit., 'sent out *horns* of light, glowed.' " See Durham, *Exodus*, 465n29c.

[39]Durham, *Exodus*, 465.

[40]See, e.g., Brueggemann, "The Book of Exodus," *NIB* 1:953-54.

[41]English translations do not translate this verb in the same way in both of these verses, thus obscuring the connection. See the discussion in McEntire, *The Blood of Abel*, 52-53.

YHWH thus absorbs the lingering lure of Egypt's wealth, and the Israelites drink the pulverized gold of the calf in 32:20. A vision of Israel's worship of YHWH, now that they have fully escaped Egypt, is established when the book of Exodus ends.

History and Exodus

The introductory chapter addressed some of the problems involved in relating the events described in Exodus to history from other sources. Some review and expansion of these issues is in order, having completed an exploration of the contents of the book. Separating historical issues related to Exodus from those related to other books leaves three important questions.

> First, was there a large group of Israelite slaves in Egypt and, if so, when?
>
> Second, did a group of Israelite slaves, under the leadership of Moses, escape from Egypt in the wake of a series of devastating disasters and, if so, when?
>
> Third, did a group of escaped slaves from Egypt travel for decades through the wilderness of the Sinai Peninsula, including a significant stop at a place they called Mount Sinai or Horeb and, if so, where is this mountain?

The immediate problem faced by an investigation of these questions is that the Bible reports all of these events, but all other sources, most significantly Egyptian records, lack any direct reference to them. The matter that is still being debated intensely is whether indirect evidence adequately supports the likelihood of these events.

In response to the first question above, it has been amply demonstrated that persons like the Israelites, seminomadic herders from the area known as "Canaan," were present in Egypt during the third and second millennia BCE. Further, there is evidence that adverse weather conditions, such as droughts, were one of the reasons they traveled there.[42] There is also significant evidence that slaves were used in Egypt during the second millennium to perform various tasks, including brick making.[43] The books of Genesis and Exodus do not mention the names of any of the pharaohs with whom the characters interact. So, while there is solid evidence for the plausibility

---

[42]See James K. Hoffmeier, *Israel in Egypt: The Evidence for the Authenticity of the Exodus Tradition* (New York: Oxford University Press, 1999, ©1996) 52-68.

[43]Hoffmeier, *Israel in Egypt*, 112-15.

of a story of slavery during the second millennium, like the story told in Exodus 1–2, it is not possible to confirm this story or to establish a more precise date for it.

The Bible itself offers two different lengths of time for the Egyptian bondage, 400 years (Genesis 15:13) and 430 years (Exodus 12:40), which are very close to each other, but these are only relative time periods which cannot be linked to a specific timetable. Something closer to a chronological designation appears in 1 Kings 6:1, which says Solomon began building the temple 480 years after the Israelites left Egypt. Since the date of Solomon's temple cannot be established with certainty, however, the biblical chronology cannot be attached to absolute dates. In addition, there is disagreement about the source of this number and its meaning.[44] The best that can be said in conclusion about this first question is that the story of Israelite bondage in Egypt generally fits what is known from other sources about the time period. This sends the question back to the burden-of-proof issue. The enslavement of the Israelite descendents of Abraham, Isaac, and Jacob cannot be proved or disproved.

The second question, concerning the historicity of Moses, the plagues, and the flight into the wilderness, faces a similar initial difficulty. No records outside the Bible make any reference to the specific events, so only indirect evidence can be gathered. The practice of bringing foreign princes into the Egyptian court for educational purposes is attested in Egyptian records,[45] so the general outline of the story of Moses' early life is plausible, even if some of the details seem unlikely.[46] There have been many attempts to associate the plague stories with observable natural events in Egypt. For some readers, this may increase the plausibility of the story, but such a practice is of little historical or theological value. Debate often centers around whether these events had a supernatural cause, and the point that is

---

[44]The Septuagint says 440 years instead, but this is not a significant difference. Some interpreters argue for a symbolic meaning for this number, based upon 12x40—that is, twelve generations of forty years each, although a generation of twenty to twenty-five years would be a better fit—and this seems likely. For a more extended discussion of the surrounding issues, see Hoffmeier, *Israel in Egypt*, 124-25.

[45]Hoffmeier, *Israel in Egypt*, 142-43.

[46]The similarity of the miraculous birth story of Moses to earlier stories from the ancient Near East, particularly the legend of Sargon, raises the possibility that it is a formulaic introduction.

often missed in such debates is that natural explanations and supernatural interpretations are not mutually exclusive. As is the case with all potential miracles, history is unable to evaluate a faith claim. Egyptian records indicate that events like those described in the plague narratives happened in ancient Egypt,[47] but, once again, only tentative conclusions can be offered about the major elements of the story of Moses and the Exodus event. They fit adequately within the picture produced by a reading of the Egyptian records, without being specifically confirmed.

Discussion of the first question above addressed the issue of chronology. The common, but uncertain, dating of Solomon's temple in the mid-tenth century, along with the 480 year notation in 1 Kings 6:1, produces a fifteenth century date for the Exodus. The name of one of the store cities built by the Israelites in the book of Exodus is "Ramses," which has generated attempts to link the story of Moses with one of the pharaohs known by this name.[48] The most commonly accepted possibility is Ramses II, who ruled Egypt in the middle of the thirteenth century. This date fits the biblical chronology fairly well, but attempts to fix a date for the Exodus always eventually become entangled with the historical problems related to the conquest events recorded in Joshua and Judges. Ultimately, this question cannot be resolved.

The third question posed at the beginning of this section is somewhat different because it lies outside of Egypt and its extensive ancient records. The biblical report of the journey in the wilderness has been measured against archaeological and geographical evidence from the Sinai Peninsula, but no identifiable evidence of a large group of slaves wandering for decades in this area has been found. Of course, one might respond by asking what kind of evidence might these people have been expected to leave behind in the first place. This is a question that eventually involves the problem of numbers in the exodus. The traditional understanding that Moses led a group of about 2,000,000 Israelites out of Egypt and into the Promised Land is based on the statement in Exodus 12:37 that the group was comprised of 600,000 adult men. Such a massive group of people would have been more likely to leave traces behind, but this number seems implausible. Not only would supplying and distributing resources for a group this large be impossible, but try to imagine any of the scenes depicted

---

[47]Hoffmeier, *Israel in Egypt*, 146-53.

[48]This tendency found popular expression in Cecil B. DeMille's film, *The Ten Commandments*, in which the Pharaoh has this name.

in Exodus involving Moses and the people using a number this large. It is possible that the number has been exaggerated for effect by adding zeroes, but a more interesting possibility involves the Hebrew word for "thousand," which contains exactly the same consonants as the military word meaning something like "troop," a group of perhaps ten or twelve soldiers.[49] "Six hundred troops of men" might be about 6,000 or 7,000, which would lead to a total number of about 20,000 people, a large, but more plausible number of people. This returns us to the question of what traces such a group might leave behind that could be found and identified 3,000 years later. The lack of archaeological evidence proves nothing one way or another about the wilderness period.

The route taken by the Israelites in the exodus and wilderness wanderings and the location of Mount Sinai present a different set of problems. The location of the mountain has been a point of significant investigation and debate. By about the fourth century CE, Christian tradition had associated "Mount Sinai" with a mountain called Jebel Musa near the southern point of the Sinai Peninsula, but there are two problems with this location. First, it is not close to a direct route from Egypt to Canaan, and second, this mountain would not have been volcanic during that time period, and many readers interpret the pyrotechnics of Exodus 19–20 with volcanic activity. A second possibility is Jebel Halal, a mountain in the northern part of the Sinai Peninsula. This mountain is on what would seem to be a more likely route from Egypt to Canaan, but would not have been volcanic, and is not a very impressive mountain. A third possible location is the mountain range in the land of Midian (modern Saudi Arabia) on the east side of the Gulf of Aqaba. The book of Exodus associates Moses' first visit to Sinai with his sojourn among the Midianites, but the extent of their territory at that time is uncertain. There would have been volcanic activity in these mountains at the time, but this would also require an unlikely route from Egypt to Canaan. Deuteronomy 1:2 says, "(It is) Eleven days from Horeb, by way of Mount Seir, to Kadesh-barnea." If this tradition is precise, then Jebel Halal is too close to Kadesh, but Jebel Musa or a Midianite location might be an appropriate distance.[50]

---

[49]See the discussion of this issue in Colin J. Humphreys, "The Number of People in the Exodus from Egypt: Decoding Mathematically the Very Large Numbers in Numbers i and xxvi," *Vetus Testamentum* 48/2 (April 1998): 196-213.

[50]See the summary of these issues related to the location of Mount Sinai in G. I. Davies, "Sinai, Mount," in *The Anchor Bible Dictionary* 6:47-49.

This inability to locate Sinai precisely reveals an important point about this Israelite tradition. It is possible that there never was a precise location connected to this tradition, but if there was, then Israel seems to have lost Mount Sinai and forgotten its location, and it is difficult to imagine that this was accidental. There would have been a good motive in ancient Israel to avoid attaching a specific location to Mount Sinai or to engage in active forgetting of that location. As a functioning pilgrimage site, Mount Sinai would have been a serious competitor with Jerusalem and other sacred sites within Israel. The Exodus journey and Sinai visit seem irretrievable as a historical event and their reenactment as a religious act is discouraged. Remember that only one person in all of the Old Testament ever tries to go back to the mountain: Elijah (1 Kings 19), and YHWH tells him to leave immediately.

Key Terms

apodictic law
casuistic law
Decalogue
Covenant Code
tabernacle
Ark of the Covenant
Passover
Yom Suph
Narrative of Oppression
Murmuring Tradition
Sinai pericope

Questions for Reflection

1. What are the problems associated with Moses as the hero of the exodus story, and how does the book of Exodus address these problems?
2. What kinds of legal texts appear in Exodus 1–18, where are they, and what function do they seem to serve?
3. What are the major bodies of legal material in Exodus 19–40, and why might they be arranged in this particular way?
4. What theological purpose(s) might the wilderness stories in Exodus serve? How do they compare to the wilderness accounts in Numbers?

Sources for Further Study

Alt, Albrecht. "The Origins of Israelite Law." In *Essays in Old Testament History and Religion*, 101-73. Translated by R. A. Wilson. Garden City NY: Doubleday, 1967, ©1966. Oxford: Blackwell, 1966. German original, 1940.

Brueggemann, Walter. "The Book of Exodus: Introduction, Commentary, and Reflections." In *The New Interpreter's Bible*, edited by Leander E. Keck et al., 1:675-981. Nashville: Abingdon Press, 1994.

Durham, John I, *Exodus*. Word Biblical Commentary 3. Waco TX: Word Books, 1987.

Britt, Brian M. *Rewriting Moses: The Narrative Eclipse of the Text.* JSOT Supplement series 402. Gender, Culture, Theory 14. London, New York: T. & T. Clark International, 2004.

Childs, Brevard S. *The Book of Exodus: A Critical, Theological Commentary*. The Old Testament Library. Philadelphia: Westminster Press, 1974.

Gowan, Donald E. *Theology in Exodus: Biblical Theology in the Form of a Commentary*. Louisville: Westminster/John Knox Press, 1994.

Hoffmeier, James Karl. *Israel in Egypt: The Evidence for the Authenticity of the Exodus Tradition*. New York: Oxford University Press, 1999, ©1996.

Pixley, George V. *On Exodus: A Liberation Perspective*. Translated by Robert R. Barr. Maryknoll NY: Orbis Books, 1987.

Propp, William H. C. *Exodus 1–18: A New Translation with Introduction and Commentary*. Anchor Bible 2. New York: Doubleday, 1999.

Sarna, Nahum M. *Exodus. The Traditional Hebrew Text with the New JPS Translation*. JPS Torah Commentary. New York: Jewish Publication Society, 1991.

Setel, Drorah O'Donnell. "Exodus." In *The Women's Bible Commentary*, expanded edition, edited by Carol A. Newsom and Sharon H. Ringe, 26-35 (same pages in the 1st ed.. 1992). Louisville: Westminster/John Knox, 1998.

Chapter 4

The Book of Leviticus

The Literary Landscape of Leviticus

It is tempting to consider the book of Leviticus the least important book in the Pentateuch. Not only do its contents seem arcane and irrelevant to modern readers, it is also buried in the middle of a five-book collection. If Genesis or Deuteronomy were removed from the Pentateuch, we would notice something missing, but if Leviticus disappeared, would we miss it? Further, it would seem impossible to remove Exodus or Numbers from the Pentateuch because each of those books transports the Israelites, first from Egypt to Sinai (Exodus), then from Sinai to the trans-Jordan (Numbers). These observations reveal that the book of Leviticus does not move the story of Israel forward, and it is not, therefore, a narrative necessity for the Pentateuch. The entire book simply sits still and talks, and we are not sure why we should care about what it is saying. Many readers have noticed that the transition directly from the end of Exodus to the beginning of Numbers would operate rather smoothly if Leviticus were absent. Exodus ends with the completion of the Tent of Meeting and the descent of the glory cloud, signaling YHWH's occupation of the new structure. The reference to YHWH's movement with Israel on their journey in the final verse of Exodus seems to have the characters in the story and the reader prepared to continue on the way through the wilderness. At the beginning of Numbers YHWH speaks to Moses in the Tent of Meeting and provides instructions for the resumption of the journey.[1] In light of this, Leviticus looks like an interruption. Even the first word of the book, from which its Hebrew name comes, sounds like an interruption. Moses has completed the manufacture of the tabernacle and suddenly *vayiqra*, YHWH "called" to (or "summoned") Moses and began to speak to him about sacrificial offerings, a subject which seems useless, or

[1]The opening chapters of the book of Numbers deal directly with the census of the Israelites, which will be discussed further in chapter 5, but Numbers 2 reveals that the structure of the census also provides the marching orders for the Israelites as they continue to move toward the Promised Land.

even counterproductive, to a group of fugitive slaves struggling to survive a perilous journey through the wilderness.

Two factors help us resist the temptation to dismiss Leviticus. First, on a small scale within individual texts, and on a moderate scale within larger sections of books, we have been observing in the Pentateuch the use of chiastic structure, a device that places emphasis on what lies at the center of a literary unit. It is possible that the entire Pentateuch operates in this way, attempting to focus our attention on its center—the book of Leviticus.[2]

Second, the idea that Leviticus is not a narrative necessity may heighten its significance in the Pentateuch, as the only book of the five that is in place largely by choice and not because the movement of the entire literary collection depends upon it. The beginning of Leviticus exhibits both continuity and discontinuity with the end of Exodus. The beginning of the book reveals that YHWH has moved. Throughout the legal portions of the book of Exodus, Moses has climbed up and down the mountain to meet and confer with YHWH. Exodus ends with the movement of YHWH, embodied in a cloud, into the Tent of Meeting, and this is where Moses is summoned to meet YHWH at the beginning of Leviticus. The connection between Leviticus and the end of the book of Exodus is emphasized grammatically by the conjunction that begins Leviticus 1:1, "*And* YHWH called to Moses. . . ."[3]

Compared to the two books that precede it in the Bible, Leviticus has a very narrow spatial and temporal scope. It all happens in one location. Very little time passes in the course of the book. As Stephen K. Sherwood has observed, the narration time, that is, the time it takes to tell the story, roughly equals the narrative time, that is, the amount of time that is passing in the story.[4] Of course, this is typical when a story is dominated by dialogue. Sherwood further notes that only twenty characters appear in the book of Leviticus, and eleven of those are mentioned only once.[5]

---

[2]The "middleness" of Leviticus is further highlighted by the longstanding observation that it contains the Pentateuch's middle verse (8:8), middle word (10:16), and middle letter (11:47). All of these middle elements are acknowledged in the marginal notes of the Leningrad Codex.

[3]See the discussion of this feature in Stephen K. Sherwood, *Leviticus, Numbers, Deuteronomy* (Collegeville MN: Liturgical Press, 2002) 3.

[4]Sherwood, *Leviticus, Numbers, Deuteronomy*, 11.

[5]Sherwood, *Leviticus, Numbers, Deuteronomy*, 20-21.

Reading Leviticus as a narrative is difficult. Both the form and content of the preponderance of legal material that makes up the book resists such a reading, but we can begin with some observations about the larger shape of the book. Leviticus falls into six major components, as follows.

Chapters 1–7	Instructions concerning sacrificial ritual
Chapters 8–10	The ordination of the Aaronide priesthood
Chapters 11–15	A collection of purity laws
Chapter 16	Observation of the Day of Atonement (*Yom Kippur*)
Chapters 17–26	The Holiness Code
Chapter 27	Laws concerning various offerings

Academic discussion of the contents of Leviticus has typically been dominated by the division of the material into what is assumed to come from the Priestly source, most of chapters 1–16, and the seemingly self-contained "Holiness Code" (H) in Leviticus 17–26. One feature that is sometimes used to distinguish these two halves of the book is that in 1–16 YHWH, through Moses, primarily addresses the priests, while the addressees in 17–26 are the people of Israel.[6] While the content of the legal material may lean in this direction, careful attention to who is being overtly addressed raises some questions about this distinction. The "Israelites" are directly addressed twelve times in 17–27, but they are directly addressed seven times in 1–15. This notion that the book of Leviticus demonstrates a sense of movement from priests to people will require further consideration as we move through the book.

One place to begin a more detailed discussion of the literary development of Leviticus is by examining the frequently occurring introductory formulae, "And YHWH spoke/said/called to Moses . . . ," which introduces the divine addresses mentioned above. Wilfred Warning has used the presence of these formulae to identify thirty-seven divine speeches in Leviticus.[7] If Warning is correct about the significance of this delineation of speeches, then it is important to note that the nineteenth speech, which is at the center of the pattern, is 16:2-34, the description of the Day of

---

[6]See, for example, Baruch Levine, *Leviticus* (Philadelphia: Jewish Publication Society, 1989) xvi.

[7]See the full list of these speeches in Wilfred Warning, *Literary Artistry in Leviticus* (Leiden: Brill, 1995) 40-42.

Atonement (*Yom Kippur*).[8] These speeches will be identified throughout this chapter at appropriate points.

Finally, it is convenient to think of the book of Leviticus as a collection of "manuals", with connecting materials: on Sacrifice (1–7), Purity (11–15), and Holiness (17–26). These terms are used frequently in the study of Leviticus and are reflected in the outline of this chapter. While this is a useful organizational scheme, the discussion below will be careful to avoid assumptions that these represent originally independent works which were brought together by an editor to form Leviticus. Evidence for and against such positions will be included in the discussion.

Instructions for Sacrifice

The previous chapter called attention to some patterns of divine speeches involved in the instructions for building the tabernacle in Exodus 25–31. The primary activity of the tabernacle, sacrificial ritual, is now prescribed in a series of divine speeches in Leviticus 1–7.[9] Table 4.1 provides an outline of these speeches.

As the second and third columns in table 4.1 indicate, there is a pattern in this "Manual of Sacrifice." Moses first speaks to the people about five different kinds of sacrifices. Terminology varies, depending on translation, so a list will help clarify the variations in name. The five sacrifices are

(1) Burnt Offering
(2) Cereal, Grain offering
(3) Peace offering, Offering of well-being, Fellowship offer(ing
(4) Sin offering, Purification offering
(5) Guilt offering, Offering of reparation.

---

[8]Warning, *Literary Artistry in Leviticus*, 39. The primary difficulty with this scheme is the identification of 16:1 by itself as a separate speech, even though it is an introductory formula followed by no actual speech content. Warning refers to this verse as a "resumptive repetition," recalling the events of chap. 10, following the long, intervening collection of purity laws in 11–15 (Warning, 43–45).

[9]Samuel E. Balentine, following Frank H. Gorman, identifies seven speeches in this sequence, which would provide an even closer match to Exodus 25–31. Neither Gorman or Balentine lists these speeches, so it is difficult to determine how they count seven. See Samuel E. Balentine, *The Torah's Vision of Worship* (Minneapolis: Augsburg/Fortress Publishers, 1999) 150-51; and Frank H. Gorman, *The Ideology of Ritual: Space, Time, and Status in Priestly Theology* (Sheffield UK: Sheffiled Academic Press, 1990) 49-50.

Table 4.1

Introductions to Divine Speeches in Leviticus 1-7[10]

Text	Command*	Sacrifice(s) Involved
1:2	Speak to the people	Burnt, Grain, Well-being
4:1	Say to the people	Sin
5:14	None	Guilt
6:1	None	Guilt
6:8	Command Aaron and his sons	Burnt, Grain
6:19	None	Anointing (given by priests)
6:24	Say to Aaron and his sons	Sin, Guilt, Well-being
7:22	Say to the people	Various sacrifices
7:28	Say to the people	Various other offerings

*For all of these, except 1:2 ("And YHWH spoke to him . . . "), the introductory formula is "And YHWH spoke to Moses. . . . "

Instructions given to the people regarding these five offerings comprise the four divine speeches in 1:1–6:7. Discussions of the details of these offerings and their meanings runs into at least two major problems. The first is that the instructions for sacrifices contain a lot of what appears to be technical language. As the list above indicates, consistent translation of this language is difficult. In addition, it is apparent at a number of places that the meanings of these technical terms shifts, even when translation is not at issue. John F. A. Sawyer has argued convincingly that terms that may have had precise technical meanings within a smaller, earlier set of instructions may not be able to retain these meanings once they become part of a large literary work like Leviticus.[11]

A second major problem, related to the first, is that too often interpreters assume that texts about sacrifice throughout the Old Testament all

[10]This list follows the introductory formulae, as identified by Warning, *Literary Artistry in Leviticus*, 40-42. Differences in chapter divisions in the Hebrew text and English text create some confusion here. In the Hebrew text, chap. 5 continues through the first seven verses of chap. 6 in the English text. The Hebrew chap. 6 begins with what the English text labels as 6:8.

[11]John F. A. Sawyer, "The Language of Leviticus," in *Reading Leviticus: A Conversation with Mary Douglas*, ed. John F. A. Sawyer (Sheffield UK: Sheffield Academic Press, 1996) 15-20.

emerge from a single, coherent system of worship, and can be used to interpret one another. This includes assuming that texts that use the same terminology, such as "burnt offerings," in narrative contexts like Genesis 8:20 or 1 Samuel 7:9, poetic contexts like Psalm 51:17 and legal contexts like Leviticus 1 can reasonably inform one another.[12] The discussion of sacrificial rituals in Leviticus 1–7 below will attempt to pay careful attention to what is in the texts, without attempting to develop precise conclusions about what is being described, or harmonizing them with distant texts to reconstruct a coherent system of sacrificial ritual in ancient Israel.

It is common to separate the first three offerings from the last two because the first three seem voluntary, while the last two are required responses to situations of sin. Within the group of three voluntary offerings, the first and third use animals, while the middle involves vegetation. The instructions for the burnt offering in 1:2-17 allows for the use of a bull (vv. 3-9), a sheep or goat (vv. 10-13), or birds (vv. 14-19). The mention of only the first two, "from the herd" and "from the flock," in the introduction in v. 2 raises the possibility that the use of birds is a later accommodation, because of logistical or economic necessity. In all of these cases, the animals are to be burned entirely upon the altar at the entrance to the Tent of Meeting, with the assistance of Aaron and his sons, the priests. The possible exception to this is the skin of the animal, which Leviticus 7:8 designates for the priests, but the relationship between these two different sets of instructions is uncertain. Although, as mentioned earlier, this is often classified as a voluntary offering, v. 5 mentions the purpose of "making atonement.' At the end of each of the three sections, the instructions state that the offering is "a pleasing odor to the LORD" (vv. 9, 13, 17). The express purpose of the burnt offering is not stated in clear terms in this passage.[13]

---

[12]Perhaps the definitive discussion to date of the "Manual of Sacrifice" is found in the magnificent commentary by Jacob Milgrom: *Leviticus 1-16. A New Translation with Introduction and Commentary*, Anchor Bible 3 (New York: Doubleday, 1991) 129-490. Still, Milgrom lacks consistency, at times admitting that sets of instructions from different sources have been mixed together in Leviticus, creating an incoherent final result (202), but at other times using information from a distant text to interpret the details of another (174-75).

[13]See Milgrom's discussion of the various meanings that might be attached to the burnt offering: *Leviticus 1-16*, 174-75.

The instructions for grain offerings in chapter 2 also list three kinds of offerings: flour (vv. 1-3), baked cakes of unleavened bread (vv. 4-10), and "first fruits" consisting of crushed, new grain (vv. 11-16). A major difference that appears in these instructions, in contrast to the burnt offerings, is that the grain items are not to be burned in their entirety. Only a "memorial portion" is burned, with the remainder retained by the priests. This reveals at least one major purpose of the grain offering: the provision of sustenance and income for the priests. Beyond that, there is no purpose provided for this kind of sacrifice, aside from the description of "a pleasing odor to the LORD."[14]

Leviticus 3 also uses a threefold pattern to describe the "(offering for a) sacrifice of well-being," again depending upon the kind of animal used: "from the herd," (that is, a cow or an ox) (vv. 1-5); "from the flock" (a sheep) (vv. 6-11); or "a goat" (from the flock) (vv. 12-17). Two major differences distinguish this offering of well-being from the burnt offering. First, the burnt offering can only be a *male* animal, while the offering of well-being can be either male or female. Second, only specific parts of the animal, such as the fat and the internal organs, are burned on the altar. While the remainder of the animal is not mentioned specifically, the presumption is that the meat serves as food and additional income for the priests. It is also possible that the meat was served immediately as part of a ritual feast, even a shared meal with the deity.

The remainder of the instructions about sacrifice, proclaimed to the people in 4:1–6:7, have a characteristic mode of address based on conditional sentences. Table 4.2 provides a list of the conditional openings of the sections in this part of Leviticus.

Table 4.2
Conditions for Sin and Guilt Offerings

4:2	If a person sins unintentionally . . .
4:13	If all the congregations sins unintentionally . . .
4:22	When a ruler sins . . . unintentionally . . .
4:27	If one person from the people of the land sins unintentionally . . .
5:1	If a person sins . . .

[14]The possible functions of the grain offerings are reviewed and evaluated by Milgrom: *Leviticus 1–16*, 195-202.

5:15	If a persons commits a trespass and sins unintentionally . . .
5:17	If a person sins . . .
6:2	If a person sins and commits a trespass . . .

The purpose of sacrificial ritual has been the subject of a great deal of scholarship. Most cultures that have practiced sacrifice, and those that still do, do not have documents defining the practice such as those like we find in the book of Leviticus. The simple, surface meaning is generally presumed to be appeasement of god(s). Outside observers, though, have often wondered if something more complex is happening in sacrificial ritual. Even in the case of the Israelites, who did produce documents that provide some explanation of sacrificial rituals, it is hard to avoid the notion that something more is going on of which the practitioners may not be fully aware.

Some of the most important of the responses to this issue have been those growing out of the work of Émile Durkheim, who has proposed that sacrificial ritual has some crucial social functions. Durkheim noted that forces of survival tend to divide societies into individuals. In contrast, rituals like sacrifice reconstitute a social group and signify an individual's place within it.[15]

A more recent, related development is found in the influential work of René Girard on the concept of "sacred violence." Girard has argued that internal conflicts build up within a society and, to keep this violence from breaking out, the society chooses and sacrifices a unanimous, innocent victim and channels its violence into the sacrifice of this victim.[16]

Further development of these kinds of proposals is not possible here, but they have sufficiently raised the possibility that much more is going on in sacrificial ritual than is immediately apparent.

The Ordination of the Priesthood

The author of the book of Leviticus has a chicken-and-egg problem. The instructions for various sacrifices in chapters 1–7 all assume the role of

[15]Émile Durkheim, *The Elementary Forms of the Religious Life: A Study in Religious Sociology*, trans. Joseph Ward Swain (London: George Allen & Unwin; New York: Macmillan, 1915) 336-49.

[16]See René Girard, *Violence and the Sacred*, trans. Patrick Gregory (Baltimore: Johns Hopkins University Press, 2005, ©1977) 78-79.

priests in the ceremonies, yet there are no priests until Aaron and his sons are ordained in chapters 8–10. On the other hand, the ordination rites of the priests in 8-10 require the use of some of the sacrificial rituals described in 1–7. This problem is only partially resolved in the final construction of the canon by the indirect introduction of the priesthood in the tabernacle passages in the book of Exodus, where the priestly vestments and ordination ceremony are described in Exodus 28–29. In fact, something of a gap exists in Exodus when the instructions for the vestments in chapter 28 are reflected by their production in chapter 39, but there is no corresponding reflection of the ordination instructions in Exodus. This gap must wait to be filled by Leviticus 8.

While Leviticus 8–10 is closely connected to the book of Exodus, particularly in the way Leviticus 8 matches Exodus 29 in almost every detail, these chapters about the ordination of Aaron and his sons are well integrated into the structure of Leviticus. Within the structure of the thirty-seven divine speeches identified by Wilfred Warning (see n. 7 above), these chapters contain speeches number 10 and 11, the latter of which, at 10:8, is notable because it is the only divine speech of the thirty-seven in Leviticus that is not addressed, at least partially, to Moses. Instead, in speech 11, Aaron is addressed by YHWH and given three commands concerning priestly behavior, which will be discussed in detail later. Divine speech number 10 begins at 8:1 and initiates the ordination procedure. Other patterns connect this section to the larger context of the Pentateuch. The priests are ordained for seven days (8:33), and the anointing oil is sprinkled on the altar seven times (8:11), which links this ordination ceremony to the seven-day creation in Genesis and to the seven speeches of the tabernacle instructions in Exodus 25–31.

Leviticus 8–10 also contains a number of internal literary features that bind its disparate components together. No less than fifteen times the reader is reminded that Moses and Aaron are doing everything as commanded by YHWH. Of the eleven occurrences of such statements in chapter 8, five use the characteristic phrase, "as YHWH commanded Moses" (vv. 9, 13, 17, 21, 29). The first and last statements, in v. 4 and v. 36, use the more complete fulfillment formula, "And X did as YHWH commanded," with slight variations, and demonstrate an important sense of movement in this chapter. In v. 4 it is Moses who does as YHWH commanded by assembling Aaron, Aaron's sons, the sacrificial animals, and other materials for the ordination ceremony. In v. 36, after all of the rites have been completed, it is Aaron and his sons who "did all of the things that YHWH commanded by the hand of Moses." The Aaronides have authority by the end of this chapter, even if it is a derivative of the authority of Moses.

Once the priests are ordained, another ceremony can take place "on the eighth day" (chapter 9). In this inaugural service a purification offering and a burnt offering are first brought for the priests themselves, then the offerings of the people are brought: a purification offering, a burnt offering, a grain offering, and an offering of well-being. The preparation of these offerings triggers the appearance of "the *glory* of YHWH" (9:23). This "glory" is not described, except for the emergence of fire from it, which consumes the sacrifices on the altar. At similar occurrences, such as the completion of the tent of meeting in Exodus 40 and the dedication of the temple in 1 Kings 8, the cloud that represents YHWH's glory is described. In the account of the temple dedication in 2 Chronicles 7, the presence of the cloud is implied, but not specifically mentioned. In the closing verses of Leviticus 9, worship has accomplished its purpose, when YHWH, Moses, the priests, and the people have all been brought together.

Leviticus 10 is the most thoroughly narrative portion of the entire book. Even the report of the first worship service in 9:8-24 still retains a sense of being a program of instruction rather than a pure story.[17] Chapter 10 begins with the deaths of two of Aaron's sons, Nadab and Abihu, and ends with an averted threat to Aaron's other two sons, Eleazar and Ithamar. In neither case is the precise nature of their offense clear, but this is especially so in the case of Nadab and Abihu. Two very different views of their deaths have developed in various traditions. In one view, they committed some kind of infraction and were punished. Perhaps the command about priests not drinking alcohol before performing their duties in v. 8 indicates the Nadab and Abihu were drunk when they entered the tent.[18] Others have viewed their deaths as an act of sanctification, a completion of the sacrificial rites that inaugurated the worship of Israel. This was the view of the ancient Jewish philosopher, Philo (*On Dreams* 2.67), and is also expressed in

---

[17]Gerstenberger has commented on this aspect of Leviticus 8–9. See Erhard S. Gerstenberger, *Leviticus: A Commentary*, trans. Douglas W. Stott (Louisville: Westminster/John Knox, 1996) 101-105.

[18]This view is expressed by one of the rabbinic voices in an ancient commentary called *Leviticus Rabba*. See James Kugel's discussion of this and other ancient interpretations in *Traditions of the Bible: A Guide to the Bible as It Was at the Start of the Common Era* (Cambridge MA: Harvard University Press, 1998) 744-45.

Leviticus Rabba. It may be supported in the text by the statement that "they died before YHWH" in 10:3 and the command that Aaron not mourn their deaths in v. 6.[19]

In the second half of chapter 10, Eleazar and Ithamar carry on with the priestly duties and fall into a dispute with Moses about the eating of offerings. Though vv. 17-18 indicate that Eleazar and Ithamar did not eat this offering properly, it is not clear whether they ate it in the wrong place or failed to eat it at all. Aaron offers an explanation that is even more cryptic, but that appears to satisfy Moses and serves to avoid any punishment of Aaron's remaining two sons.

In this kind of literary construction, where two similar stories frame a set of instructions, one would expect that the stories help to interpret the laws. The instructions come in four sets of commands:

(1) Not to mourn the deaths of Nadab and Abihu.[20]
(2) Not to drink alcohol before going into the tent of meeting.
(3) To distinguish between holy and common, clean and unclean.
(4) To teach the statutes to the people of Israel.

Certainly the handling of the bodies of Nadab and Abihu (10:4-5) is related to the instructions concerning mourning (vv. 6-7). The intricacies of ritual and the high cost of an error in both of the framing stories would explain the need for sobriety and careful instruction, as in vv. 8-11. The commands about handling and eating sacrifices in vv. 12-15 seem to have some relation to the story of Eleazar and Ithamar, although, as Erhard Gerstenberger notes, their mistake seems more likely a violation of the instructions in 6:26 and 29.[21] Aaron's satisfactory explanation (10:19-20), however it may have been so, demonstrates his abilities to distinguish and instruct.

By fulfilling or completing both the tabernacle construction from Exodus 35–40 and the Manual of Sacrifice in Leviticus 1–7, the stories of the ordination of the Aaronides and their inauguration of worship

---

[19]See Kugel, *Traditions of the Bible*, 745-46.

[20]It is unclear whether this instruction is a more extensive prohibition against priests mourning any death, a command which would have had some practical benefit since contact with dead bodies would have rendered the priests "unclean" and unable to perform their duties.

[21]Gerstenberger, *Leviticus*, 120.

synthesizes two traditions and prepares the way for Leviticus to continue to move on to other issues in the life of the Israelite community.

The Purity Laws

The ordination texts in Leviticus 8–10 end with a concern about proper eating, providing a transition into the dietary laws of chapter 11, which begin the section of legal material in chapters 11–15. There is enough of a sense of cohesion in this collection of legislation on diverse issues to have earned the section the designation, "The Manual of Purity." The current chapter divisions in Leviticus 11–15 follow the pattern established by the concluding statement, "This is the law/ritual for ______," which appears near the end of each chapter (11:46, 12:7, 13:59, 14:54, and 15:32), producing sections with fairly distinct concerns as each relates to purity:

Chapter 11. Diet
Chapter 12. Childbirth
Chapter 13. Skin Diseases
Chapter 14. Purification after a Skin Disease
Chapter 15. Genital Discharges

In many ways, the concerns of this chapter flow out of the command given by Moses to Aaron and his sons in 10:10 to "divide/distinguish between the holy and the common/profane, and between the unclean and the clean." The language of this verse recalls the creative acts of God in Genesis 1, and the echoes of Genesis 1 continue throughout these chapters that make up the Manual of Purity. The concern for order in creation is reflected in the concern for order in the daily lives of the Israelites. This section contains six divine speeches, numbers 12-17 (see n. 7 above) in Leviticus, which are listed in table 4.3, along with their opening addresses.

Table 4.3
Introductions to Divine Speeches in Leviticus 11–15

11:1	And YHWH spoke to Moses and Aaron . . .
12:1	And YHWH spoke to Moses . . .
13:1	And YHWH spoke to Moses and Aaron . . .
14:1	And YHWH spoke to Moses . . .
14:33	And YHWH spoke to Moses and Aaron . . .
15:1	And YHWH spoke to Moses and Aaron . . .

While these introductory formulae are not perfectly consistent, it is apparent that the status of Aaron has been elevated in the wake of the ordination ceremony.

Many of the issues raised by the dietary laws at the head of this section will persist throughout chapters 11–15. While the discussion of eating at the end of chapter 10 makes for a sensible transition into the dietary laws, the presence near their conclusion of the dramatic statements in 11:44-45 may provide another reason that they appear first in the collection. The command to "be holy, for I am holy" is often understood to express the central theme of the entire book of Leviticus.[22] Interpretive discussions of the dietary laws typically center themselves around the origins and purpose of these regulations which sound so strange to the modern ear. A basic question to begin with ought to be whether these laws precede or succeed the behaviors they describe. This question may be expressed clearly in relation to the dietary laws. Do these regulations set forth a consciously developed, new diet for their audience, or do they describe and codify a diet already in existence? One important, if obvious, observation is that the dietary laws address only the eating of animals, so all plant life must have been considered clean and acceptable for eating.[23]

There have been a number of different lines of argument attempting to explain the dietary laws. One possibility is that they were intended to keep Israel from being corrupted by its neighbors. For example, Israelites may have been forbidden from eating pigs because these were used in sacrificial rituals and eaten among surrounding Canaanite and Hittite groups. While it seems likely that issues of cultural identity are involved in the purity laws, this approach fails as a comprehensive way of understanding the dietary regulations. Surely, most of Israel's neighbors also sacrificed and ate cows, sheep, and goats, and these are not forbidden. Another possible approach is that these laws had something to do with health and hygiene. The law

[22]Variations on this central theme as stated in 11:44, 45 also occur at 19:2, 20:7, 26.

[23]This may relate back to the creation account in Genesis 1, which assumes that the initial diet of humans was vegetarian, and that meat was only added after the flood. In Genesis 1:29 God gives to humans and animals "all plants bearing seed upon the face of all the earth, and all trees which bear seed in the fruit of the tree." Of course, in light of the wording of Genesis 1:29, we might wonder why there were not dietary regulations defining exactly which plants qualified as "seed bearing."

forbidding the eating of blood required meat to be prepared in a certain way that might have avoided the spread of disease. In addition, the extension of this law that disallowed eating any animal that eats blood might have prevented the spread of disease from carrion. Interpreters who have taken this course, however, have not established a clear, medical rationale that explains this entire system of laws.[24]

A more thorough attempt to explain the dietary laws has come from a prominent anthropologist named Mary Douglas, whose famous essay, "The Abominations of Leviticus," which appeared in her 1966 book, *Purity and Danger*, has had significant influence on the interpretation of this part of Leviticus over the last few decades. Douglas relates purity to holiness and, ultimately, to wholeness or completeness, the completeness of creation. Using the three animal categories from Genesis 1—water, land, and sky—Leviticus 11 declares unclean the animals that do not fit into this sense of wholeness by matching their categories: for example, fish without fins, or birds that do not fly, or "swarming things" that do not move in a definite direction.[25] It is not always clear in Douglas's essay whether the dietary laws had an external purpose corresponding to this internal purpose of defining wholeness. In her words:

> To be holy is to be whole, to be one; holiness is unity, integrity, perfection of the individual and of the kind. The dietary laws merely develop the metaphor of holiness along the same lines.[26]

Douglas's proposal makes significant progress against another common assumption, that the dietary laws are entirely arbitrary, but falls short of determining how they accomplish their purpose. Did a significant number of people in ancient Israel really eat this way, or is Leviticus 11 primarily a literary construct that "develops a metaphor"?

Of course, these dietary laws did become a major component of Judaism, and they persist into the modern era in the system of *Kashrut*, the Jewish dietary system that was developed out of Leviticus 11 and the related set of regulations in Deuteronomy 14. But our primary concern is

---

[24]See the discussion of these proposals and others in W. H. Bellinger Jr., *Leviticus, Numbers* (Peabody MA: Hendrickson, 2001) 71-72.

[25]Mary Douglas, *Purity and Danger: An Analysis of Concepts of Pollution and Taboo* (New York: Routledge, 1970) 65-70.

[26]Douglas, *Purity and Danger*, 66.

how these laws function within the world of Leviticus.[27] By speaking about food, which became an issue in sacrificial ritual in chapter 10, the book of Leviticus enters into the world of the daily life of Israelites in chapter 11, a chapter that ends with the resulting discussion of how contact with unclean animals should be handled.

The application of this notion of purity to the daily life of Israel continues in chapter 12 with issues surrounding the birth process. The dietary laws in chapter 11 were stunningly silent about their own rationale, never explaining why chewing cud or a split hoof makes an animal clean. The regulations concerning childbirth are equally reticent. Why does giving birth make a woman "unclean." Why is she unclean for twice as long after giving birth to a female child? This may have been the result of a general sense of mystery and fear surrounding life-and-death issues, like childbirth. It may have served to provide the mother with a period of recovery by separating her from the normal activities of life for a while. Such explanations are never fully satisfying, though. Milgrom has demonstrated that the regulations surrounding birth in Leviticus are consistent with widespread practices in other ancient Near Eastern cultures of the time, so no explanation peculiar to Israelite culture or religion can suffice.[28]

From childbirth, the text moves on to skin diseases in chapters 13–14, an aspect of life in which the priests, whose absence in the previous two chapters is surprising, play a major role, inspecting, diagnosing, and quarantining victims. Leviticus 13 discusses what appears to be a wide range of skin diseases and, concerning the issue of purity, it is difficult to deny the obvious, commonsense explanation of purpose. Many skin diseases are highly contagious and extremely dangerous. The closing verses of this chapter even extend to the treatment of clothing that has been potentially contaminated by such diseases. Chapter 14 follows logically by describing processes for returning to clean status and normal life within the community. The role of the priests and the use of various offerings that had

---

[27]For more on the later development and use of dietary laws within Judaism, see Harry Rabinowicz, "Dietary Laws," in *Encyclopedia Judaica Jerusalem*, 16 vols. (Jerusalem: Keter Publishing House, 1972) 6:120-40; or Harry Rabinowicz and Rela Mintz Geffen, "Dietary Laws," *Encyclopedia Judaica*, 2nd ed., 22 vols. (New York: Macmillan, December 2006) 5:650-59. The 2nd ed. "Dietary Laws" article also is available online: <http://www.encyclopaediajudaica.com/efiles/Dietary.pdf>.

[28]See Milgrom, *Leviticus 1-16*, 749-65.

been described in Leviticus 1–7 serve to integrate this chapter into the world of the book of Leviticus.

An important issue arises at 14:21 more overtly than in previous regulations concerning sacrifice. The various requirements for sacrificial offerings, whether related to purification or ordinary services of worship, assume significant economic means. In Leviticus 1 the procedures for burnt offerings are listed for animals of descending value, but there is no explicit statement about the differing abilities of worshippers to afford these offerings. In the childbirth regulations in chapter 12, v. 8 appends the use of birds instead of sheep, with a more explicit acknowledgement of economic hardship, "If she cannot afford. . . . " After the instructions for purification of disease in 14:1-20, the next verse opens with, "But if he is poor and cannot afford so much," then proceeds through a list describing less costly offerings in vv. 21-32. The remainder of chapter 14 then addresses procedures for purifying a house that is contaminated by skin disease.

The final chapter in the Manual of Purity deals with the uncomfortable subject of genital discharges. This subject has already been raised to a minor extent in chapter 12, where the regulations about childbirth were surely connected in part to the continuing discharges that follow the birth process. Chapter 15 begins with the effects of a genital discharge on a man's purity status. Interpreters have long noticed a pattern in the four primary sections of this chapter. The outer sections, vv. 1-15 and vv. 25-30, deal with prolonged, abnormal discharges of men and women respectively. Such discharges are presumably related to disease, and the extent of their effects is great. Sacrifices are required in order to restore purity once the discharge has ended (vv. 14-15 and vv. 29-30). The two middle sections, vv. 16-18 and vv. 19-24, deal with normal emissions, the emission of semen from a man during sexual intercourse and the emission of blood from a woman during menstruation. Both of these activities bring about a state of impurity, but purity is restored more easily by bathing and a brief waiting period. Chiastic constructions like this, on a variety of scales, are common in Leviticus and have been cataloged extensively.[29] The text provides no sense of how these regulations, regarding what would seem to be intensely private matters, might be enforced.

[29]See, e.g., Warning, *Literary Artistry in Leviticus*, 82-100; and Milgrom, *Leviticus 17-22*, 1319-25.

The Day of Atonement

Leviticus 16 is the most well-known chapter in the book, because of the use of the Day of Atonement (*Yom Kippur*) traditions in both Judaism and Christianity. The relationship of this chapter to the rest of the book is an issue of some complexity. Wilfred Warning identified 16:1 as the eighteenth divine speech in Leviticus and 16:2-34 as the nineteenth, and central, speech of the thirty-seven total (see n. 7). The problems involved in identifying 16:1 by itself as a divine speech were mentioned above. There is no actual content of a divine speech here to accompany the introductory formula.[30] Further, this verse functions to resume the narrative flow of the book following the lengthy diversion into the Manual of Purity (chapters 11–15). As the most important of all priestly functions, presiding over the Day of Atonement, is about to be addressed, the recalling of the deaths of Aaron's two elder sons is a reminder that the priestly function is serious, deadly business. The introductory formula in 16:2 is also a point of difficulty because it differs from all others except 21:1.

The position of the Day of Atonement ritual in 16:2-34 is curious, given the presence of a full festival calendar in chapter 23, which includes a significantly different presentation of the Day of Atonement (23:26-32).[31] Internally, however, 16:2-34 provides a fascinating and powerful display of religious ritual. Understanding this description requires some awareness of the temple/tabernacle layout, as described in Exodus 25–40. The Ark of the Covenant sits in the innermost part, which is only to be entered by the high priest on this particular day. The Hebrew word for "atonement," *kippur*, does not appear in this text, but the name for the "mercy seat" or cover of the ark (16:14), *kapporet*, is derived from the same root word. The sacrifices involve separate sin offerings and burnt offerings for the high priest and the people.

Two features distinguish this ritual from other sacrifices in Leviticus. First, the blood of the bull that is a sin offering for Aaron is taken inside the inner room and sprinkled on the mercy seat itself. Second, two additional goats are brought for a unique ritual act. After being designated by casting lots, one of these goats is assigned to "Azazel," a character (?) mentioned nowhere else in the Old Testament except here at 16:8, 10, and 26. The

[30]See the discussion in Warning, *Literary Artistry in Leviticus*, 42-46.

[31]See the discussion of this issue in Gerstenberger, *Leviticus*, 213.

identity of this being has been a point of much discussion but few useful conclusions. This goat, traditionally called the "scapegoat" (that is, "escape-goat"), is used in vv. 20-22 to carry away the sins of Israel.[32] A full understanding of this aspect of the Day of Atonement seems hopelessly lost in antiquity.

Leviticus 16 becomes even more complicated and difficult to follow in vv. 15-28. It is not clear that all of the components of this chapter come from a unified source and fit easily together. The conclusion in vv. 29-34 speaks to the perpetual observation of the Day of Atonement and uses the language of Sabbath (v. 31) to describe it in a way that connects this chapter more closely to the parallel text in 23:26-32. This could be seen as the hand of the final author of Leviticus weaving together diverse materials into a coherent whole.

The Holiness Code

The notion that Leviticus 17–26 is a distinct, unified literary work, and the eventual attachment of the label "Holiness Code" (H) to it, developed through the work of several German scholars in the second half of the nineteenth century, notably Karl Heinrich Graf and August Klostermann.[33] Since then, this assumption and the terminology that accompanies it have become commonplace in Old Testament scholarship. The most certain aspect of this position is the sense that 26:46 is bringing something to a close. This verse uses three synonyms, sometimes translated as "statutes," "ordinances," or "laws," to summarize what has come before it. Two of these words, "statutes" and "ordinances," appear at the beginning of chapter 18 and frequently throughout chapters 18–26. "Statutes" appears in chapter 16 and "laws" appears exclusively in chapters 11–15. The use and arrangement of these words in 26:46 brings to a close a section that may begin at either 17:1 or 18:1, and it also appears to draw together all of the material from chapters 11–26.[34] So, even if 17–26 or 18–26 is an originally independent unit, it has been woven into the book of Leviticus with deliberate care.

---

[32]It should be noted that the specific instructions for sending off the "goat" in vv. 20-22 do not mention "Azazel."

[33]See the very through review of the history of scholarship on this subject in John E. Hartley, *Leviticus*, Word Biblical Commentary 4 (Waco TX: Word Books, 1992) 247-60.

[34]See the discussion of this feature in Hartley, *Leviticus*, xxxiii.

Leviticus 17–26 contains seventeen divine speeches, which are marked by introductory formulae as demonstrated in table 4.4. (The divine speech introduced at 27:1 is included in the table.)

Table 4.4
Introductions to Divine Speeches in Leviticus 17–27

17:1	And YHWH spoke to Moses: Speak to Aaron and his sons
18:1	And YHWH spoke to Moses, . . . Speak to the people of Israel
19:1	And YHWH spoke to Moses, . . . Speak to . . . the people of Israel
20:1	And YHWH spoke to Moses, . . . Say . . . to the people of Israel
21:1	And YHWH *said* to Moses: Speak to the priests, the sons of Aaron
21:16	And YHWH spoke to Moses, . . . Speak to Aaron
22:1	And YHWH spoke to Moses, . . . Direct Aaron and his sons
22:17	And YHWH spoke to Moses, . . . Speak to Aaron and his sons
22:26	And YHWH spoke to Moses, . . .
23:1	And YHWH spoke to Moses, . . . Speak to the people of Israel
23:9	And YHWH spoke to Moses: Speak to the people of Israel
23:23	And YHWH spoke to Moses, . . . Speak to the people of Israel
23:26	And YHWH spoke to Moses, . . .
23:33	And YHWH spoke to Moses, . . . Speak to the people of Israel
24:1	And YHWH spoke to Moses, . . . Command the people of Israel
24:13	And YHWH spoke to Moses, . . .
25:1	And YHWH spoke to Moses . . . Speak to the people of Israel
27:1	And YHWH spoke to Moses, . . . Speak to the people of Israel

A number or formal elements link various groupings of these units together, and will be observed throughout this section. One feature that is extensive enough to note at the beginning is a sequence of five "exhortations"[35] which fall at the ends of various chapters in the current divisions.

[35]This term is used by Blenkinsopp, who divides Leviticus 17–26 into sections based on the use of these exhortations as "homiletic conclusions." See Joseph Blenkinsopp, *The Pentateuch: An Introduction to the First Five Books of the Bible* (New York: Doubleday, 1992), 224. It should be noted that Blenkinsopp argues against the independent existence of H before the placement of these chapters in Leviticus.

These appear at 18:24-30, 20:22-26, 22:31-33, 25:18-24, and 26:3-45, building to a crescendo at the end of this portion of Leviticus.

Leviticus 17 has long been a matter of dispute, even among those who support the idea of a distinct "Holiness Code." The preoccupation with sacrifice in this chapter, for example, causes Gerstenberger to associate it more closely with chapter 16.[36] The primary issues in chapter 17 are improper sacrifice and improper killing of animals, and in some ways the chapter looks like a case-law addendum to Leviticus 1–7. The major concern is the consumption of blood, which is completely forbidden for Israelites. The repeated notion that "the life of the flesh is in the blood" (17:11) or "the life of all flesh is its blood" 17:14) runs counter to the notion elsewhere in the biblical tradition that breath is the animating force (Genesis 1–2).

A more regular pattern begins in Leviticus 18, and chapters 18–20 are often treated as a cohesive unit. In this diverse collection of laws concerning everyday issues, two grammatical forms dominate, negative commands beginning with "You shall not . . . " (18:11, 19; 19:11, 13; etc.) and conditional statements beginning with "If/when a person. . . . " The former is more common at the beginning of the section and the latter at the end. Some prominent clusters require special mention.

First, most of chapter 18 contains a long list of negative commands related to sexual impropriety, including incest (vv. 6-18), sexual relations during menstruation (v. 19), adultery (v. 20), sexual relations between two men (v. 22), and sexual relations with animals (v. 23). The condemnation of child sacrifice in v. 21 in the midst of this list is something of a surprise.

Second, chapter 19 is marked by the repeated punctuating remark, "I am YHWH" (eight times) or "I am YHWH your God" (eight times). This phrase is dispersed within a diverse set of commandments, which interpreters for many centuries have attempted to connect to the Ten Commandments. The list does address idolatry (v. 4), using God's name falsely (v. 12), honoring parents (v. 3), keeping Sabbath (v. 3), killing (v. 18), stealing (v. 11), and false testimony (vv. 11, 16). Still, there is much additional material in the chapter that does not relate easily to the Ten Commandments, and it would be very difficult to explain the rationale for such rearrangement.[37]

---

[36]Gerstenberger, *Leviticus*, 234-40.

[37]See the discussion and evaluation of various proposals in Milgrom, *Leviticus 17-22*.

Finally, 20:10-21 moves this section toward its end with a list of conditional laws concerning inappropriate sexual relations, which closely matches those at its beginning in 18:6-23.

A shared concern for the function of priests and the conduct of sacrifices link chapters 21 and 22 together, but these chapters are also linked to the preceding ones by the commands to holiness found in 19:2, 20, 26 and 21:6, 8. Chapter 22 does not contain one of these commands, but the word "holy" appears a remarkable fourteen times in its thirty-three verses.[38] As this chapter gives careful attention to the appropriate nature and use of offerings, it makes use of the punctuating phrase, "I am YHWH"—so common in chapter 19—six times, at 22:9, 16, 27, 31, 32, and 33.

As mentioned earlier, Leviticus 23 contains a festival calendar, one of four such "calendars" in the Pentateuch, which are difficult to reconcile with one another. A summary of their contents is presented in table 4.5

Table 4.5
Festival Calendars in the Pentateuch

Festival	Ex. 23	Lev. 23	Num. 28-29	Deut. 16
Sabbath	vv. 12-13	v. 3	28:9-10	---
Passover/ Unleavened Bread	vv. 14-15	vv. 4-8	28:16-25	vv. 1-8
Weeks	v. 16	vv. 15-21	28:26-30	vv. 9-12
Trumpets	---	vv. 23-25	29:1-6	---
Atonement	---	vv. 26-32	29:7-11	---
Booths	v. 16	vv. 33-36	29:12-38	vv. 13-15

The existence of multiple calendars in the Pentateuch is a puzzling feature.[39] There seems to be one for each of four major law codes: the Covenant Code (Exodus 23), the Holiness Code (Leviticus 23), the Priestly Code (Numbers 28-29), and the Deuteronomic Code (Deuteronomy 16). As the table demonstrates, the Covenant Code contains the briefest calendar, with three festivals, and the Deuteronomic calendar looks like an expanded version of this three-festival calendar. The H and P calendars both contain six

[38]English translations often use the word "sanctify" to translate the verbal form of this word, which can be rendered "to make holy."

[39]For a more thorough discussion, see James C. Vanderkam, "Calendars," in *The Anchor Bible Dictionary* 1:814-20.

festivals and are quite close in detail, with the festival of Booths as their greatest point of departure. Historical-critical arguments have attempted to explain the similarities and differences among these calendars and to establish their origins, but have not yielded results with reasonable certainty.

The festival calendar in Leviticus 23 is followed by a diverse collection of materials, as the contents of the book of Leviticus begin to look more like an appendix. Instructions about the lamp (24:1-4) and the bread (24:5-9) may be something of a corrective to religious practices that focus too intensely on the festivals in the previous chapter, because these are items that require daily or weekly attention throughout the year. Gerstenberger described the intent of 24:1-9: "The uninterrupted light and perpetually present bread are to be observed in addition to the holiday events themselves."[40]

The following text, 24:10-23, is more of an anomaly in this position. The story of a blasphemer, who is brought to Moses and subsequently stoned (24:10-12 and v. 23), serves as a narrative framework for a set of laws in 24:13-22 that includes instruction about blasphemy. The legal core of this passage also addresses property damage, injury, and murder, in a way that echoes the "Law of Retaliation" (*lex talionis*) in Exodus 21:12-27. The idea that holds this legislation together is that the laws should be applied equally to Israelites and non-Israelites. The framing narrative is partly on point because the blasphemer is half Israelite and half Egyptian.

Leviticus 25 contains another unit, legislation concerning the Sabbath year and the Jubilee year, which does not fit easily into its context. The introductory formula in 25:1, "And YHWH spoke to Moses on Mount Sinai, . . . " stands out in Leviticus, because the setting for all of the divine speeches to Moses thus far has been the tent of meeting (Leviticus 1:1).[41]

---

[40]Gerstenberger, *Leviticus*, 355.

[41]"Sinai" is mentioned as a general location for the book of Leviticus at 7:38, 26:46, and 27:34 ("*on* Sinai"). Milgrom discusses several proposed solutions to this problem. The text could be indicating that the content of this speech was given to Moses earlier, an idea reflected in a pluperfect translation: "And YHWH *had spoken* to Moses on Mount Sinai." The verb form here, however, matches that used in all of the other divine speeches in Leviticus. The setting of the preceding story of the blasphemer could be understood as a different location, requiring the narrator to bring the reader back to Sinai at 25:1. See Milgrom, *Leviticus 23-27*, 2151-52. Perhaps, in conjunction with this second possibility, the ambiguity of the preposition—which also could mean "*at* Mount Sinai" or "*by* Mount Sinai"—should be noted.

These laws also have much more to do with the social and economic obligations of the community, rather than just the behavior of individuals. The Sabbath year legislation in 25:1-7 might seem fairly practical and realistic, but a purpose is not provided here, and a thorough application of this law could be extremely problematic. Is the rest during the seventh year supposed to benefit YHWH, the land, or the people who cultivate the land? The references to the land Sabbath in Leviticus 26:34 and 2 Chronicles 36:21 raise the possibility that this idea is primarily a theological explanation for the Exile, rather than realistic legislation.

The Jubilee legislation in Leviticus 25:8-55 seems even more unrealistic. Interpreters have long noted that the provisions of the Jubilee, such as releasing of slaves, return of property, and erasing of debts would be difficult to carry out, and historians have found little evidence that they were applied.[42] It seems more likely that the Jubilee year is intended to provide an imaginative vision of a world that emphasizes economic justice and continuing deliverance from oppression.[43] On the other hand, Gerstenberger has pointed to "edicts of release and remissions of debt" issued by Babylonian kings during periods of economic crisis,[44] while Milgrom has argued more extensively that Jubilee years may have been observed in Judah around 688, 638, 588, 538, 488, and 438 BCE.[45]

Leviticus 26 contains a list of rewards and punishments (vv. 3-13 and 14-39) that can be expected as a result of obedience or disobedience to God's commands. Ending a law code or covenant with a list such as this was common in the Ancient Near East.[46] Leviticus 26 begins with a repetition of the commands not to make idols and to keep the Sabbath. These commands are punctuated at the end of v. 2 with the statement, "I am YHWH," which connects this text to such statements in chapters 19, 22, 23, 25, and 26. The blessings of obedience are described in vv. 3-13, followed by a more detailed set of potential punishments in vv. 14-39. Some interpreters have divided these two sections into five distinct rewards and

[42]See the discussion in Bellinger, *Leviticus, Numbers*, 149.

[43]This is how the synagogue sermon of Jesus in Luke 4:18-19 seems to make use of this tradition.

[44]Gerstenberger, *Leviticus*, 393.

[45]See Milgrom, *Leviticus 23-27*, 2257-69.

[46]A more complete treatment of this issue will appear in chap. 6 below, in the discussion of Deuteronomy 29–30.

five distinct punishments.[47] The punishments are laid out in a pattern of ascending severity (vv. 18, 21, 24, and 28), which ends with the destruction of Israel and the dispersal of the Israelites in vv. 32-33. Along with the continuing sense of choice described in vv. 34-35, this passage demonstrates an awareness of the Exile and restoration, which now serve as an object lesson.[48] Before the concluding statement in 26:46, a final occurrence of the punctuating phrase, "I am YHWH," appears in v. 45.

Leviticus 27 is the thirty-seventh, and final, divine speech in the book, and the content of this chapter forms an even more diverse and disconnected appendix than previous chapters. The dissolution of coherence at the end of Leviticus returns us to the challenge of reading it as a complete and unified book, but the beginning of the chapter discusses vows, and this discussion moves into instructions concerning various offerings, so the book of Leviticus ends on the same subject with which it began, demonstrating a sense of circularity that has been observed on many scales throughout this literary work.

History and Leviticus

The few events described in Leviticus, such as the ordination of Aaron and his sons or the stoning of the blasphemer (24:10-23), are not the kind of events that would leave behind extrabiblical evidence, either in the form of texts or artifacts. The encampment of the Israelites at a place called Mount Sinai for about a year might, but the problems related to this were addressed at the end of the previous chapter. The only evidence that YHWH actually spoke these words to Moses, while the Israelites were camped in the wilderness sometime in the first half of the second millennium BCE, is precisely these texts themselves.[49] This position falls victim to the assumption that the only way the Bible can be authoritative is if the formula, "And YHWH spoke to Moses," is a literal description of a historical event. This attachment of authority to history refuses the possibility that the

---

[47]See, e.g., Milgrom, *Leviticus 23-27*.

[48]Milgrom has argued, based on the reference to plural "sanctuaries" in 26:31 and other factors, that this does not refer to the Babylonian invasion. Milgrom, *Leviticus 23-27*, 2321.

[49]See Hartley, *Leviticus*, xli-xlii, for a modified, traditional position which accepts divine revelation to Moses as a starting point of Leviticus, but relegates later developments in the book to the status of "scars of a long history of transmission."

Sinai setting and the presentation-to-Moses framework were used for dramatic purposes, and that the genre of literature such a process might yield need not be any less authoritative than a simple historical account.

Once the composition of Leviticus is detached historically from Moses and the Sinai setting and evidence, rather than *a priori* assumptions, is used to try to determine a date for its composition, the arguments become somewhat diverse. Milgrom, for example, has argued for a preexilic date for most of Leviticus, perhaps in the seventh or eighth century.[50] Thus, much of Leviticus reflects worship practice in Solomon's temple. Gerstenberger, on the other hand has proposed a sixth century, exilic date for the production of most of Leviticus, though some of the materials in the book may be considerably older.[51] Neither Milgrom nor Gerstenberger gives as much attention to a historical setting for the final form of the book of Leviticus as they do for the composition of 1–16 and 17–26, though in Milgrom's argument for a preexilic date for H, he assigns small portions to a postexilic redactor, who might be assumed to be the one who brought the full book together.[52] This would admit a postexilic date for the final form of Leviticus.

The book of Leviticus would have done two important things for a community that had suffered exile. First, with the curses in chapter 26, it explains the cause of exile. This explanation even accounts for the long delay of this ultimate punishment through its succession of the intensifying results of disobedience. Included along with this explanation of the Exile is a way to experience worship through the act of reading, during a period when the actual performance of worship was not possible, and a program for reestablishing worship after the Exile comes to an end.

A second, and lesser task, performed by the book of Leviticus is the legitimization of the priestly descendents of Aaron, who were likely in conflict with other groups of priests, particularly in the postexilic period. One of the questions that many arguments seems to ignore is why a book

---

[50]See Milgrom, *Leviticus 1-16*, 3-34. This argument is based primarily upon vocabulary and a perceived dependence of Deuteronomy on P material in Leviticus.

[51]See Gerstenberger, *Leviticus*, 10-17. An exilic or postexilic setting for the formation of Leviticus is also supported in the work of Balentine, *The Torah's Vision of Worship*, 39-47, and Blenkinsopp, *Introduction to the Pentateuch*, 237-42. In fact, both of these interpreters push the final formulation of the books of the Pentateuch into the Persian period, while not denying the existence of older materials within the books.

[52]See Milgrom, *Leviticus 17-22*, 1361-64.

like Leviticus would be produced. Did priests in ancient Israel really follow a written manual like this when conducting ritual activity, or might it have been used in their training? This seems very unlikely. A more likely purpose of these intricate, written descriptions of ritual is to replace the actual performance of the ritual. This idea would place the primary activity of constructing Leviticus in the exilic period, when the performance of these rituals in the temple was not possible, while allowing for the inclusion of smaller pieces of earlier, preexilic material and some continuing shaping of the book in the postexilic period.

Key Terms

Azazel
Levite
Holiness Code
Yom Kippur
Tent of Meeting
Kashrut
burnt offering
offering of well-being
purity
mercy seat
festival calendar
Festival of Booths
Festival of Weeks

Questions for Reflection

1. What kinds of roles might laws like those found in Leviticus have played in an ancient culture like Israel?
2. How should modern readers understand and make use of the laws found in Leviticus which do not fit their contemporary context?
3. Does the prolific use of violence in Israel's worship, that is, killing animals and performing rituals with blood, raise problems for modern readers of Leviticus?
4. Is the law as it is expressed in various parts of Leviticus a force for liberation or oppression?

Sources for Further Study

Balentine, Samuel E. *The Torah's Vision of Worship*. Overtures to Biblical Theology. Minneapolis: Augsburg/Fortress Publishers, July 1999.

Bellinger, W. H., Jr. *Leviticus and Numbers*. New International Biblical Commentary: Old Testament series 3. Peabody MA: Hendrickson, 2001.

Douglas, Mary Tew. *Purity and Danger: An Analysis of the Concepts of Pollution and Taboo*. London, New York: Routledge and Kegan Paul, 1970, ©1966; second edition, 2000.

Gerstenberger, Erhard S. *Leviticus: A Commentary*. Translated by Douglas W. Stott. The Old Testament Library. Louisville: Westminster/John Knox, 1996.

Hartley, John E. *Leviticus*. Word Biblical Commentary 4. Waco TX: Word Books, 1992.

Levine, Baruch A. *Leviticus. The Traditional Hebrew Text with the New JPS Translation*. JPS Torah Commentary. Philadelphia: Jewish Publication Society, 1989.

Milgrom, Jacob. *Leviticus. A New Translation with Introduction and Commentary*. Three volumes. Anchor Bible 3. New York: Doubleday, 1991–2001. (1) *Leviticus 1–16*, AB-3 (1991). (2) *Leviticus 17–22*, AB-3A (2000). (3) *Leviticus 23–27*, AB-3B (2001).

Sawyer, John F. A., editor. *Reading Leviticus: A Conversation with Mary Douglas*. JSOT Supplement series 227. Sheffield UK: Sheffield Academic Press, 1996.

Sherwood, Stephen K. *Leviticus, Numbers, Deuteronomy*. Berit Olam [(The) Everlasting Covenant]: Studies in Hebrew Narrative and Poetry. Collegeville MN: Liturgical Press, 2002.

Warning, Wilfred. *Literary Artistry in Leviticus*. Biblical Interpretation series 35. Leiden, Boston: Brill Academic Publishers, June 1999.

Chapter 5

The Book of Numbers

The Literary Landscape of Numbers

The introductory chapter of this volume describes the pathway followed by the name of the fourth book of the Pentateuch, from its Jewish designation, *bemidbar* ("In the Wilderness"), to its English name, derived from the Greek and Latin names, *Arithmoi* and *Numeri*. The progress of this name reveals much about the content and organization of the book. While the Jewish name for the book is taken from the first common noun, the fourth word, in the Hebrew text, it also describes the setting of the entire book, and while the wilderness is the setting for other portions of the Pentateuch, it is in the book of Numbers that this setting becomes so prominent that the wilderness might even be understood as a character in the story.

The change in title reveals, however, that later readers began to recognize the important literary role that the Israelite census plays in the book. As earlier chapters of this book have recognized, the division of the Pentateuch into separate books at this point is problematic. The so-called Sinai Pericope began at Exodus 19 when the Israelites arrived at the holy mountain, and they will not leave Sinai until Numbers 10:10. Just as this conception of a block of material in the Pentateuch pulls the second half of the book of Exodus forward, away from the narrative of the exodus itself, so the first nine chapters of Numbers are pulled back away from the collection of wilderness stories that fill much of the final three-fourths of this book. Thus, the two acts of taking a census, in chapters 1 and 26, are the strongest elements of cohesion holding together the book of Numbers.

The initial census in Numbers 1 serves to identify all of the adult male Israelites who had been in the group that left Egypt. The second census in Numbers 26 occurs after the forty years of wandering in the wilderness. It confirms that all of the adult males in the first census, except for Moses, Joshua, and Caleb, are dead. The forty years of wandering and death are most clearly explained in Numbers 14 as punishment for the disobedience of the Israelites when they heard the report of the spies who had been sent into Canaan. Difficulties surrounding this tradition, including its inability to explain the initial census, will be discussed further below.

Careful attention to the position of the two census texts leads to the realization that the entire book of Numbers can be divided into two sections, chapters 1-25 and 26-36, which are parallel to each other in a number of ways. That parallel structure is demonstrated in table 5.1.

Table 5.1
The Census Structure of Numbers

Numbers 1-2	The first census and the arrangement of the camp
Numbers 3:1–10:10	Laws and instructions[1]
Numbers 10:11–25:18	Travel and battle narratives[2]
Numbers 26	The second census
Numbers 27–30	Laws and instructions
Numbers 31–33	Travel and battle narratives
Numbers 34–36	Instructions for settling Canaan

The parallel nature of these two large sections is not the only way to look at the structure of the book of Numbers. The earlier chapter on the book of Exodus discussed the idea of an alternation, within much of the Pentateuch, between the disorder of life in the wilderness and the orderliness and structure provided by the legal materials. On a large scale, we can observe that the first series of wilderness stories in Exodus is followed by the massive collection of legal materials at Mount Sinai in the second half of Exodus, all of Leviticus, and the early part of the book of Numbers. The Pentateuch returns to a focus on life in the wilderness in the remainder of the book of Numbers, which is then followed by another large legal collection in Deuteronomy. On a smaller scale, this kind of alternation is also present in the book of Numbers, and provides another way of looking at the outline of the book presented above. The ultimate frame of the book, its first and last verses, seems to be a deliberate connection to its canonical position. Numbers 1:1 appears to assume the presence of Exodus before Numbers,

[1]The census of the Levites is treated separately and is included in this section. This feature serves to connect the first two sections, 1–2 and 3–10:10, more closely.

[2]The strange story of Balaam (chaps. 22–24) and the seemingly related incident at Baal Peor (chap. 25) are included within this section. It is also possible to view these four chapters as an interlude between the two parallel sections. This role of these chapters in the book of Numbers will be discussed more fully below.

and Numbers 36:13 seems to point consciously to Deuteronomy. Jacob Milgrom has outlined an alternating pattern of law and narrative that extends throughout the entire book of Numbers, which is illustrated in the left column in table 5.2.[3] (On Douglas's Law/Story outline in the right column, see below.)

Table 5.2
Two Possible Patterns of Alternation in Numbers

Milgrom's Law/Narrative Pattern		Douglas's Law/Story Pattern	
1:1–10:10	Law	1:1–4:49	Story
10:11–14:45	Narrative	5:1–6:27	Law
15:1-41	Law	7:1–9:23	Story
16:1–17:13	Narrative	10:1-10	Law
18:1–19:22	Law	10:11–14:45	Story
20:1–25:18	Narrative	15:1-50	Law
26:1–27:11	Law	16:1–17:13	Story
27:12-23	Narrative	18:1–19:22	Law
28:1–30:16	Law	20:1–27:23	Story
31:1–33:49	Narrative	28:1–30:16	Law
33:50–36:13	Law	31:1–33:49	Story
		33:50–35:34	Law
		36:1-12	Story

One significant aspect of Milgrom's outline is that the legal material seems to provide the framework for the book. Not only do legal sections form the beginning and end of the book, but they constitute more than half of its contents.

Using the same general idea of alternation, Mary Douglas has produced a somewhat different outline, which is displayed in the right column in table 5.2.[4] While there are many points of contact between this scheme and

[3]The outline demonstrated in table 5.2 appears in Jacob Milgrom, *Numbers*, JPS Torah Commentary (New York: Jewish Publication Society, 1990) xv. See a similar discussion of alternation in Stephen K. Sherwood, *Leviticus, Numbers, Deuteronomy* (Collegeville MN: Liturgical Press, 2002) 110.

[4]The outline presented in the right-hand column of table 5.2 comes from Mary Douglas, *In the Wilderness: The Doctrine of Defilement in the Book of Numbers* (Sheffield UK: JSOT Press, 1993) 103.

Milgrom's, some striking differences are immediately apparent. Douglas's outline identifies the opening and closing sections of the book as story, rather than law. Along with the first section, which contains the first census, she also classifies the second census in Numbers 26 as narrative, while Milgrom includes it in a legal section. Likewise, Douglas identifies the two sections concerning the daughters of Zelophehad (chapters 27 and 36) as story rather than law. This is a good indication that these ways of classifying texts are not always obvious.

Douglas's conclusions seem to fit the text more precisely. The criteria that she uses to distinguish law and story include observations about how they treat space and time. In her own words, "The law sections are not circumscribed by present chronology, nor does the internal development of a law section have a temporal order."[5] In contrast to this, "The story sections always mark out their temporal and spatial structure." For Douglas, the narrative sections can still contain divine commands because "If events in the story are activated by divine commands, the commands are instructions for tasks to be carried out at once, not to be confused with ordinances to be observed forever."[6] This more nuanced assessment of what constitutes narrative as opposed to law, produces an outline in which narrative is in greater control of the book of Numbers, framing the book at the beginning and the end and comprising a significant majority of the overall content.[7]

In addition to the possible alternating pattern of law and narrative, the book is framed by texts concerning particular issues. Along with the census, the beginning of the book also describes, in chapter 2, the camping arrangement the Israelites are to use as they journey through the wilderness. This spatial arranging of the wilderness camp is reflected in the spatial arrangement of the Promised Land provided in chapters 34–35. These additional observations establish that while the book of Numbers appears to be made

---

[5]Douglas, *In the Wilderness*, 102.

[6]Douglas, *In the Wilderness*, 102.

[7]Douglas has developed her understanding of the structure of Numbers significantly further, based on these observations. Her proposal that the sections in her outline can be matched in pairs forming a chiastic structure is appealing, and will be discussed occasionally in relation to specific texts later in this chapter. The idea that the first twelve sections in her outline can be placed in six pairs which form a ring construction, corresponding to the Jewish calendar, with the thirteenth section returning the reader to the beginning of the book, seems more speculative. Douglas, *In the Wilderness*, 113-22.

up of two large sections that match each other in many ways, the book does not merely repeat itself, but makes significant narrative progress. At the beginning of the book, the Israelites are still encamped around Sinai, having stayed still since Exodus 19, but the final verse (36:13) finds them in Moab, across the Jordan River from Jericho, prepared to enter the land of Canaan. Geography has often been a basis for ways of understanding a more general outline of Numbers. The three major locations in the book can be matched with sections of the text as follows.

1:1–10:10	Sinai
10:11–21:35	Kadesh and the surrounding wilderness
22:1–36:13	Moab

While such outlines are somewhat simplistic, they do reveal the sense of movement that characterizes the book of Numbers, and that places it in significant contrast to the books of Leviticus and Deuteronomy, which precede and follow it.[8]

Interpreters of Numbers have identified many other literary features in the book. Numbers contains a relatively large number of rhetorical questions. Sherwood has identified fifty-three of these, with as many as seventeen each posed by Moses and Balaam.[9] Numbers also contains many instances of chiastic construction, inclusions, and repetitive resumptions.[10] These features indicate that the book of Numbers, on both a large scale and a small scale, is a carefully crafted literary work. These features will receive more attention as they arise in the discussion of individual texts throughout the rest of this chapter.

The results of source-critical study of the book of Numbers have been varied and somewhat contentious, but some broad areas of consensus may be helpful. The bulk of the legal material in Numbers has typically been identified as part of the Priestly Code, and is more concentrated in the outer portions of the book. Much of the middle of the book has been identified with other sources which are older than the P material. Passages like the Balaam narrative (22–24) have the appearance of great antiquity and are difficult, sometimes simply because of their oddness, to associate with one

---

[8]For an example of this kind of outline and its application, see Thomas B. Dozeman, "The Book of Numbers: Introduction, Commentary, and Reflections," in *The New Interpreter's Bible*, vol. 2 (Nashville: Abingdon Press, 1998) 23.

[9]Sherwood, *Leviticus, Numbers, Deuteronomy*, 101-103.

[10]See the extensive lists in Milgrom, *Numbers*, xxii-xxxi.

of the traditional sources like J or E. This has led to a frequent practice of referring to these texts that dominate the center of the book as "pre-Priestly."[11] While precise identification of sources and dates is not possible, the important part of this observation is that much of the book of Numbers has an ancient "feel" to it.

Israel Defined Numerically

Numbers 1–4 contains a diverse mixture of material, but two basic concerns dominate. These chapters contain the first census in the book of Numbers, and some delineation of the duties of various groups of priests. Numbers 1:1 demonstrates immediately both a sense of continuity and discontinuity between the books of Leviticus and Numbers. While the standard introductory formula from Leviticus, "And YHWH spoke to Moses,"[12] opens the book, the specific geographical and spatial designations, "in the wilderness of Sinai" and "in the Tent of Meeting," differentiate this divine address that opens Numbers.

The first census is commanded and defined in Numbers 1:2-3, after which most of chapter 1 is shaped by two different lists of the tribes of Israel. The first list, in vv. 5-15, designates a leader or "head" of each tribe. The tribe of Levi is not included in this list, but the number of tribes is twelve because of the separation of Joseph into two tribes, Ephraim and Manasseh. The second list, in vv. 20-43, describes the counting of each of the tribes in steady, repetitive fashion. Again, the omission of the Levites and division of Joseph yields twelve tribes, with numbers of men of fighting age ranging from 32,200 (Manasseh) to 74,600 (Judah), for a total of 603,550 (v. 46). The order of the tribes in the two lists is the same, except for the surprising movement of Gad from eleventh place in the first list to the third position in the second. This movement inserts Gad into Levi's place in the common Reuben-Simeon-Levi-Judah opening of such lists and splits Gad away from its typical pairing with Asher, the other Zilpah tribe. These lists also split Dan and Naphtali, the Bilhah tribes which are typically

---

[11]See this usage in Milgrom, *Numbers*, xxxii; and Dozemann, "The Book of Numbers," 9-10.

[12]Like the beginning of Leviticus and each of the other divine speeches in that book, Numbers 1:1 opens with a conjunction.

placed together.[13] A descriptive comparison of all lists of the tribes in the book of Numbers is presented in table 5.3.

Table 5.3

Lists of the Twelve Tribes of Israel in Numbers

Numbers 1:6-15. List of the men who are to assist Moses in the first census, one from each tribe. Levi is not included in this list, nor in the census, but the tribe of Joseph is subdivided into Ephraim and Mannaseh, to retain the number twelve. The list begins with the characteristic birth order—Reuben, Simeon, Judah—then Issachar and Zebulun are in the fourth and fifth positions, Ephraim and Manasseh sixth and seventh, Benjamin is eighth, and the list concludes with Dan, Asher, Gad, Naphtali. This is the first time the Bilhah tribes (Dan and Naphtali) are separated.

Numbers 1:17-47. The actual census list. The order is very close to the previous list, with Levi excluded, and Ephraim and Manasseh mentioned individually. The Levites, who are not counted at this point, are treated separately in 1:48-54. The major difference is the movement of Gad into the third position, entirely separate from Asher, which is eleventh, the first separation of the Transjordan, Zilpah tribes.

Numbers 2:1-34. The list of positions of the tribes in the military encampment. The list contains four groups of three tribes, posted on the four geographical directions, each with a lead tribe. Levi is placed in the middle of the list, camped between the second and third groups, and with Ephraim and Manasseh listed separately with no mention of Joseph. The result is: East—Judah, Issachar, Zebulun; South—Reuben, Simeon, Gad; the Levites with the Tent of Meeting: West—Ephraim, Manasseh, Benjamin; North—Dan, Asher, Naphtali.

Numbers 7:12-83. A list of offerings brought by the leaders of each tribe for the dedication of the altar. The order is the same as the previous list in Numbers 2 with Levi excluded of course.

Numbers 10:1-36. The "marching orders" provided as the Israelites set out from Mount Sinai. The tribes are listed in the same four groups of three as

[13]Compare to the five lists described in table 3.1. The variations in these lists make it obvious that the status and relationships among the tribes in ancient Israel were a matter of constant negotiation. The order of these lists in Numbers may reveal that by this point in the story of Israel, the birth order of the patriarchs and their identification with their mothers is declining in importance while other factors are gaining.

in the encampment positions in Numbers 2. The Levites are not mentioned as a group by name, but subgroups are identified and assigned to carry the tabernacle and accompanying equipment.

Numbers 13:1-16. The list of spies sent into Canaan by Moses. The pattern developed in the previous three lists is discontinued here, and the order is closer to the census list in Numbers 1, but still with some significant differences: Reuben, Simeon, Judah, Issachar, Ephraim, Benjamin, Zebulun, Manasseh (also identified as the tribe of Joseph), Dan, Asher, Naphtali, Gad. This is the first time Ephraim and Manasseh are separated in a list.

Numbers 26:5-51. The second census, taken at the end of the forty years in the wilderness, with a significant amount of genealogical material. The Levites are identified in an entirely separate section in 26:57-62, and Ephraim and Manasseh are listed under Joseph, though a slight grammatical anomaly gives preference to Ephraim. Important aspects of birth order and maternal groupings are still present, but with some differences. The Rachel tribes are in the center of the list, and Gad is moved to the third position, between Simeon and Judah.

Numbers 34:16-29. A leader from each tribe is selected for the purpose of apportioning the land. The Levites are omitted, as usual, but this list also omits Reuben and Gad, who have already been assigned land on the east side of the Jordan in 34:13-15. Oddly, Mannaseh is included in the Transjordan allotment in 34:13-15, but also in the primary list in 34:16-29, preceding Ephriam. The latter list presents this order: Judah, Simeon, Benjamin, Dan, Joseph (Mannaseh and Ephraim), Zebulun, Issachar, Asher, and Naphtali.

The separate tasks and camping position of the Levites are provided in a separate divine speech to Moses in 1:48-53, again introduced by, "And YHWH spoke to Moses." A fulfillment formula ends the chapter in v. 54: "The Israelites . . . did just as YHWH commanded Moses."

Numbers 2 begins with an introduction to a new divine speech, this time addressed to Moses and Aaron. This chapter is given its primary shape by a single list of the tribes. The primary purpose of this list is to identify the camping positions of tribes, but numbers are included once again. The most distinctive feature of this list is the placement of the twelve tribes into four groups of three, headed by Judah, Reuben, Ephraim, and Dan. The same numbers of troops are provided for each of the individual tribes as in chapter 1, but now totals are provided for each of the four divisions. This arrangement has also necessitated some movement of the individual tribes, which are described in table 5.3. One final, striking feature is the placement of the Levites and the Tent of Meeting precisely at the center of the list. Like chapter 1, this list ends with a statement of fulfillment in v. 34: "And the children of Israel did according to all that YHWH had commanded Moses."

The book of Numbers appears to take a different turn at 3:1 with a genealogical notice reminiscent of Genesis: "These are the generations of Aaron and Moses." The inclusion of Moses is odd here, since the genealogy includes only the four sons of Aaron and then stops. A sequence of three divine speeches in vv. 5-10, 11-13, and 14-15 suddenly addresses the duties of the Levites, however, revealing that the purpose of 3:1-4 is not to provide genealogical information, but to define the duties of the Levites in relation to those of the sons of Aaron. The text is very specific in 3:9 that "You shall give the Levites to Aaron and his sons. They are surely given to him from among the Israelites." So the placement of the Levites under the genealogy of Aaron is fitting here.[14] The remainder of chapters 3–4 will be concerned with the functions of the Levites, which are presented within a census framework.

The intertwining of the census tradition, which seems to have primarily a military purpose, and the encampment tradition, which seems primarily cultic in focus, is an important development in the preparation of the Israelites to move away from Mount Sinai.[15] The identity of this group of people seems to be at stake here. The book of Leviticus designated them as "holy" and defined that designation in terms of commitment to worshipping YHWH, but this takes place in a stationary context. Moving through the wilderness and toward the Promised Land will be a military endeavor, so the worshipping identity must be embedded within a military one.

The Levitc census in Numbers 3 is framed by an odd story, which begins at v. 11 when YHWH tells Moses that the Levites are to replace the firstborn Israelite males, who belong to YHWH, in exchange for the killing of the Egyptian firstborn. After the counting of all of the males one month or older in each of the three houses of Levites—Gershon, Kohath, and

---

[14]Conflicts between rival groups of priests were intense at certain points in Israel's history. It is possible that one function of a text like this one is the attempt to influence the outcome these conflicts.

[15]See the explanation of this feature in Baruch A. Levine, *Numbers 1-20*, Anchor Bible 4 (New York: Doubleday, 1993) 144-51.

Merari—a total of 22,000[16] is recorded in v. 39. A corresponding count of all the Israelite firstborn males in vv. 40-43 yields 22,273.[17] The planned redemption of the firstborn by the dedication of the Levites thus falls 273 short, and this problem is addressed in vv. 44-51, by replacing the shortage of Levites with a monetary offering of five shekels each. The offering is given to Aaron and his sons at the end of the chapter, which closes with a typical completion formula.

A new census of the Levites begins in 4:1, again using the three houses, but this time in the order Kohath, Gershon, and Merari. Another major difference is that only those between thirty and fifty years of age are counted. Apparently, it is this group which is understood to be eligible to perform their service in the tabernacle. This count yields 8,580 such Levites, who are meticulously assigned various duties throughout the chapter. Once again, these numbers create some problems, especially if they are put together with the numbers from the previous chapter. The overall proportion of Levite males who are between thirty and fifty is thirty-eight percent (8,580/22,300), but for the individual levitical houses the proportions range from tirty-two percent of Kohathites (2,750/8,600) to fifty-two percent of Merarites (3,200/6,200). Such wide demographic variations seem very unlikely. Such difficulties reveal the need to acknowledge that the writer of the book of Numbers is probably dealing with a wide variety of traditions and sources of information which do not easily fit together.

Chapter 4 closes with the usual completion formula, which illustrates the role of such elements in the attempt to unify these disparate traditions within a single work of literature.

---

[16]The three separate numbers provided for the houses of Levi, 7,500 Gershonites (v. 22), 8,600 Kohathites (v. 28), and 6,200 Merarites (v. 33), actually adds up to 22,300, which would make the entire correction passage in vv. 44-51 unnecessary. Some interpreters have proposed a mistake of a single consonant in the number given for the Kohathites, which would account for this discrepancy. See Levine, *Numbers 1-20*, 161.

[17]This number presents significant problems for the tradition of 2,000,000 Israelites participating in the exodus, a number reaffirmed by the count of 603,550 adult males in Numbers 1. If this total included approximately 1,000,000 males, then combining it with 22,273 firstborn males would mean that only one out of every forty-five males was a firstborn, a seemingly unrealistic number.

Laws and Instructions I

The book of Numbers shifts its attention significantly at 5:1 and begins to address community issues with a set of legal instructions similar to those found in Leviticus 12–15. The chapter is divided into three divine speeches with introductory formulae at vv. 1, 5, and 11. Issues such as leprosy, genital discharges, contact with corpses, and restitution for harmful actions are addressed in fairly brief fashion in vv. 1-10, leading up to a lengthy set of instructions in vv. 11-31 describing what can be done with a woman suspected of adultery. This ritual is shocking to modern readers because of the inequity and brutality to which it exposes the woman, and because it cannot be separated from its magical elements. It is apparent that the ancient Israelites who took this ritual seriously believed that writing down curses and washing them off into the water which the woman drinks carries the curses and their effects into her body, and the text can only be understood in light of that premise. The ritual is purely the prerogative of the husband, and the woman in this case is forced to endure the ordeal, with no repercussions for the husband should the accusations prove false. The nature of the effects on the woman is not clear in the text. The suspicion of adultery here does not seem limited to pregnancy, but such a condition would certainly be included. The "swelling" of the body and "falling" of the thigh would include a miscarriage, but could also refer to permanent anatomical damage, both in cases when the woman is pregnant and when she is not.[18] The implication of v. 29 is that this damage would prevent future childbearing. An innocent woman is cleared, according to v. 29, with a promise of no ill effects, but v. 31 assures no punishment for a man who makes a false accusation.[19]

Numbers 6 is also dominated by a lengthy set of legal instructions in vv. 1-21. This time the subject is the procedures and obligations surrounding Nazirite vows, a subject that has not yet appeared in the Pentateuch, though this text seems to assume some prior knowledge. This is not a widespread tradition in the Bible. The instructions here indicate that both men and

---

[18]See the thorough discussion of these issues in Levine, *Numbers 1-20*, 202-206.

[19]There have been some attempts to explain away the gender inequity of this text. See the discussion and dismissal of these in W. H. Bellinger, Jr., *Leviticus and Numbers* (Peabody MA: Hendrickson, 2001) 198.

women can take the vow (v. 2), leading to days of separation which include abstaining from certain foods and drinks (vv. 3-4), refraining from cutting the hair (v. 5), and no contact with corpses (vv. 6-12).[20] The days of separation are followed by an offering at the tent of meeting (v. 17), and the shaving of the head in order to dedicate the hair (vv. 18-19). Nowhere in the text is a purpose given for the Nazirite vow, nor is any benefit derived from it mentioned. Once the concluding ritual is completed, the restrictions of the days of separation are lifted. The only specific case of a Nazirite in the entire Old Testament is Samson in Judges 13–16, whose specific situation differs from what is described in Numbers 6, because his mother makes the vow for him, before he is born, and he follows some of the restrictions all of his life. Within the narrative of Samson, of course, the primary role of the Nazirite tradition is to explain his long hair and its special qualities. The only other mention of Nazirites in the Old Testament is in Amos 2:11-12, which seems to imply that only males can be Nazirites and that abstaining from wine is the defining characteristic.[21] Dozemann has presented a scheme by which the subject of purity is brought from outside the camp to the inside through progressive stages, with the Nazirite passage forming the innermost zone, with its culminating offering taking place in the tent of meeting.[22]

Chapter 6 closes with a separate, brief divine speech, which contains the most well-known text in the book of Numbers, the little poem sometimes called the "Aaronide Blessing" (vv. 24-26). There is no apparent connection between this blessing and the Nazirite material which precedes it, but there may be a significant connection to what follows it in chapter 7. This blessing has found a significant place in Jewish tradition into the modern period, and in Christian liturgy.

Numbers 7 is the longest chapter in the book, and its opening is confusing for a couple of reasons. First, this account of tribal offerings does not open with the type of divine speech that dominates this part of Numbers. It

---

[20]Only in this last case is there a procedure for correcting a violation, provided that the contact with a corpse is inadvertent.

[21]See the thorough discussion of the Nazirite tradition in Levine, *Numbers 1-20*, 229-35.

[22]See Dozeman, "The Book of Numbers," 60.

[23]Bellinger argues that the Aaronide Blessing is a conclusion to the purity laws in chaps. 5–6. See Bellinger *Leviticus, Numbers*, 204.

is possible to understand that the preceding Aaronide Blessing performs this function,[23] but standard, introductory formulae followed by brief divine speeches do appear in vv. 4 and 11. Second, the opening in v. 1 is retrospective in nature, recalling the completion of the tabernacle in Exodus 40 and its anointing and consecration in Leviticus 8. The retrospective nature of Numbers 7 is enhanced by its connections to the next two chapters. The introduction in 9:1 identifies its date as "the first month of the second year." Numbers 1:1 has already placed the events at the beginning of the book of Numbers on "the first day of the second month of the second year." So, the closely connected events in chapters 7–9 occur in the month previous to those in chapters 1–6, which places the former with the description of setting up the tabernacle in Exodus 40:17 "on the first day of the first month of the second year."[24]

After the Levites are properly equipped with wagons and teams in Numbers 7:1-9, representatives from each of the tribes bring offerings, one on each day for twelve days. The twelve offerings are presented in vv. 12-83 in repetitive fashion, each account consisting of six verses arranged in identical form. One result of this description of the offering procession is the literary production of another list of the twelve tribes (see table 5.3). The ceremony concludes in v. 89 when Moses enters the tent and hears the voice of God coming from the ark.

As these instructions continue to accumulate, it is possible to get the impression that the departure from Sinai is being stalled deliberately by the narrator. Recall that the Israelites were ready to go at the end of the book of Exodus.[25] Numbers 8 depicts the dedication of the Levites, an event toward which the book of Numbers seems to be oriented for much of the time up to this point, having given extensive attention to the special tribe in chapters 1–4 and 7.

Chapter 8 is divided into three sections by the appearance of three introductory formulae, "And the LORD spoke to Moses," in vv. 1, 5, and 23.

---

[24]See the discussion of this timing in Katherine Doob Sakenfeld, *Journeying with God: A Commentary on the Book of Numbers* (Grand Rapids MI: Eerdmans, 1995) 46-47.

[25]Bellinger has proposed that the purpose of the lengthy chap. 7 is to slow the narrative in order to emphasize the divine presence at its center. Bellinger *Leviticus, Numbers*, 204. It is difficult to determine a logical purpose for the offerings at this point in the story. If the Israelites have forty years of traveling through the wilderness ahead of them, why transfer possession of all this property now?

The opening section, vv. 1-4, concerns the setting up of the lamps in the tabernacle. These are the lamps Moses was instructed to make in Exodus 25:31-37, and which were constructed in Exodus 37:17-23. It is not clear how the consecration of the Levites is connected to the lamps, but the process begins in 8:5 and proceeds with washing and shaving, before the sequence of offerings starts in v. 8. Included in these are a grain offering, a sin offering, and a burnt offering, as described in Leviticus. The Levites themselves are now part of the offering, though. In vv. 16-18 they are dedicated in place of the Israelite firstborn, as described in Numbers 3. The third divine speech, in 8:23-36, provides an additional instruction concerning the Levites, that they are to serve as assistants to the priests from age twenty-five to age fifty, but no explanation is provided for these boundaries. Surely, these men would have been capable of such work at a much younger age than twenty-five, and some would likely have been capable of serving beyond the age of fifty. This text is in conflict with the Levite census in chapter 4, which used an age range of thirty to fifty. The presence of these boundaries and their differences may reflect times in Israel's history when there were more Levites than could reasonably be used at the temple, so some limitations on their numbers were required.

Numbers 9 opens with instructions for the first Passover celebration after the completion of the tabernacle, which is, of course, the first Passover celebrated outside of Egypt. The initial instructions in vv. 1-8 do not provide many details, but seem primarily concerned with determining who may participate. Some of the Israelites lacked the purity status to join in the festival.[26] This example of a specific case, which must be addressed by the law, is similar to the case of the blasphemer in Leviticus 24:10-23 and forms a type of text that will be prominent in the latter portions of Numbers, when the case of the daughters of Zelophehad arises in chapters 27 and 36. The members of the community who come to Moses in 9:7 cite defilement by a corpse as the reason they cannot participate in Passover.[27] The subsequent ruling, which Moses receives from YHWH, also addresses those who miss the celebration on the fourteenth day of the first month because they were on a long journey and the application of Passover rules to

[26]This situation closely reflects the Passover celebration led by King Hezekiah in 2 Chronicles 30.

[27]Based on numerous rabbinic sources, Milgrom has argued that this cause of impurity was used to designate all others, such as discharges and diseases. See Milgrom, *Numbers*, 68.

resident aliens. Obviously these added cases do not fit the Passover observed in the wilderness setting, and the pronouncement in vv. 10-14 has the feel of a perpetual ordinance rather than a one-time ruling. The presence of a Passover celebration may help explain the retrospective placement of this and the surrounding material. As the Israelites get ready to leave Sinai, they observe Passover, ready to travel just as in Exodus 12.

The remainder of chapter 9, vv. 15-23, addresses an entirely different subject, one more pertinent to the approaching departure. The reference in 9:15 to "the day the tabernacle was raised" refers back to 7:1, which opens with a similar phrase, and the two verses together are connected to the construction of the tabernacle in Exodus 35–40. More specifically, the description of the cloud covering the tabernacle, and lifting in order to signal the Israelites to depart their current location, expands upon a similar passage in Exodus 40:36-38. These two cloud passages in Exodus 40:36-38 and Numbers 9:15-23, therefore, bracket the entire Priestly legislation from Leviticus 1:1 to Numbers 9:14.[28]

The description of the entire section in chapters 7–9 reveals a point of difficulty for Douglas's outline, which was presented in table 5.2. She identified this whole section as "story" despite the presence of legal material within it. This is largely explained by her emphasis on the use of space and time in these texts.[29] Still a section like 9:9-14 operates outside of specific space and time, like a law section, according to Douglas's dichotomy, but it is tied to the specific incident in 9:6-8, which has the space and time qualities of a story. An important question in a case like this may be whether one of these texts is in control of the other. This would explain how a small piece of "law" might fit into a section designated "story," or vice versa.

One final delay fills the first ten verses of Numbers 10. In order to indicate the departure, following the cloud, there must be a trumpet signal. The making of the trumpets is described in v. 2, followed by a more elaborate set of instructions for their use, which includes much more than just the departure signal. A final mark of punctuation appears at the end of v. 10, putting an appropriate end to the long stay at Mount Sinai with "I am YHWH your God."

---

[28]Milgrom, *Numbers*, 70-71.

[29]See the discussion in the introductory section to this chapter and in Douglas, *In the Wilderness*, 102.

Travel and Battle Narratives I

The opening section of this chapter described the literary analysis of Mary Douglas, which divides the book of Numbers into thirteen sections that alternate between story and law (see table 5.2). The departure from Sinai is the fifth of these sections and brings a new narrative quality to the text. While Douglas's designation of the census account in 1:1–4:49 as "story" is appropriate, the content of this section is dominated, in quantitative terms, by nonnarrative documents, specifically, the census lists. The movement into the wilderness, beginning at 10:11 is a much less encumbered story, and is the beginning of what will be treated as a long section at the heart of the book of Numbers (10:11–27:23), which is dominated by narrative material.

Over this alternating pattern of story and law lies another, larger pattern, which was mentioned briefly in chapter 3. The portion of the Pentateuch after the flight from Egypt can be divided into four large segments:

Wilderness I	Exodus 14–18
Law I: Sinai	Exodus 19–Numbers 10
Wilderness II	Numbers 10–36
Law II: Moab	Deuteronomy

Of course, there are legal texts embedded within the large wilderness complexes and, likewise, stories within the large, legal collections. These contours may be more clearly drawn using other dichotomies, such as movement versus stasis or disorder versus order. This last dichotomy is an essential element of thc theology of the Pentateuch. It is commonplace for contemporary readers to view the legal material in the Bible as rigid and restrictive. In Christian traditions, this is partly due to the caricature of first-century Judaism that emerges from the New Testament and its interpretation. It is unlikely that the disadvantages of an overly strict enforcement of the law would have been lost on the Israelites, even the most ancient ones. The juxtaposition of law and wilderness here, as the ultimate depictions of order and chaos, reveal the liberating aspect of law. In the face of a chaotic environment, which is life-threatening in its severity, law offers a livable way of being, even a liberation of sorts. Earlier discussion in this book linked the creation story of Genesis 1 with the building of the tabernacle in Exodus 25–40 as matching processes of order. Even in the wilderness, a disordered space, the ordered space of the tabernacle, a seed of creation just like Noah's ark floating on the face of the chaotic waters, sits at the center of the Israelite community, which struggles to stay ordered around it.

In the large collection of wilderness stories that fills much of the middle of the book of Numbers, a pattern that began in the early wilderness stories of Exodus 14–18 is raised to a higher register. Again and again a situation arises in which the Israelites complain about some hardship, God becomes angry and decides to destroy them, Moses intervenes and convinces God not to destroy the Israelites, the punishment is mitigated, and the Israelites receive some comfort from the initial hardship. These stories often end with a place-name etiology which is connected to either the actions of the people or the actions of God in response. Examples of this narrative pattern are listed in table 5.4, though every story does not contain every element of the pattern.

Table 5.4
Wilderness Complaint Narratives in Numbers

11:1-3	General complaining at Taberah
11:4-35	Craving for meat
12:1-16	Aaron and Miriam challenge Moses' leadership
14:1-38	Reaction to the report from the spies
16:12-40	The rebellion of Korah
16:41-50	Complaints about the killing of the Korah group
17:1–18:7	The selection of the Levites
20:1-13	The waters of Meribah
21:1-9	The bronze serpent

As noted in our chapter on Exodus, this set of stories forms part of what has traditionally been called the "murmuring tradition," because of the translation in the King James Version of the word now more commonly rendered as "complain." This word itself does not appear in every story (see, for example, Numbers 11:1). The eight occurrences in Numbers are confined to chapters 14–17, so they are at the core of the collection. The word appears in Exodus in chapters 15–17, but does not appear anywhere else in the Pentateuch outside of these two limited sections.

While these stories are often remembered as a negative reflection on the Israelites during the wilderness experience, something more nuanced seems to be going on in the book of Numbers. A complex relationship is developing between God, Moses, and the Israelites, in which Moses acts as the mediator. Some important observations need to be made about this set of stories. First, the provisions received by the Israelites in the wilderness always follow their complaints. Thus, they are not always punished for complaining; sometimes they are rewarded. This also reflects their initial deliverance from Egypt which is the result of their "crying out" to God (Exodus 2:23 and 3:7). Second, the Israelites are never provided with food and water in the wilderness unless they complain. This raises questions about what would have happened to them had they not complained. Third, many of these stories end with place-name etiologies, like *Meribah* ("quarreling" in 20:13) and *Taberah* ("burning" in 11:3). There seems to be a need to explain the origins of these negative and contentious names of places. Finally, the Israelites' complaints about God and Moses seem to match the complaints about them made by God and Moses.[30]

Some of these stories appear to be alternative versions of stories found in the smaller collection of wilderness narratives in Exodus 14–18. This raises questions about whether multiple sources of tradition remembered the stories differently or whether such events might have actually happened twice. It may be more important to ask how the stories are alike and how they are different, and what it means for similar stories to sit on either side of the giving of the law at Mount Sinai. The relationship of this phenomenon to the law and the figure of Moses will be discussed extensively in other places.

The wilderness stories in 10:11–21:36 are centered around the story of the spies sent into Canaan (chapters 13–14), and the outcome of this central conflict will determine the destiny of this generation of Israelites. The orderly departure from Mount Sinai is reported in 10:11-36. The date in v. 11, "in the second year, in the second month, on the twentieth day," would appear to have allowed time for the late Passover observers from chapter 9 to complete their celebration. The "marching orders" in the departure story present another list of the Israelite tribes (see table 5.3). The initial leg of the journey is three days in duration, according to vv. 33-34, and the departure account culminates with the fascinating little "Song of the Ark" in vv.

---

[30]The symmetry of this relationship of complaint has been observed and brilliantly described by Jack Miles in *God: A Biography* (New York: Vintage Books, 1996) 32-33.

[31]See the discussion of the "Song of the Ark" in Milgrom, *Numbers*, 81. Torah

35-36. The origins of this song are uncertain, but parts of it also appear in Psalms 68:2 and 132:8.[31] In the context of Numbers 10, it is part of the departure scene in vv. 29-36, which follows the more formal marching orders. This section is commonly identified by source critics as the first part of the "prepriestly" material, a collection that makes up much of the wilderness tradition in the middle part of the book of Numbers, sometimes with parallel Priestly material like vv. 11-28 in this case.[32]

The first "murmuring" story arrives quickly at 11:1. The lack of specific content in the Taberah account in vv. 1-3 makes it possible to consider this a paradigmatic introduction to all of the murmuring stories, but it is tied to a specific place and form of punishment. Though 11:3 provides a place-name etiology tied to the form of punishment, it is not clear at 11:4 that a new story begins, because there is no report of travel from Taberah.[33] The complaint about a diet restricted to manna, which continues in vv. 4-6, sounds as if it could be an expansion of the small complaint story in vv. 1-3, but the conclusion of the story, which provides a separate place-name etiology (*Kibroth-hattaavah*) in vv. 34-35 makes clear that this is a separate story. The presence of manna is assumed here and not explained, leaving two possible ways to understand the relationship between the wilderness narratives in Exodus and those in Numbers. Either an awareness of the stories in Exodus is presumed, and the reader is supposed to know that the Israelites have already complained of hunger and God has responded by sending the manna, or the wilderness traditions in Numbers do not understand the manna as a response to a complaint. Of course, the latter view may also be more reasonable, since it is not clear in Exodus 16:1-8 what the Israelites were supposed to eat in the wilderness before the manna came in response to their hunger complaint. The quails, which are the response to complaints about the manna according to Numbers 11:18-20 and 31-33, are mentioned in Exodus 16:13, but only in a brief manner that does not make it clear that they are provided as a food source.

The complaint story in Numbers 11:4-35, which is resolved by the sending of the quails, surrounds three other important elements in this chap-

---

scrolls commonly mark off the Ark Song with special symbols, indicating that this is a questionable place for it to sit in the text of the Pentateuch.

[32]See the discussion of these sources in Dozeman, "The Book of Numbers," 92-97.

[33]Those who complain in 11:4 are referred to as "the rabble among them." See the discussion of this description in Dozeman, "The Book of Numbers," 105.

ter, all related to the leadership of Moses. First, the triangular relationship which has been formed between YHWH, Moses, and the Israelites is addressed again in vv. 10-15. Moses makes clear that the Israelite project belongs to YHWH and that the burden of leadership has become so great that he would welcome death. Second, the expression of frustration by Moses leads to a system of delegating authority and responsibility to seventy elders (vv. 16-25).[34] Third, the presence of other prophets in the camp (vv. 26-31) puts to rest any notion that such activity is a threat to Moses' authority. These leadership issues are tied to the quail tradition by the imbedding of information about the ongoing complaint story at vv. 13 and 18-23. The account comes to a conclusion in vv. 31-35 with a double punishment. The arrival of the quails, which might seem to be an unmitigated blessing, is overwhelming, as vv. 19-20 have already indicated. The quail come in piles that are waist deep (two cubits), making the notion of "gathering" (v. 32) satirical. As soon as the Israelites begin eating the meat, the punishment comes upon them in full force as a plague (v. 33).

The next story again raises issues about Moses' leadership. The travel note in 11:35 takes the Israelites to a new place, one designated at 12:1 as the site of the next episode. The Cushite wife of Moses, who is at least the surface cause of the conflict that arises between him and his siblings, is a mysterious figure.[35] Zipporah is mentioned by name three times in the Bible, all in Exodus (2:21, 4:25, and 18:2). When Jethro meets Moses in the wilderness (Exodus 18), Jethro brings Zipporah and her two sons with him, because Moses had "sent her." Exodus 18:2 uses the characteristic language of divorce, and this is the most obvious meaning, though it is possible to argue that he sent her back to her father's house to keep her and the children away from the rigors and dangers of the plagues and the exodus. When Jethro departs from Moses (Exodus 18:27), the text does not mention Zipporah, so she may or may not have stayed with Moses. The Cushite wife is obviously not Zipporah, who is always described as a Midianite.[36] The complaint story in Numbers 12 does not identify the specific issue that

[34]This account reflects the story in Exodus 18:13-24, which is different in some details and is separated to a greater extent from the complaint stories.

[35]The parenthetical statement in v. 12b seems to be placed here to assure the reader that this element of the accusation is true.

[36]Though Moses' father-in-law has a different name, Reuel, in Numbers 10:29, he is still called a Midianite, and Reuel is the name associated with Zipporah in Exodus 2.

generates the objection from Aaron and Miriam. It may be because the woman is Cushite, or because Moses has divorced Zipporah to marry this Cushite, or because Moses had not divorced Zipporah and had taken a second wife, or for some entirely different reason.

This is an interesting point at which to examine the traditions known as the *Targumim*, translations of the Hebrew scriptures into Aramaic, probably originating a century or so before the turn of the eras and continuing a few centuries into the Common Era. These translations are quite free in form, offering interpretations and revisions of the Hebrew text, particularly at points of difficulty or confusion. There are three primary *Targumim* of the Pentateuch, known as Onqelos, Neofiti, and Pseudo-Jonathan. All three of these renderings of Numbers are obviously bothered by this tradition of the Cushite wife of Moses. Onqelos resolves the difficulty, in part, by translating the word "Cushite' as "beautiful," perhaps making it easier to assume that this is still Zipporah. Neofiti acknowledges that she is a "Cushite woman," but specifically identifies her as Zipporah, and also comments on her rare beauty and character. Pseudo-Jonathan refers to a "Cushite woman" and does not identify her by name, but claims that Moses married her during his "flight from Egypt," which is when he had married Zipporah in Exodus 2. There is also some implication that Moses may have been forced to marry her. None of these textual revisions fully resolves the difficulty, but they are all good indications of ways that interpreters 2,000 years ago struggled with a difficult issue in the text.

Moses' marriage turns out to be only a curious diversion, as the story moves on in 12:2-9 to revel that the authority of Moses is the real issue. In vv. 10-16 Miriam, but not Aaron, is punished with leprosy. Aaron quickly prays, admits fault, and asks God to heal Miriam, and, as a result of Aaron's prayer, the period of Miriam's illness is reduced to seven days. After waiting for Miriam to recover, the Israelites move on from Hazeroth to Paran (12:16). This time there is no connection drawn between the events and the name of the place.

The spy story in chapters 13–14 is a long, complex narrative, that does not begin as a complaint story. Notice that the three stories immediately preceding this one have moved the point of conflict and rebellion from the outer part of the camp (11:1) to the main part of the camp (11:10) and then to the very center (12:4).[37] The disruption over the spies' report will now address the identity of this people and its reason for being. The command

---

[37]See Bellinger, *Leviticus, Numbers*, 224-25.

to send spies into Canaan comes from YHWH and requires another list of the tribes in 13:4-16 (see table 5.3). The story of the spying itself is straightforward. Its forty days mirror the forty days Moses stayed on Mount Sinai, and will lead to the upcoming forty years of wandering in the wilderness. The collective report of the spies in 13:27-29 provides a geographic and ethnographic tour of the Promised Land. Disagreement breaks out in vv. 30-33 as only Caleb supports immediate invasion, while the others object, expanding upon the cryptic reference to "descendants of Anak," in v. 28, to describe the *Nephilim* (v. 33)[38] and others in the land as "giants" (v. 32).

Chapter 14 reports the response of the people to the spies, and takes the form of another complaint story. An added element appears in 14:5-10, when Joshua and Caleb join Moses and Aaron to plead with the people, but they are threatened with stoning and the story moves into the usual conference between YHWH and Moses. In this case, YHWH wishes to kill the Israelites and begin nation building anew with Moses, but Moses appeals to YHWH's international reputation and eventually uses the creedal formulation from Exodus 34:6-7 to remind YHWH of the commitment to forgiveness. The mitigated punishment is not allowing the present generation of adults to enter the land and the death by plague of all the spies except for Joshua and Caleb. The story concludes when the people, distraught over their punishment, attempt an invasion into the hill country of Canaan, but are soundly defeated.

Elements of the spy story generate geographical difficulties which persist for the remainder of the book of Numbers. When the Israelites first leave Sinai, they travel to the "wilderness of Paran" (10:12). This is not a precise location, but seems to be the name given to the northern part of the Sinai Peninsula by some of the biblical sources. According to 13:26, the episode concerning the spies occurs at "in the wilderness of Paran, at Kadesh."[39] Numbers 32:8 is even more precise, using the fuller name "Kadesh-barnea" to designate the place from which the spies were sent.

Additional complications arise at 20:1, which describes the travels of

---

[38]The obscure term *Nephilim* (KJV "giants") occurs in the Old Testament only here, Numbers 13:33, and at Genesis 6:4.

[39]The more general "wilderness of Paran" is used at 13:3 as the location from which the spies were sent. One should keep in mind that these biblical narratives are often the only source of information available to those who draw the maps in Bible atlases, so such maps do not resolve the difficulties, but simply represent them graphically.

the Israelites as they "enter the wilderness of Zin" and "dwell in Kadesh." Zin is also an imprecise term, which some biblical sources use to describe the southern part of the Negeb, which would be the area immediately north of the wilderness of Paran. Are the wilderness areas called Paran and Zin different enough that Kadash cannot be in both, and, therefore, one set of texts must be locating it incorrectly? Are these two wilderness regions overlapping, in which case Kadesh might be located within a vague boundary zone, making either location correct to some extent? A third possibility is that different parts of the Bible, written by different people at different times use varying names to identify places and areas. These geographical problems cannot be resolved here. It becomes apparent that the writer of the book of Numbers is using multiple sources about the spy story, and that these sources speak about places and locations differently.[40] Readers should be wary of any attempts to explain these issues with too much precision, based on the travel narratives in the book of Numbers.

At this devastating point, the narrative is interrupted by a collection of cultic regulations that fill chapter 15, providing a welcome break from the conflict and punishment of the spy story. The two major sections are introduced by similar clauses in v. 2 and v. 18. Though the preposition in v. 2 is ambiguous, and could mean anything from "When you come into the land" to "If you come into the land," the occurrence of this introduction in v. 18 switches prepositions and provides an unambiguous temporal clause, "When you come into the land." The eventual entry is thus reasserted, and instructions are given for offerings, both spontaneous (vv. 3-16 and 19-21) and as a response to sin (vv. 22-31).[41] The closing sentences of the latter section distinguish between unintentional sins, for which atonement may be offered, and sinning "with a high hand," for which it may not. An example of such a sin is provided in vv. 32-36, in which a man is discovered gathering firewood on the Sabbath and is subsequently stoned to death. This horrifying account is followed by a remedy for forgetfulness or temptation when YHWH commands Moses to have the Israelites make fringes with a blue chord on the corners of their clothes as a constant reminder to keep the law. Like an earlier set of instructions at 10:10, this one ends at 15:41 with an emphatic statement, "I am YHWH your God."

---

[40]See the extensive discussion in Levine, *Numbers 1-20*, 53-55.

[41]These offerings reflect those in Leviticus 1–3, but additional elements are included, suggesting that this text is likely a later development. For a more detailed discussion, see Levine, *Numbers 1-20*, 385-93.

The brief respite offered by the legislation in chapter 15 comes to a sudden halt with another rebellion story in chapters 16–17. Like the spy account in chapters 13–14, the passage often designated as "Korah's Rebellion" is a lengthy and complex narrative, with two lengthy complaint stories contained within it at 16:1-40 and 16:41-50. No location is given in chapters 16–17, so this section offers no help in resolving the geographical difficulties raised by chapter 13, and this episode is merely assumed by most interpreters to take place at Kadesh. The beginning of chapter 16 seems somewhat confused, and Levine has argued effectively that an original story, from the J and E sources, of a rebellion by a group of Reubenites, represented by Dathan and Abiram, has been expanded and revised by the P source to portray a conflict within the tribe of Levi.[42] The primary culprit in the final form of the story is Korah, a Levite of the Kohathite clan. So, the end product is a combined story of protest by some Reubenites against Moses, and by a Levite subgroup against Aaron and his family. There is also a double punishment. First, the earth opens up and swallows the protesters (16:32), while fire destroys a few others (16:35) and, second, a plague kills 14,700 Israelites (16:46-50). In the recollection of this event at Deuteronomy 11:6 it is the Reubenite households of Dathan and Abiram who are swallowed by the earth, so it is once again apparent that multiple traditions of rebellion against the leadership of Moses and Aaron have been woven together.[43]

Chapter 17 offers a resolution to the rebelliousness in the previous chapter, with a story that seems to address both aspects of the rebellion to some extent, but which fits neither perfectly. The two questions presupposed by the "budding-staff" story are whether the tribe of Levi has a special role among the Israelite tribes and whether the family of Aaron has a privileged status within the tribe of Levi. YHWH, through Moses, decides the second question by fiat, simply declaring that Aaron's name be written on the staff representing the tribe of Levi. The first question, on the other hand, is answered by the miraculous, overnight transformation of Aaron's rod into an almond tree bearing ripe fruit. Aaron's rod is to serve as a warn-

---

[42]The story in its present form probably addresses issues of conflict among priestly families at a later time. Proposals about these issues are too complex and speculative to present here. See Levine, *Numbers 1–20*, 423-32.

[43]See the attempts to untangle these narrative traditions in Dozeman, "The Book of Numbers," 134-40; and Levine *Numbers 1-20*, 405-406.

ing against rebellion.[44] Apparently it works, as the chapter ends with a direct question from the Israelites, who fear that they will all die.

The legal regulations in chapter 18 serve both as an answer to the question that ends chapter 17, and as another break from the exhausting wilderness narratives. The chaos of Korah's rebellion presents a need for order, which a set of instructions concerning the responsibilities of the Levites fulfills. There is nothing entirely new in this chapter, since the issues have already been addressed in Numbers 8, but the statement in 18:1—"And YHWH said unto Aaron"—makes this set of commands unique as the only case in the entire Pentateuch where YHWH addresses the brother of Moses alone. This is reaffirmed in v. 8 with the similar introductory formula—"And YHWH spoke to Aaron"—and in v. 20 when the form in v. 1 is repeated. The distinct duties of Aaron's family and those of the rest of the Levites are identified in vv. 1-7, and the former are elaborated in vv. 8-20. In vv. 21-24 the role of the Levites is explained more fully, and these privileges are confirmed in vv. 25-32 by a divine speech to Moses. The careful delineation of these responsibilities should serve to protect the Israelites from the danger of improper cultic behavior and rebellion against authority, as experienced in the previous narrative.

Legal material continues in chapter 19 with a vivid description of an unrelated but fascinating ritual. The issue of defilement by a corpse has been mentioned previously in Leviticus (21:2, 11; 22:4) and Numbers (5:2; 6:6-11; 9:6-12), but has not been addressed thoroughly. The ritual of the "red cow" provides a more complete set of instructions to remedy this type of impurity. In 19:1 YHWH addresses Moses and Aaron. Unlike other sacrificial rituals defined in the Pentateuch, the red cow procedure takes place outside the camp (v. 3). The process described in vv. 2-10 provides the materials necessary for purification in the production of cleansing water, using ashes from the burned cow. The use of the ashes and water are described more fully in vv. 11-21, and the chapter concludes by addressing the uncleanness of those who officiate in the purification ceremony.

Numbers 20 introduces a difficult tradition that will hang over the remainder of the Pentateuch. Moses cannot live forever, and both the Israelites in the story and those telling and hearing or reading the story have become accustomed to following him. The geographical difficulties created

---

[44]Many interpreters have noted that the word for "almond branch" in Hebrew is very similar to the verb for "watch." This is the subject of a famous wordplay by the prophet Jeremiah in Jeremiah 1:11-12.

by 20:1, and its report of a second arrival at Kadesh, now located in the wilderness of Zin, were discussed above. A more ominous note is sounded by the sudden death of Miriam in this same verse. The death of Moses' sister at the beginning of the chapter is matched by the account of the death of Aaron, which closes the chapter in vv. 22-29. Death brackets a complaint story about water, which is a reflection of the pre-Sinai episode in Exodus 17:1-7. The place where the Israelites "contend" with YHWH over water in Numbers 20:2-13 is still called Meribah, as in Exodus. This time the resolution involves Moses and Aaron, and something goes wrong when the water is once again obtained miraculously from a rock, but the narrator is frustratingly vague about the offense. Were they not supposed to hit the rock at all this time (v. 8), or was the second strike (v. 11) a display of impatience or unbelief, or did they attempt to take too much credit for themselves (v. 10)? Whatever the mistake, the punishment is harsh, and it falls almost immediately upon Aaron, who dies and is replaced by his son, Eleazar, at the close of the chapter.

In the meantime, Israel is on the move, but an old rivalry reappears when the Edomites, whom the Bible understands to be the descendants of Esau, refuse passage through their territory, sending the Israelites on an even more circuitous route that includes Mount Hor, the site of Aaron's death.[45] The report of the death of Aaron matches the report of Moses' death (Deuteronomy 34) in many ways. It happens on a mountain in secrecy, no burial site is mentioned or remembered, and the death is followed by thirty days of mourning.

The composite nature of Numbers 21 is a glaring reality, and reading all of its parts together coherently is a significant challenge. The chapter is characterized by movement and battles, and the brief report of a first victory over the Canaanites in vv. 1-3 is difficult to reconcile with the resumption of the tradition that Israel had to circumvent Edom (v. 4).

The last of the complaint stories in vv. 4-9 presents a major theological problem. The bronze serpent that Moses fashions so the Israelites can look up at it and be healed of their snakebites is an obvious violation of the commandment against making images (Exodus 20:4), but the story does not pause to ponder this issue. Instead, in the remainder of chapter 21, the Israelites rapidly pass through at least seven locations, defeat the armies of two kings, and occupy areas and cities designated as Sihon, Heshbon, Jazer,

---

[45]On the difficulties and possibilities of locating this mountain, see Ray L. Roth, "Hor," in *The Anchor Bible Dictionary* 3:287.

and Bashan.[46] It may even seem that the composer of the story wanted to hurry away from the scene before any objection might be raised.

In the flurry of travel and battle accounts that fill Numbers 21:10-35, a subtle thing happens, which might go unnoticed until it becomes suddenly obvious in the confusing story of Balaam in chapters 22–24. After the serpent incident, Moses begins to recede from view. He is mentioned in an offhanded recollection at 21:16 and twice in the brief spy narrative in vv. 31-35. His absence from verses 17-30 presages his total disappearance during the entire Balaam narrative. This is made more obvious by the stunning shift in point of view in these three chapters. Once the Israelites arrive "in the fields of Moab" (22:1), where they will remain for the rest of the Pentateuch, the narrator's eye shifts onto the Moabites and, more specifically, onto their king, Balak, and the mysterious prophet named Balaam.

The long Balaam narrative falls into two distinct parts. First, 22:1-40 describes in fascinating detail the attempts of King Balak to acquire the services of Balaam. Many interpreters have rightly noticed the emphasis upon "seeing" in this chapter, from v. 2 when Balak sees all of the activities of the Israelites in relation to the Amorites, as recorded in chapter 21, to 22:41 when Balaam arrives at Bamoth-baal and sees the people who pose a threat to Balak.[47] The humorous irony of the story occurs in the middle of the chapter when the donkey is able to see the angel which the professional seer cannot see.

In the second section of this narrative, the first three of Balaam's four oracles are presented in formulaic fashion. Each time Balak brings Balaam to a high place (Bamoth-baal in 22:41, Pisgah in 23:14, and Peor in 23:28), builds seven altars, and offers a sacrifice at Balaam's request. Each time Balaam meets with YHWH and receives a message which he returns to speak in Balak's presence. Following each of the oracles, which bless rather than curse Israel, Balak responds angrily to Balaam. The first two oracles, in 23:7-10 and 23:18-24, are introduced in the same manner and speak to or about Balak by name. The third oracle, in 24:3-9, which is placed in the same narrative framework as the first two, matches the fourth (24:15-24)

[46]Based on the itinerary here in Numbers and the chronology of Deuteronomy 2:14, Levine has argued that the Exodus generation dies out at Zered (Numbers 21:12), and the subsequent narrative reflects the adventures of the new generation. The narrator of Numbers, however, does not acknowledge this. See Levine, *Numbers 21-36*, 79-80.

[47]On this feature, see Bellinger, *Leviticus-Numbers*, 264-66.

more closely in form, using the same introductory formula and speaking to issues much broader than the immediate concerns of Balak. After the angry response of Balak to the third oracle, the narrative framework does not point them to another place, but indicates the upcoming departure of Balak and Balaam, each to his own people. After the fourth oracle, this parting of the ways takes place and the story ends.[48]

The figure of Balaam is a great enigma in the biblical tradition. Though he is hired by a foreign king to curse Israel, he instead always faithfully reports the blessings of God upon the chosen people. He is, at worst, a neutral character in Numbers 22–24, but in most other places in the Bible where he appears, he is cast in a negative light. Most significantly for this context, he is blamed in 31:16 for the sins of Israel at Peor.[49]

Just as 22:2 lightly connects the long Balaam complex to the preceding Amorite battles in chapter 21, the location of Balaam's third oracle at Peor links the story to the shocking Baal-peor incident recorded in chapter 25. Three issues related to this incident merit some attention. First, the account of the worship of "Baal-peor" or "Baal of Peor"[50] by the Israelites resembles the golden calf episode in Exodus 32. All of the adults from the prior incident should now be dead, so this indicates that idolatry is a perpetual problem, yet the second census will proceed in the next chapter.

Second, this story is surprising in its use of personal names of individuals, particularly the names of the slain man and woman, Zimri and Cozbi. The other named individual, Phinehas, emerges as the heroic figure

---

[48]Numbers 24:20-24 may be understood as three brief, independent oracles attached to the end of the fourth main oracle. See the discussion in Levine, *Numbers 21-36*, 204-209.

[49]Numbers 31:8 reports that Balaam is killed by the Israelites. Deuteronomy 23:4-5 implies that Balaam did curse the Israelites, but that YHWH did not listen to him and turned the curse into a blessing. This tradition is reaffirmed in Joshua 13:22, 24:9-10, and Nehemiah 13:2. Micah 6:5 mentions Balaam in neutral fashion, but the New Testament references in 2 Peter 2:15, Jude 1:11, and Revelation 2:14 present Balaam as a negative character. See the discussion of this extensive tradition in James L. Kugel, *The Bible as It Was* (Cambridge MA and London: Belknap Press of Harvard University Press, 1997) 482-95.

[50]"Baal-peor" (KJV) is both a place-name and the name of a (pagan) deity. In most modern English translations the "Baal-peor" of KJV, ERV, and ASV has become "Baal *of* Peor" (e.g., NRSV). (Apparently, "Peor" is a shortened form of "Baal-peor," "Baal-peor" is a variant of "Beth-peor," and the full name of the place was "Beth-Baal-peor.")

in the story, but his reward of an "eternal priesthood" is unclear in light of all of the previous promises to Aaron and his descendents.

Third, while there is no complaint here, the story still resembles the earlier complaint narratives in Numbers, with disobedience followed by a deadly plague, which is abated by the actions of a leader. This time, however, the leader is not Moses, who, although he has returned to the narrative in this chapter, still acts in a diminished fashion.

The second census finally arrives, filling most of chapter 26. The list includes all of the tribes, though not in exactly the same order as the initial census list in 1:17-47 (see table 5.3). The concluding verses (26:64-65) reiterate that all of the previous generation of adult males is dead except for Caleb and Joshua.

The final ten chapters of the book of Numbers are bracketed by two texts concerning a group of women identified as "the daughters of Zelophehad" (27:1-11 and 36:1-12). In both cases, the primary issue is the inheritance of land by women. The alternating story-and-law pattern developed by Douglas (see table 5.2) identifies chapter 27 as the end of a long story section, which began at chapter 20, so this pair of texts and the and the material they enclose extend across some significant boundaries in the book of Numbers. The appearance of the daughters of Zelophehad in 27:1-11 provides an occasion to observe Moses in all of his roles—leader, administrator, and lawgiver. Bringing Moses back to the center of the reader's view prepares the way for the remaining events in the chapter.

Despite the proclamation of Moses' coming death in chapter 20, and the subsequent reports of the deaths of Miriam and Aaron, it still comes as something of a shock when it suddenly seems that Moses' death is imminent in 27:12-14, and this development may seem even more confusing to readers who are aware that Moses will not die until the end of the book of Deuteronomy. Moses' request for a new leader (27:16), however, seems to forestall his death and he returns to the camp to commission Joshua. The introduction to the new generation of Israelites in the second census is now appropriately followed by an introduction to a new leader.

Laws and Instructions II

The lengthy legal section in Numbers 28–30 begins with a presentation of a cultic calendar. This ritual calendar closely resembles the one in Leviticus

23, but seems to be slightly less developed.[51] The instructions for various offerings progress from the most frequent—the daily offerings described in 28:2-6—to the least frequent—the annual festivals outlined in 28:16–29:39. The calendar is neatly introduced and concluded in 28:1 and 29:40 by the standard introductory and completion formulae, which have become the norm throughout the middle of the Pentateuch. In light of the previous chapter, with Moses' near-death experience and his apparent replacement by Joshua, it is interesting to see Moses return to his old form as receiver and deliverer of divine legislation.

The regulations concerning vows are introduced separately in 30:1. The passing reference to "votive offerings" in 29:39 is the only visible link between this section and the cultic calendar that precedes it. Gender issues arise again in this chapter and dominate the discussion of vows. This is a good place to be reminded to whom the laws of the Pentateuch are directed. From the opening of the Sinai Pericope, the narrative framework (e.g., Exodus 19:15) and the language of the laws themselves (e.g., Exodus 20:17) make clear that the law is directed toward men. This tradition continues in Numbers 30, where women are the object of much of the legislation about vows, but are never truly the subject. Sakenfeld has observed that concern about male responsibilities frames the passage in vv. 1-2 and 16. The intervening material reads much like a collection of case laws in which male responsibility for vows made by women under their control is delineated, according to the relationship of the woman to the man.[52]

Travel and Battle Narratives II

Once again the mixture of law and narrative in Numbers produces an interlocking system that extends across what may be perceived as major divisions in the book. Determining whether law or story is in control of the book at any point is the key issue, but this is not always easy. Casuistic law also fills much of chapter 31, but this time the laws are introduced by an actual story, rather than hypothetical situations. The book of Numbers returns to the Israelite itinerary of travels and battles, but the victory of the Midianites in 31:1-12 provides the occasion to address some legal issues when the victorious Israelite soldiers return from the battle with the typical

[51]For a thorough comparison of the two ceremonial calendars, see Dozeman, "The Book of Numbers," 228-34.

[52]See the discussion in Sakenfeld, *Journeying with God*, 160-64.

spoils of war, including women, children, and livestock. The conflict with the Midianites is connected to the Balaam affair, in which Midian was accused of being allies of the Moabites (22:4-7). The Midianites appear as enemies of Israel in the Baal-peor incident in chapter 25. Both of these offenses are reiterated in 31:16, and this tradition stands in some tension with the story of Moses marrying into a Midianite family.[53]

The Israelites have already fought a number of battles earlier in Numbers, but the issue of spoils does not arise in those texts. On this occasion, however, Moses, Eleazar, and other leaders meet the returning soldiers and a dispute erupts. The instructions from Moses concerning spoils are lengthy and complex. They continue to be worked out specifically for this case with the Midianite spoils, using a lot of numbers, but a procedure is produced that could be applied to other situations with mathematical precision. A few other points arise here which should not go unnoticed. Moses is concerned that women who are not virgins and male children are among the captives, and he orders them to be killed (31:17). This still leaves an enormous number of young, female captives, 32,000 according to v. 35.

This text does not describe the more rigorous ban (*herem*), that would become part of Israelite tradition, as described, though not in great detail, in Deuteronomy 7:1-7 and as employed in Joshua 6. Not only are young female captives and metal objects (vv. 22-23) retained, but livestock are looted in massive numbers, and the division of these animals occupies most of the attention of the second half of chapter 31.

The events of Numbers 32 mark a momentous occasion. The tribes of Reuben, Gad, and Mannaseh decide to settle on the east side of the Jordan and, thus, become known as the "Transjordan" tribes. So, the wilderness period would seem to be over for some Israelites and the settlement has begun, but this appears to be a disputed tradition, both internally in this text and externally in its relation to others. In chapter 32, the controversy is fairly simple. The Transjordan territory has already been taken, and is described as it is apportioned in vv. 33-42 as primarily the lands taken in battles against kings Sihon and Og (21:21-35). Why should these tribes be allowed to settle here while the others still have to cross the Jordan and fight the Canaanite for land? Moses resolves this dilemma by negotiating a deal with the Transjordan tribes, whose men agree to settle their families

---

[53]Levine has argued that the Priestly source develops this tradition of animosity toward the Midianites as a backdrop for the wars with the Midianites in Judges 6–8. See Levine, *Numbers 21-36*, 445-46.

and then cross the Jordan to battle the Canaanites with the other tribes before returning back home.

One other internal detail points toward some serious external issues. In 32:1-2, 6, 25, 29-31 the Reubernites and Gadites are identified as Transjordan tribes, but only vv. 33-47 include Manasseh with them. Careful attention to these difficulties reveals much about the nature and design of the book of Numbers.

The external difficulties created by this text are not so easily resolved. While Numbers 21 records the taking of the Transjordan territories in battle, the material in chapters 22–30 consistently treats all of the tribes as a single unit, preparing to cross the Jordan into Canaan together. The problem is most visible in the conflicting traditions of the location of Manasseh. While this "half-tribe" of the house of Joseph is allotted land on the east side of the Jordan, along with Reuben and Gad in chapter 32, and this location is confirmed in Deuteronomy 3 and Joshua 13, Manasseh is also connected to territory west of the Jordan in Joshua 17. Levine contended that Numbers 32 plays a critical role in the book of Numbers, picking up the Transjordan tradition which was initiated in chapter 21, then vanishes, preparing the way for the important uses of this tradition in Deuteronomy and Joshua.[54]

The last major narrative section of Numbers begins with a lengthy retrospective in 33:1-49. These verses record, in considerable detail, the stages of the Israelite journey through the wilderness, and are introduced by the claim in v. 2 that Moses wrote them down. A close look at the itinerary provided here produces a variety of observations. This is by no means a summary of the Israelite travels as reported by Numbers up to this point. Several important places along the journey are on the list, such as Ramses, Succoth, Rephidim, Kadesh, and Mount Hor, but several important sites in the complaint tradition, such as Taberah (Numbers 11:3 and Deuteronomy 9:22) and Meribah (Numbers 20 and Deuteronomy 32:51) are missing from the list, while others like Kibroth-hataavah (Numbers 11:34-35) are found in it (33:16-17). Some place names like Alush (33:13-14) and Mithkah (33:28-29) occur only in this one place in the entire Bible. This Priestly itinerary clearly follows a different tradition and has a different purpose than what is commonly understood to be the "JE Travel Narrative," which largely agrees with the Deuteronomic version in Deuteronomy 1–2.

---

[54]See Levine, *Numbers 21-36*, 482-94. Levine labels this chapter as J and E source material, while the rest of Numbers 25–36 is from P.

Instructions for Settling in Canaan

If the book of Numbers was primarily a book about traveling, then chapter 33 should have brought it to a close with its review of the journey. The book began, however, with more than nine chapters of narratives and laws which put Israel in order while still encamped at Mount Sinai. This beginning is matched at the end by material that organizes Israel in the land, even though it has not yet been fully occupied. Chapter 34 accomplishes two of these organizing tasks. First, it draws the boundaries of the entire land by delineating its borders on the south, west, north, and east. The second half of the chapter lists the leader for each tribe who will participate in the apportionment of the land. This provides the final occasion in Numbers for a list of the tribes (see table 5.3). This list designates a leader for ten tribes, with Reuben and Gad excluded because of their Transjordan assignment, and with Levi excluded because the priestly tribe received no land. Mannaseh is included, along with Ephraim, even though Mannaseh is assigned Transjordan land (above in vv. 13-15).

The issue that holds chapter 35 together is the designation of cities of refuge. These cities, to which a suspected murderer may flee for protection until the case is adjudicated, are also defined in Exodus 21:12-14 and Deuteronomy 19:1-13. Numbers 35 commands six such cities among the total of forty-eight given to the Levites, while Exodus assumes only one and Deuteronomy has three.[55] Neither of these other texts associates cities of refuge with the Levites. Together, these three passages show a clear sense of growth and development in the Israelite legal traditions. As territory and population expanded, more cities would have been required, and Levite management appears to have been a later development. The definition of the cities of refuge in 35:9-15 leads to a legislation concerning murder and revenge in vv. 16-34. This legislation distinguishes between deliberate, premeditated murder (vv. 16-21) and accidental killings (vv. 22-28), with cities of refuge provided for cases of the latter. The closing passage of the chapter commands capital punishment for murder, describes the need for

[55]The Levite city assignments in Joshua 21:13-38 names five such cities: Hebron, Shechem, Golan, Kedesh, and Ramoth. 1 Chronicles 6:57-67 names six cities: Hebron, Libnah, Jattir, Eshtemoa, Shechem, and Gezer. Obviously, this is a complex and convoluted tradition. See the discussion in Levine, *Numbers 31-36*, 550-53.

multiple witnesses, and forbids the freeing of murderers by payment of a ransom. Murder is singled out here as a defilement of the land, not just an individual violation of the law.

Mary Douglas has identified three significant places in Numbers that address laws concerning women. These are the testing of the wife suspected of adultery in chapter 5, the set of regulations concerning vows in chapter 30, and the pair of texts involving the daughters of Zelophehad in chapters 27 and 36. Douglas argued that this strikingly incomplete set of laws does not deal with women in Israel, but with one woman, who is Israel. Particularly the unfaithful wife of chapter 5 and the woman making vows in chapter 30 represent Israel, who may have been found unfaithful and in violation of her vows, but will be taken back because her husband (YHWH) has pronounced her vows void (30:15).[56] While this argument is not always convincing, it may help to explain why the book of Numbers comes to a close with a seemingly trivial return to the situation of the daughters of Zelophehad in chapter 36, which may address Israel's inheritance in the turbulent and tumultuous world in which Numbers was composed. Israel is forgiven and should stay together as one people and hold on to its inheritance.[57] On the other hand, Numbers 36 may be just an appendix which clarifies issues raised in chapter 27, particularly in light of the land allotment passages in chapters 32 and 34.[58]

The final verse of Numbers (36:13) is an obvious editorial note, bringing the book to a close. It resembles Leviticus 27:34, but the language of the two verses does not match precisely.

History and Numbers

It is essential to remember that historical questions concerning the Pentateuch continue to operate on at least two major levels. These are, first, questions concerning the events depicted within the books; second, questions concerning the historical circumstances surrounding the production of the book. The results of asking and answering the first kind of question about Numbers differ little, if any, from the discussion of history and Exodus. The pertinent issues were raised in the final section of

---

[56]Douglas, *In the Wilderness*, 160-71.

[57]Douglas, *In the Wilderness*, 235-45.

[58]For an example of this more traditional reading, see Levine, *Numbers 21-36*, 575.

chapter 3 above, so that discussion will not be repeated here. It is sufficient to remember that there is no evidence from outside the Bible that can be applied to the wilderness period of Israel's story described in the Pentateuch. The inscription on the Merneptah Stele, from about 1200 BCE, continues to be the central datum, but all it can tell us is that at that time something called "Israel" existed in the land known as Canaan.[59]

Issues and questions raised in the final sections of previous chapters about the production of the Pentateuch and its books also apply to the book of Numbers. Most interpreters identify two basic kinds of material in the book, Priestly legislation and pre-Priestly narrative material. Some material in the book of Numbers, however, helps to reveal the simplistic nature of such a division. The legislation concerning the "red cow" ceremony in chapter 19 certainly does not fit easily within a collection of priestly laws,[60] and the strange Balaam narrative in chapters 22–24 defies easy categorization into an early narrative source like J.

Historians are on somewhat firmer footing when asking questions about the production of the final form of the book of Numbers. The consistent concern with the role of the Levites and the priesthood descending from Aaron, and the competing claims of various groups and subgroups point to a period of controversy over such issues. As with the book of Leviticus, the reestablishment of worship in the second temple, after the chaotic experience of Exile, seems to be the most likely setting. On the other hand, compared to Leviticus, Numbers contains a lot more material that looks considerably older, and this gives the fourth book of the Pentateuch a much different feel, even if these two books in their final form were produced at similar times under similar circumstances.

Key Terms

Arithmoi	Kadesh (Kadesh-barnea)
Baal-peor	Murmuring Tradition
Balaam	oracle
Bemidbar	Phinehas
census	seer

[59]See the section on "History and the Pentateuch" in chap. 1 above.

[60]Douglas called this text "an archaic exorcism retained from pre-Israelite times in the liturgy of Judaism." See Douglas, *In the Wilderness*, 165.

Questions for Reflection

1. How are the orderliness of law and the disorder of wilderness related in the text of Numbers, and how do they relate to one another as theological concepts?
2. How does the character of Moses develop through the book of Numbers? What major events form and change his character? How does this fit with the character of Moses in other parts of the Pentateuch?
3. In what ways is the Balaam narrative unique to the Pentateuch? What seems to be its internal meaning and its purpose within the larger context of Numbers, and how do these two compare?
4. Is the book of Numbers a narrative book that contains law or a law book that contains narrative? What are the implications of this distinction for reading and understanding the book?

Sources for Further Study

Douglas, Mary. *In the Wilderness: The Doctrine of Defilement in the Book of Numbers*. JSOT Supplement series 158. Sheffield UK: JSOT Press, 1993.

Dozeman, Thomas B. "The Book of Numbers: Introduction, Commentary, and Reflections." In *The New Interpreter's Bible*, edited by Leander E. Keck et al., 2:1-268. Nashville: Abingdon Press, 1998.

Knierim, Rolf P. and George W. Coats. *Numbers*. The Forms of the Old Testament Literature 4. Grand Rapids MI: Eerdmans, 2005.

Lee, Won W. *Punishment and forgiveness in Israel's Migratory Campaign*. Grand Rapids MI: Eerdman's, 2003.

Levine, Baruch. *Numbers: A New Translation with Introduction and Commentary*. Two volumes. Anchor Bible 4. New York: Doubleday, 1993, 2000. (1) *Numbers 1–20*, AB-4 (1993). (2) *Numbers 21-36*, AB-4A (2000).

Milgrom, Jacob. *Numbers. The Traditional Hebrew Text with the New JPS Translation*. JPS Torah Commentary. Philadelphia: Jewish Publication Society, 1990.

Noth, Martin. *Numbers: A Commentary*. Translated by James D. Martin. The Old Testament Library. Philadelphia: Westminster Press, 1968.

Sakenfeld, Katherine Doob. *Journeying with God: A Commentary on the Book of Numbers*. International Theological Commentary. Grand Rapids MI: Eerdmans, 1995.

Sherwood, Stephen K. *Leviticus, Numbers, Deuteronomy*. Berit Olam [(The) Everlasting Covenant]: Studies in Hebrew Narrative and Poetry. Collegeville MN: Liturgical Press, 2002.

Chapter 6

The Book of Deuteronomy

The Literary Landscape of Deuteronomy

Deuteronomy is the most clearly defined and homogeneous book in the Pentateuch. Among the "books of Moses," it is most definitively *the* "book of Moses." The bulk of the book is made up of two extended speeches given by Moses to the Israelites on the "plains of Moab" as they awaited instructions to cross the Jordan River into Canaan, so Moses' presence dominates Deuteronomy. A simple concordance search, however, might not reveal this aspect of the book. Table 6.1 displays the number of appearances of Moses' name in the books of the Pentateuch, along with the chapters from which his name is absent.

Table 6.1
Moses' Name in the Pentateuch[1]

Book	Number of Occurrences	Chapters Lacking Moses' Name
Exodus	290	1, 21–23, 26–29, 37
Leviticus	86	2–3
Numbers	233	22–24
Deuteronomy	38	2–3, 6–26, 28, 30

This word distribution points out some important features of the Pentateuch, including some of the extended collections of law and instruction that cross chapter boundaries, and might lead the reader to draw some prelimi-

[1]Moses' name appears 767 times in the entire Hebrew canon; 647 of these are in the Pentateuch. These statistics are from Francis I. Anderson and Dean A. Forbes, *The Vocabulary of the Old Testament* (Chicago: Loyola Press, 1993) 236. For others, textual issues suggest slightly different counts. English versions produce greater numbers because, for the sake of clarity, the third-person, singular pronoun is quite often replaced by Moses' name. (E.g., in the RSV, *Moses* and *Moses'* occur 869 and 18 times, respectively; in the NRSV, 870 and 16 times.)

nary conclusions about the relative importance of Moses in different part of the Pentateuch. The absence of a character's name, though, does not indicate the absence of that character. The long gap in Deuteronomy 6–26, in which Moses' name is absent, is made up entirely of speech uttered by Moses. This indicates a very different structural pattern than Leviticus, for example, where much shorter divine speeches to Moses are continuously introduced by the narrator, always using Moses' name.

In the introductory chapter of this volume, we identified some of the problems related to the position and presence of Deuteronomy in the Pentateuch. As indicated in the previous chapter, the book of Numbers ends with the Israelites virtually settled in the Promised Land, even though there is no account of crossing the Jordan. The legal texts and narratives in Numbers 34–36 provide boundaries for the land, produce sample legislation for a settled people, and demonstrate the application of law in a settled community. The sense that Deuteronomy starts something new has led some interpreters to think of Genesis through Numbers as a "Tetrateuch" (lit., "four books"). This tendency also points to the strong connections between Deuteronomy and the books that follow it, suggesting an original, unified work, the so-called "Deuteronomistic History." This connection contributes to the possibility of a "Hexateuch" (lit., "six books"), which extends through Joshua and provides a more satisfactory conclusion to the Exodus story. In the end, the figure of Moses is too powerful for all of these forces to overcome. His life provides the defining shape of the Torah, and the position of Deuteronomy as its fifth and final book is secure.

In Numbers 27 it appears that Moses is about to die, but some quick maneuvering forestalls the divine intent to take his life at this point, and Moses reasserts himself in the closing chapters of the book of Numbers, playing a leading role in the beginning of the settlement. It is clear enough at the end of Numbers what Moses has been kept alive to do, but as we back off and look at the entire Pentateuch it also becomes clear that Moses has survived in order to speak the book of Deuteronomy into existence. Historical issues will be addressed more extensively at the end of this chapter. For now, it is enough to say that some form of Deuteronomy emerged as a "second law" during the seventh century in Israel. Who else but Moses could speak such a law into existence. In the story line created by the Pentateuch, we are transported back out of the Promised Land, where Numbers 34–36 placed us, at least symbolically, so that Moses can speak this second law on the doorstep of the Promised Land.

Even though Moses does not die until the final chapter of Deuteronomy, the death of Moses is a major literary feature of the book, as the work of Dennis T. Olson has demonstrated. Explicit references to Moses' death occur at 1:37, 3:23-27, 4:21-22, 5:25-27, 18:15-19, 31:2, 31:14, 31:16, 31:27, 31:29, 32:48-52, and 34:1-9.[2] Again, a large gap shows up in the lengthy legal speech in 12–26. The death of Moses turns out to be a significant feature of almost every other part of Deuteronomy, however, providing an important sense of shape to the whole book and becoming a serious preoccupation as it draws to a close.

The observation above of two different literary features of Deuteronomy revealed the unique character of chapters 12–26, and there appears to be a consensus among modern interpreters that these chapters form the core of the book of Deuteronomy. Careful attention to this center and the framework that forms around it reveals multiple layers of complexity to the literary landscape of Deuteronomy. One way of seeing its design is based on the existence and nature of a series of superscriptions in the book, which are tabulated in table 6.2

Table 6.2
The Superscriptions of Deuteronomy

1:1	These are the words that Moses spoke to all Israel beyond the Jordan—in the wilderness. . . .
4:44-45	This is the law that Moses set before the Israelites. These are the decrees and the statutes and ordinances that Moses spoke to the Israelites when they had come out of Egypt.
6:1	Now this is the commandment—the statutes and the ordinances—that YHWH your God charged me to teach you to observe. . . .
12:1	These are the statutes and ordinances that you must diligently observe in the land that YHWH, the God of your ancestors, has given you to occupy. . . .
29:1	These are the words of the covenant that YHWH commanded Moses to make with the Israelites in the land of Moab, in addition to the covenant that he had made with them at Horeb.
33:1	This is the blessing with which Moses, the man of God, blessed the Israelites before his death.

[2]Dennis T. Olson, *Deuteronomy and the Death of Moses: A Theological Reading* (Minneapolis: Fortress Press, 1994) 17-22.

Four of these superscriptions are in the narrator's voice and refer to Moses in the third person. The superscriptions at 6:1 and 12:1 are in the first-person voice of Moses, and help to identify the core of legal instruction at the center of the book. The complex layers of development in Deuteronomy, however, make the production of a precise outline a troublesome task. One layer of organization is provided by the speeches of Moses, which are introduced by these superscriptions.

Fretheim has identified another factor in the organization of the book of Deuteronomy, based upon the reappearance of the Decalogue in chapter 5. In the Pentateuch as a whole, Fretheim points to two "major complexes of law," the Sinai complex (Exodus 21–23 and Leviticus) and the Deuteronomic complex (Deuteronomy 6–26). Each of these collections is introduced by the Decalogue, in Exodus 20 and Deuteronomy 5.[3] While this scheme does not give attention to all of the components of Deuteronomy, and therefore cannot account fully for this book's organization, it describes important aspects of the book and its participation in the larger, pentateuchal narrative. These observations should also encourage careful consideration of the connections between Deuteronomy 12–26 and the Covenant Code in Exodus 21–23.[4]

A final layer of organization identified by Fretheim is the identity of Deuteronomy as a "book of the covenant." In 29:1, Deuteronomy itself recognizes two covenants between YHWH and Israel, the one made at Horeb (Sinai) and the one made in Moab.[5] The study of Deuteronomy has been heavily influenced for several decades by comparisons to various types of treaties in the Ancient Near East. George E. Mendenhall was a pioneer in this comparative study and his work has been the most influential. Based primarily on ancient Hittite treaties, Mendenhall identified a basic covenant outline, which he associated with "suzerainty" treaties, those made between a powerful entity, typically a king, and a group with far less power, typically a vassal state. The six components of this form are (1) Preamble; (2) historical prologue; (3) stipulations; (4) instructions for keeping and

[3]Terrence E. Fretheim, *The Pentateuch*, Interpreting Biblical Texts (Nashville: Abingdon Press, 1996) 157-58.

[4]See further discussion of this point in Ronald E. Clements, "The Book of Deuteronomy: Introduction, Commentary, and Reflections," in *The New Interpreter's Bible*, vol. 2 (Nashville: Abingdon, 1998) 273.

[5]Fretheim, *The Pentateuch*, 158-60.

public reading of the covenant; (5) a list of gods as witnesses; and (6) a list of blessings and curses resulting from performance of the stipulations.[6]

Mendenhall's primary interests were the covenant passages in Exodus 19–24 and Joshua 24, and their failure to fit the pattern. It was left to others to apply his observations about treaties to the whole book of Deuteronomy.

Moshe Weinfeld not only succeeded in linking the major portions of Deuteronomy to Mendenhall's treaty outline, but was able to trace this outline from its Hittite expression in the second millennium BCE down to its continuing influence in seventh-century Mesopotamia, a chronological setting very close to Deuteronomy.[7] It is not difficult to see much of Mendenhall's outline in the book of Deuteronomy, yet not all parts of the book are explained by this model. The correspondence of chapters 1–3 to the notion of a "historical prologue" and chapters 27–28 to the blessing and curse formula is most striking and, while the divine nature of the Deuteronomic covenant and the monotheistic tendencies of the Israelite religion expressed in the Bible would prevent calling gods as witnesses, in Deuteronomy 32:1 Moses seems to be calling the heavens and the earth as witnesses to this covenant.[8]

Table 6.3 illustrates two different outlines of Deuteronomy. The first is based heavily on the identification of superscriptions as the beginning of each section. The second depends more upon the identification of chapters 12–26 as a unified center of the book, with a concentric structure surrounding it.

---

[6]Gerorge E. Mendenhall, "Covenant Forms in Israelite Tradition," *Biblical Archaeologist* 17 (1954): 58-61.

[7]See Moshe Weinfeld, *Deuteronomy and the Deuteronomic School* (Oxford: Oxford University Press, 1972) 59-61.

[8]Weinfeld provides a full list of correspondences. See Weinfeld, *Deuteronomy and the Deuteronomic School*, 63-66. Weinfeld's work on Deuteronomy and treaty forms built on the work of a number of other scholars between him and Mendenhall (59-61).

Table 6.3
Two Outlines of Deuteronomy

Olson's Five Superscription Outline[9]

1:1	These are the words . . .
4:44	This is the law
6:1	This is the commandment
29:1	These are the words of the covenant
33:1	This is the blessing

Christensen's Concentric Design[10]

A The Outer Frame: A Look Backwards (Deuteronomy 1–3)
B The Inner Frame: The Great Peroration (4–11)
C The Central Core: Covenant Stipulations (12–26)
B' The Inner Frame: The Covenant Ceremony (27–30)
A' The Outer Frame: A Look Forward (31–34)

All attempts to read Deuteronomy and determine some sort of outline or structure eventually return to Moses. The death of Israel's deliverer and lawgiver as the final event looms over the whole book and demands careful consideration. The book opens with Moses speaking, and the first three chapters remind the reader why Moses is important. Perhaps the most illuminating feature of this account of the journey through the wilderness is Moses' use of first-person-plural language. In communicating with Pharaoh in Exodus 5–11, Moses had spoken of himself and the Israelites as "we," but such speech is rare throughout the wilderness accounts.[11] The book of Numbers, particularly, serves to draw a line of separation between Moses and the Israelites, but Moses' own speech in Deuteronomy 1–3 brings them back together. Moses shapes the story throughout by speech and action, thus the outline in this chapter takes some of the features from each of those in table 6.3 and follows the work of Moses, as he remembers, instructs, preaches, and dies.

---

[9]Dennis T. Olson, *Deuteronomy and the Death of Moses*, 15.

[10]Duane L. Christensen, "Deuteronomy in Modern Research: Approaches and Issues," in *A Song of Power and the Power of Song: Essays on the Book of Deuteronomy*, ed. Duane Christensen (Winona Lake IN: Eisenbrauns, 1993) 9.

[11]One small exception is in Numbers 10:29-32 when Moses speaks to his brother-in-law, Hobab, about himself and the Israelites as "we."

Deuteronomy is the most self-consciously theological book in the Pentateuch, and this aspect provides one final set of observations that should be carried along on a journey through the book. The most prominent theological feature of Deuteronomy is its concern for the centralization of worship. This was likely part of Josiah's reform, which generated the production of the book and has the temple in Jerusalem in view, though it cannot say so explicitly. To avoid this anachronism, Deuteronomy consistently refers to Jerusalem as "a dwelling place for his name." Variations on this phrase appear at 12:5, 11, 21; 14:23, 24; 16:2, 6, 11; 26:2, 6, and 15. It is immediately apparent, of course, that all of these references appear in the central core of the book, chapters 12–26. A related theological issue of great importance is idolatry. Deuteronomy sees Israel's movement into the Promised Land as a temptation to take up worship of the gods of Canaan, including the fashioning of idols. Centralizing worship in Jerusalem is one way to exert greater control on religious practices and enforce monotheism. Other theological themes include holy war, land, blessing and curse, and care for the poor, but all of these revolve around this central concern for proper worship.

Moses Recalls the Israelite Story

The opening recollection in Deuteronomy 1–3 obviously presents a different way of remembering the Israelite story. It is not interested in Egypt, the Exodus, or the journey to Sinai, but begins with the departure from the mountain that Deuteronomy consistently calls "Horeb." A direct connection is drawn between the journey from Horeb to Canaan and the promises to the ancestors. The remainder of chapter 1 corresponds roughly to events in Numbers. The selection of judges from the tribes is similar to the story in Numbers 11:10-30, but in some ways it looks more like the one in Exodus 18:13-26. The account of the spies in Deuteronomy 1:22-33 is obviously referring to the same basic tradition as Numbers 13, but this time the sending of the spies is the people's idea (v. 22), rather than God's, and Joshua and Caleb do not appear as a dissenting minority when the report is given. Both of them are present in the following pronouncement of the penalty (vv. 34-45), but Joshua is not identified as one of the spies. The different recollection raises some questions about the purpose of recalling. Obviously, the book of Deuteronomy was written originally to stand alone, and predates the formation of the Pentateuch, so a context for Moses' upcoming speeches must be provided.

Moses Establishes a Second Law

Deuteronomy 4 is a difficult unit to characterize, partly because of its transitional nature. As a transitional passage it belongs both with what comes before and after. The opening, "And/So now . . . " connects this chapter to the preceding recitation of Israel's story of deliverance. The next two words, "Israel, hear" links this opening verse to 5:1, 6:4, 9:1, and 20:3, but this linkage is sometimes disguised in English translations.[12] Another pair of words in 4:1, routinely translated as "statutes and ordinances," also begins a chain of repetition. These two words will appear together in Deuteronomy a total of twelve times, all but one of which are in chapters 4–11. The speech in chapter 4 urges obedience as a result of, or response to, God's act of deliverance. The principle concern of the chapter is idolatry, and the "Baal of Peor" incident (Numbers 25) is recalled in vv. 3-4 and vv. 15-20 to remind the Israelites that because they "saw no form" of YHWH at Horeb, they are not to make idols or worship visible things. This concern with the making of idols continues to consume vv. 21-31, which seem to assume that eventually Israel will succumb to this temptation.

Deuteronomy 5 appears as a self-contained oration that includes its own version of the Ten Commandments. Many interpreters have argued that what follows in chapters 6–26 is a lengthy expansion on the Decalogue, so this use of it as an introduction is significant to the development of much of the rest of the book. The notion of a Decalogue is most explicit in 10:4-5 where Moses recalls God writing "the ten words" on the tablets, which Moses then placed "in the ark." As noted in the discussion of the Ten Commandments in Exodus, there is not one obvious way of dividing this set of laws and counting them as ten, with the greatest sense of ambiguity involving the clear identification of the first and last commandments.

The experience of Horeb (Sinai) is recalled in 5:1-5. Though the generation that was present there is now gone, the current generation is understood as the recipient of the covenant that God spoke, and Moses now commands them to "Hear" again. The Decalogue itself is in vv. 6-21, and differs in only a few ways from the version in Exodus 20. The greatest

---

[12]These other four uses of "Israel" with the imperative "Hear!" all place the verb first, while in 4:1 the verb is second and is followed by a preposition, prompting translations such as "Israel, listen to . . . " (NASV, REB, NJB) or "Israel, give heed to . . . " (RSV, NRSV, NJV).

difference is in the rationale provided for the observance of sabbath in v. 15. Here in Deuteronomy the purpose of sabbath observance is to remember the days of Israel's bondage in Egypt and YHWH's deliverance of Israel from slavery, while in Exodus 20:11 sabbath observance is connected to the seven-day creation story.

A minor grammatical difference occurs in the series of short, negative commands in the second tablet, which Deuteronomy 5 connects with conjunctions. This is reflected in English translations by the use of "neither" at the beginning of these commands (vv. 18, 19, 20, 21a, 21b), or by the absence of the conjunction altogether.[13] This feature points to an identification of six commandments in the traditional "second tablet" in vv. 17-21, with v. 21 divided into two commandments, one not to "desire" (NRSV "covet") a neighbor's wife and the other not to "covet" (NRSV "desire") a neighbor's property. This division would force the combination of vv. 6-10 into one commandment in order to achieve a count of ten, or the designation of v. 6 as an introduction and vv. 7-10 as the first commandment.[14]

The remainder of the Sinai Decalogue experience is recalled in Deuteronomy 5:22-33, as Moses is put in the position of mediator between YHWH and Israel, in an account that is close to that found in Exodus 20:18-21, though it is significantly expanded. This role of Moses is highlighted by the structure of the Pentateuch as a whole, as it moves from the book of Leviticus, which is filled with speeches of YHWH to Moses, to Deuteronomy, where Moses produces all of the speech.[15]

All of Deuteronomy 6–11 is dominated by the presence of the "greatest commandment," the *Shema*, in Deuteronomy 6:4-5. It is given the same hortatory introduction, "Hear, Israel," with which the Decalogue itself is introduced (5:1), and it is from this opening word that the most important commandment in Jewish tradition receives its name.[16] The full command

---

[13]This Hebrew conjunctive-vav is rendered as "neither" in the KJV tradition (KJV, ERV, ASV, RSV, NRSV) but is left untranslated in virtually every other English translation (e.g., 1560/1599 *Geneva Bible*, NEB/REB, JB/NJB, NAB, NIV/TNIV, NKJV, NASV, ESV, even NJV/*TaNaKh*).

[14]See in table 3.3 the lists of various ways to count the Ten Commandments, and for further discussion of this issue, see Olson, *Deuteronomy and the Death of Moses*, 42-45.

[15]On this observation, see Thomas W. Mann, *The Book of the Torah: The Narrative Integrity of the Pentateuch* (Atlanta: John Knox Press, 1988) 143-44.

[16]*Shema* is a transliteration of the Hebrew imperative verb form, "Hear!" The translation of the remainder of 6:4-5 has been a puzzle for millennia. See the discus-

ment contains the famous tripartite exhortation to love God (v. 5). This part of the commandment is familiar in the Christian tradition because of its appearances in the gospels (Matthew 22:37, Mark 12:30, and Luke 10:27), but its contents vary in the many places it appears. Table 6.4 illustrates the various versions of this commandment.

Table 6.4
Comparing Versions of the "Greatest Commandment"

All versions begin with, "You shall love the LORD (YHWH) your God will all your. . . . "

The versions continue with the list as follows:

Hebrew text of Deuteronomy 6:5	heart, soul, strength
Greek text of Deuteronomy 6:5	mind, soul, strength
Matthew 22:37	heart, soul, mind
Mark 12:30	heart, soul, mind, strength
Luke 10:27	heart, soul, strength, mind

The Greek text reveals the changing cultural understanding of the seat of human volition from the "heart" to the "head" ("mind"). The gospels then struggle with the choice either to harmonize the Greek and Hebrew traditions, producing a list of four aspects of humanity (Mark and Luke), or retain the more rhythmic threefold pattern and leave something out (Matthew).

The verses that immediately follow this commandment offer ways to remember and make use of it, including recitation to children, regular discussion, binding it to one's hand and forehead (in phylacteries), and writing it on one's doorpost.

A curious clause introduces Deuteronomy 7, which begins with a preposition most translations render as "When." This same type of grammatical construction, identifying the time of entry into the land, is repeated numerous times in the middle section of Deuteronomy.[17] This occurrence

sion in Richard D. Nelson, *Deuteronomy: A Commentary*, The Old Testament Library (Louisville: Westminster/John Knox Press, 2004, ©2002) 89-91.

[17]Nelson identifies such "temporal markers" at 7:1, 12:20, 17:14, 18:9, 19:1, 26:1, and 27:2, though 27:2 lacks the defining preposition. See the discussion in Nelson, *Deuteronomy*, 96. The preposition that marks all but the last of these clauses could be translated as "because" or even "if."

in 7:1 is the fullest expression of this type of construction. It begins with the phrase, "When YHWH your God brings you into the land which you shall enter," and goes on to list the nations Israel will conquer and describes some of the regulations of "holy war."

The list of seven nations is not repeated precisely anywhere else in the Pentateuch. The closest matches are a list of six of the same nations in Exodus 23:24 and four of them in Numbers 13:29. A closer look at the former of these two passages reveals that Deuteronomy 7 looks very much like Exodus 23:20-33, the end of the Covenant Code. The most significant difference between the two passages is the development of the harsh "ban" against foreigners in 7:2-5, requiring their total destruction. The contradiction between this order and the command not to intermarry with foreign groups, in vv. 3-4, reveals an important aspect of this and other "temporal" passages. For the characters in Deuteronomy, including Moses who is speaking these words, the entry into the Promised Land and the accompanying destruction is in the future, but for the writers and the original audience of Deuteronomy it is in the distant past. Thus, the commands against social interaction with foreigners would make sense to the original audience precisely because Israel is not the only group around, and the eradication of all other groups from Canaan was never accomplished.[18]

The ban of the past is merged in v. 6 with the program of eliminating alternative worship sites in order to centralize the Jerusalem cult. The remainder of chapter 7 expands the exhortation to enter the land, take it, and drive out the inhabitants, and it ends with commands to avoid idols and other inappropriate religious practices (vv. 25-26).

Another literary feature links Deuteronomy 7 with chapters 8 and 9. Each of these three chapters contains a phrase similar to the "When you say in your heart . . . " of 7:17 ("If you say to yourself . . . " NRSV). The three sections introduced by these phrases contain warnings against being afraid that Israel is incapable of defeating the nations of Canaan (7:17-24); taking credit for success because of one's own power (8:17-20); or believing that God chose and blessed Israel because of its righteous character (9:4-6). These warnings hold this section of Deuteronomy together by focusing on issues of "remembering" (or "not forgetting") what YHWH has done for Israel in the past and has promised Israel in the future. Moses' audience is being prepared to hear the commands that will bring the blessings of obedience or the destruction that comes from disobedience. Verb forms from the

---

[18]See the discussion of this issue in Nelson, *Deuteronomy*, 98-99.

roots "remember" and "forget" appear a total of ten times in chapters 7–9 out of a total of approximately twenty-eight appearances in the entire book of Deuteronomy.

Within this extended section which is so concerned with remembering, chapter 9 stands out because of its vivid recollection of the Israelite rebellion at Horeb. This chapter is carefully connected to the preceding material with the familiar "Hear O Israel" at v. 1, "Do not say in your heart, when YHWH your God thrusts them out from before you" in v. 4, and "Remember and do not forget" in v. 7. This recollection of rebellion receives internal cohesion from the fourfold repetition of "forty days and forty nights," the period of time Moses spent on the mountain (vv. 9 and 11), and the period of time Moses spent praying to YHWH to convince him not to destroy the Israelites (vv. 18 and 25). Moses also makes four references to "the two stone tablets" (vv. 9, 10, 15, 17) that God gave him and that he smashed upon seeing the Israelites worshipping the calf.

The emphasis upon the two tablets leads into chapter 10 where Moses recalls making the replacement tablets and taking them up the mountain. The memory of the golden calf incident and surrounding events in chapter 9 matches Exodus 32–34 fairly well, but there is a departure in 10:1-5. Moses connects the construction of the Ark of the Covenant to the making of the second set of tablets, rather than to the larger project of constructing all of the implements of the tabernacle, as in Exodus 37. Along with the recollection of making the two new tablets (10:3) and writing the "ten words" on them (v. 4), this chapter is also connected back to chapter 9 by Moses' description of the period of forty days and forty nights on the mountain the second time. Deuteronomy 9:8–10:11 might be seen as a microcosm of the entire Exodus experience. The forty-day periods of receiving the first and second sets of tablets on the mountain surround the forty-day trial in the valley below when Moses intercedes to prevent YHWH from destroying the rebellious Israelites. In the same way, two grand law experiences on Sinai/Horeb and on the plains of Moab surround a forty-year period of trial in the wilderness where such intercession by Moses repeatedly saves the Israelites from YHWH's intended destruction.

This sense of coherence running through chapters 9 and 10 is accompanied by a great deal of confusion and complexity. It is apparent that multiple literary layers have been combined to produce the final form of the text, but some of the literary confusion is partially masked in translation, either deliberately or unavoidably, due to a peculiar feature of English grammar when compared to Hebrew grammar. While English uses the pronoun, "you," for all forms of the second-person pronoun, Hebrew has four different forms which distinguish gender and number. Most significant in this text is the alternation between singular and plural forms of the second-person pronoun. Similar variation between singular and plural forms of third person is also frequently disguised in English translation by the imprecise use of plural forms.[19] This variation of pronouns is so prominent throughout Deuteronomy that German scholarship has given it the name *Numeruswechsel* or "Number Alternation."[20] Attempts to use this feature to unravel the literary layers of Deuteronomy, however, have not proven successful.

The long exhortation to keep the law begins to draw to a close at 10:12 with a weaving together of command and narrative. The reminder to judge fairly and to take care of orphans, widows, and strangers (vv. 18-19) is connected to the story of bondage in Egypt and the deliverance that followed (vv. 21-22).[21] In 11:1-7 Moses recalls this deliverance even more vividly, especially the event at the "Red Sea."

As Moses brings this part of the speech to a close, he reminds the Israelites of the blessings of the covenant (vv. 8-12) and the punishment which will come from unfaithfulness (vv. 16-17). The instructions that followed the *Shema* in 6:6-9 are repeated almost verbatim in 11:18-21. The most explicit language of blessing and curse appears in v. 26 and points forward to the other side of the Deuteronomic Code, where they will be spelled out in greater detail in chapters 27–28. Chapter 11 closes with the tenth and final reference to "statutes and ordinances" in chapters 4-11, and 11:32 provides a direct link to 12:1.

Moses Speaks the Deuteronomic Code

The discussion of Deuteronomy thus far has frequently called attention to what has been perceived as the center of the book—the legal collection in chapters 12–26, often called the "Deuteronomic Code." The catch phrase, "statutes and ordinances," has already appeared ten times in the book from 4:1 to 11:32, and the repetition of this phrase seems to be preparing the

---

[19]Nelson has called attention to this feature and the difficulties it creates. See Nelson, *Deuteronomy*, 119-20.

[20]See the discussion of this issue in Christensen, "The *Numeruswechsel* in Deuteronomy 12," in *A Song of Power and the Power of Song*, 394-402.

[21]For more on this connection between narrative and the motivation to keep the law, see Mann, *The Book of the Torah*, 153-54.

reader for the long legal "speech" of Moses, which is not nearly so much like a speech as what comes before it. Chapters 12–26 are bound by the remaining two appearances—of the twelve total in Deuteronomy—of "statutes and ordinances," in 12:1 and 26:16. Between these two defining statements lies a legal code that appears to many interpreters to be organized along the lines of the Decalogue, and the discussion that follows will make use of this organizing principle as an aid in presenting what might otherwise be a bewildering collection.

The introduction to this chapter identified centralization of worship as a primary concern of Deuteronomy. While the consolidation of Israel's religious life within the Jerusalem temple clearly had political and economic aspects, Deuteronomy keeps its focus on the theological facet of this effort. Worship sites in outlying areas are perceived as a threat to the commandment(s) against the construction of idols and worship of other gods. The Deuteronomic code addresses this issue directly at the outset, and names the central worship site with the typical circumlocution, "The place that YHWH your God will choose . . . to put his name there" (12:5). All other worship sites are understood to be inherited from the Canaanites who previously occupied the land and are to be destroyed and eliminated (12:2-3).

The statements against improper worship and idolatry in 12:2-12 and 12:29-32 surround a discussion in vv. 13-28 of a problem generated by centralization of worship. The sacrificial system serves not only as a means of worship, but also, presumably, as a slaughtering industry. In order to keep sacrificial worship confined to one place in a nation that was expanding in territory and population, a system of nonsacrificial meat processing was necessary, and here is where Deuteronomy's practical side emerges. In vv. 13-28 ordinary slaughtering of animals is separated from sacrificial offerings, with the minimal requirements of proper draining and disposal of blood retained. These stipulations are in line with those in Leviticus 17:10-14.

After the statement on idolatry in 12:29-32, a seemingly diverse collection of laws fills chapters 13–14. The argument that the Deuteronomic Code follows the Decalogue would require that something in this section correspond to the improper use of YHWH's name, and this is probably the weakest part of such a scheme. One of the more intensive efforts to place chapters 12–26 within a Decalogue outline is found in the work of Georg Braulik, who identifies 14:1-21 with taking YHWH's name in vain. Table 6.5 is based on Braulik's outline as adapted by Dennis Olson.

Table 6.5
The Deuteronomic Code and the Decalogue[22]

First Commandment	The one God of Israel	12:2-13:18
Second	Taking YHWH's name in vain	14:1-21
Third	Keeping the Sabbath holy	14:22–16:17
Fourth	Honoring parents	16:18–18:22
Fifth	Preserving life	19:1–22:8
Sixth	Rape and family	22:9–23:18
Seventh	Property	23:19–24:7
Eighth	Truth and judgment	24:8–25:4
Ninth/Tenth	Coveting	25:5–26:15

In the opening section, 13:1-5 brings up prophecy, an important issue in Israelite tradition. The command acknowledges the existence of false prophets and diviners and orders that they be executed. False prophecy might be an example of inappropriate use of God's name. This command is extended in vv. 6-18 to any person who encourages false worship. The prohibitions against self-mutilation and shaving one's hair in mourning for the dead, and eating unclean animals, all in 14:1-21, seem more like an appendix, though these practices may have been associated with foreign worship practices.

The command concerning unclean animals requires a list, which is produced in vv. 4-20 and is similar to the list in Leviticus 11:2-23.[23] The list is closed by the more general prohibition against eating animals that have already died from other causes and the odd injunction against "boiling a kid in its mother's milk," also found in Exodus 23:19b and 34:26b.

---

[22]This outline is based on that of Georg Braulik, "The Sequence of Laws in Deuteronomy 12–26 and in the Decalogue," in *A Song of Power and the Power of Song*, ed. Duane L. Christensen, 321-22, as adapted by Dennis T. Olson, in his *Deuteronomy and the Death of Moses: A Theological Reading*, OBT, (Minneapolis: Fortress Press, 1994).

[23]See the discussion of these two lists and how they are alike and different in Jeffrey H. Tigay, *Deuteronomy. The Traditional Hebrew Text with the New JPS Translation*, JPS Torah Commentary (Philadelphia: Jewish Publication Society, 1996) 137-38.

This latter law provides an interesting illustration of the various ways that law functions. First, why would such a thing be forbidden? A common guess is that this was a regular practice among Israel's "pagan" neighbors, but surely Israel's neighbors practiced animal sacrifice and many other activities not forbidden by the law. The use of this command at the end of the list may connect it to the general context of foreign worship practices in chapters 12–14, but this does not explain the reference to an act which is so specific. Second, how specific is this law? Does it allow boiling meat in milk that does not come from the animal's mother? Later Jewish law forbade cooking meat in milk entirely, presumably in order to prevent accidental violation of this law.[24]

A more direct connection to the Decalogue is immediately apparent in 15:1, which begins a set of instructions concerning the seventh, sabbatical, year. Hints of the sabbatical year appear in the Covenant Code in Exodus, which commands the release of Hebrew slaves after six years (21:2-11) and letting the land lie fallow every seventh year (for the sake of the poor and the wild animals, 23:10-11).

A more developed set of regulations for the land Sabbath has already appeared in the Holiness Code in Leviticus 25:1-7, but Leviticus is much more concerned with the "seven sabbaths of years [forty-nine]," the Jubilee Year. The Sabbath provisions in Deuteronomy 15:1-18 include remission of debts and releasing of slaves, but not land Sabbath. The procedure for keeping a slave who does not wish to go free, in vv. 16-17, shows an almost certain dependence on Exodus 21:5-6, but Deuteronomy expands the law to include female slaves (15:17b).[25]

Deuteronomy also stands apart in the ways it addresses the appropriate attitude of the ones keeping the law (v.18). They are not to consider compliance with requirements like those in this section to be a burden. This seems in keeping with the great commandment, which describes love of God with one's whole being as the foundation of the law, and contradicts the common assumption that the Torah is legalistic and onerous.

The little text about consecration of firstborn animals in 15:19-23 may at first seem out of place, but the discussion of the sabbatical year has carried the reader away from the world of the sanctuary out into the world of commerce, and the sacrifice of the firstborn brings us back to "the place

[24]Tigay, *Deuteronomy*, 140-41.

[25]See the discussion of this expansion in Nelson, *Deuteronomy*, 190-200.

that YHWH will choose" (v. 20). This relocation is vital to the upcoming discussion of festivals.

Israel's festal calendar has already been the subject of texts in Exodus 23:14-17, Leviticus 23:1-44, and Numbers 28:1–29:40, so it is apparent that this was a subject under constant negotiation, and that it likely varied from time to time and place to place. The focus in Deuteronomy 16:1-17 is on three festivals, so the Deuteronomic Code again displays an affinity with the Covenant Code, which defines three festivals in Exodus 23:14-17. More detail is provided here in Deuteronomy about the festivals of Passover, Weeks, and Booths, but the most significant change is the relocation of these festivals to the central sanctuary, "the place that YHWH your God will choose" (vv. 7, 11, and 15). What had been family or local celebrations have now become grand pilgrimage festivals, which will bring all of Israel to Jerusalem.[26]

Most interpreters recognize a fairly distinct shift in the Deutronomic Code from laws that concern worship to those that deal with civic behavior and responsibility. Again, this is a shift that reflects the character of the Decalogue, but it is not so easy to draw precise boundaries, which is a good reminder that our easy distinctions between ritual behavior and ethical behavior probably do not reflect the convictions of ancient Israel.

Ultimately, 17:2-7 establishes a judicial procedure and rules for administering the death penalty, but the example of a capital crime that it uses is idolatry. The dispersed civic life of Israel continues to be tied to the sacred center of Israel's worship in 17:8-13 where cases too difficult to adjudicate on the local level are referred to the "levitical priests and the judge" at "the place that YHWH your God will choose" (vv. 8-9).

This move back to the center, and linking of civic and religious procedures finds its ultimate expression in the surprising discussion of the monarchy in 17:14-20. Discussion of the historical implications of this text will be deferred until the final section in this chapter. In the literary development of Deuteronomy it is important to acknowledge at least two things. The Deuteronomic Code has worked its way to this point as a center. Perhaps nothing holds together the concerns of ritual life, reflected in the first tablet of the Decalogue, and the issues of civic life, illustrated in the second tablet, like the king, who is at once an accommodation to the political patterns of Israel's foreign neighbors (17:14) and the adopted son

---

[26]For a more detailed discussion, comparing this festival legislation with that found in other texts, see Tigay, *Deuteronomy*, 152-59.

of God ("a king whom YHWH your God will choose," 17:15). Deuteronomy must accept the presence of the king, of course, but retains the right to be suspicious of royal power (vv. 16-17) and to establish itself as the ultimate check on that power (vv. 18-20).[27]

The collection of laws in chapter 18 still lies close to the center of Israel's life. Regulations concerning the role of priests (vv. 1-8) and prophets (vv. 15-22) surround a list of unaccepted religious practices, particularly the type that might be influential in alternative worship sites, like sorcery and divining (vv. 9-14).

The laws in this chapter govern interactions between the general population and religious professionals, both approved and unapproved. Table 6.5 suggests that this chapter may be the last one that is related to the commandment about honoring parents. Within the Decalogue this commandment plays a transitional role between those focused upon the ritual sphere and those concerned with civic affairs. The family helps to link those two areas of life, and the commandments concerning provision for the Levites, child sacrifice, and evaluation of prophetic proclamations address that same juncture. Deuteronomy displays here some awareness of the impact of its centralization program. The Levites who would have been supported by the worship activities at outlying sites now need support from the central sanctuary.[28]

The legislation concerning cities of refuge in Deuteronomy 19:1-13 moves more clearly into the civic arena, and is closely related to the commandment against killing. The designation of cities where a suspected murderer can flee while the case is being adjudicated has arisen previously in the Pentateuch at Exodus 21:13, Numbers 35:9-15, and Deuteronomy 4:41-43. The earlier passage in Deuteronomy designated three such cities on the east side of the Jordan, while this one commands three on the west side, with the possibility of three more should the Israelite territory expand (vv. 2-3). The Exodus passage speaks of a single place, while Numbers designates three on each side of the Jordan.

The most significant distinction of the text in Deuteronomy 19 is the portrayal of an example of an accidental killing, a story about a group of men cutting wood in a forest, one of whom is killed by the loose ax head of another (vv. 4-5). The other major section in chapter 19 addresses the use of witnesses in a trial, so it is related to the eighth/ninth commandment(s)

---

[27]See the interpretation of this text in Nelson, *Deuteronomy*, 222-25.

[28]For more on this issue, see Nelson, *Deuteronomy*, 230-31.

of the Decalogue, but the examples given in this text have to do with bodily harm, so there is still a connection to the commandment against killing.

Deuteronomy 20 is composed entirely of laws concerning warfare, so the direct connection to killing continues. After allowances for anyone who has recently built a house, or planted a vineyard, or become engaged, or anyone who is so frightened as to leave the ranks before a battle, a surprising distinction is drawn concerning the conduct of war. When fighting against the six ethnic groups (20:17) whose land YHWH is giving to the Israelites, the full ban (that is, complete destruction) is commanded, but vv. 10-15 allows for peace treaties, the taking of slaves, and the taking of humans, animals, and other materials as spoils of war when fighting against others.

Further surprise is added by vv. 19-20 which commands kinder and gentler rules for the treatment of *trees* during warfare than for the treatment of human beings. The commandment against killing does not seem to apply in any way during wartime.

A strange ritual is described in Deuteronomy 21:1-9, relating to the discovery of a dead body that appears to be the result of a killing, but the assailant is unknown. In such a case, the nearest city is determined by measurement and the elders of that city must bring to a nearby wadi a cow, which is killed by breaking its neck. These elders then wash their hands and proclaim the innocence of their city. Two things about this ritual are worth noting. First, though the Levites are to be present, the text seems careful not to portray the killing of the cow as a sacrificial ritual, since this does not take place at the central sanctuary. Second, though v. 8 hints that this process might identify the killer, it is not clear how this would work.[29]

The collection of laws relating to the duties and treatment of public officials comes to an end at 21:9, and the next several chapters of Deuteronomy are composed of a more diverse collection of laws. The movement from centralized worship activities to the sphere of civic interaction to the lives of ordinary Israelite families and individuals continues. This flow is well illustrated by 21:10-14, which returns to the situation of the handling of spoils and captives of war, a subject addressed already in 20:10-20. While the earlier text dealt with the general behavior of the Israelite army, 21:10-14 raises a more specific, individual case in which an Israelite soldier, addressed here in the second-person singular, sees among the captives a woman he wishes to marry. The regulations concerning the arrange-

[29]See the discussion of this problem in Tigay, *Deuteronomy*, 191-93.

ment and conduct of such a marriage leads into requirements governing other family issues.

A most surprising regulation appears in 21:15-17, which forbids giving the firstborn privileges to the nonfirstborn son of a favored wife, a law that stands in direct opposition to the behavior of Abraham, Isaac, and Jacob.

The remainder of Deuteronomy 21 reveals how these miscellaneous laws are arranged like a chain. A problematic marriage in vv. 11-14 leads to a case involving the sons of a favored and a less-favored wife in vv. 15-17, which leads to the disciplining of a rebellious son in vv. 18-21. The application of capital punishment in this last instance points toward the regulations for the hanging of a criminal in vv. 22-23.

A new chain of laws begins in chapter 22, beginning with care for a neighbor's livestock (vv. 1-4), then an explanation of what to do with a fallen bird's nest (vv. 6-7), and instructions for building the roof on a new house so that nobody will fall off of it (v. 8). The apparent misfit law in v. 5 concerning cross-dressing seems to point ahead to the set of laws about improper mixing of grape seeds, work animals, and fabrics in vv. 9-11, all of which leads to the instruction about putting tassels on the corners of a garment (v. 12), which is related to the regulations in Numbers 15:37-41, but is not as detailed.[30]

The next set of laws, in 22:13-30, is related to marriage. When combined with the previous section, these laws address the three standard activities of establishing a home: building a house, planting a vineyard, and getting married, a sequence that also occurs in 20:5-8 when the Levites are offering the troops reasons to leave an impending battle.[31] This sequence also helps to form the foundation for the preaching of Jeremiah to the exiles (Jeremiah 29:5-6). The series of laws about marriage in Deuteronomy 22:13-30, which addresses adultery at a number of points, brings the Deuteronomic Code back into close contact with the Decalogue. A specific commandment against adultery, which demands capital punishment for an offense, is at the center of this section in v. 22.

After a set of laws in 23:1-6 forbidding admission into the "congregation of YHWH" for eunuchs, illegitimate children, Ammonites, and Moabites, vv. 7-8 specifically disallow feelings of abhorrence toward

---

[30]See the further explanation of the connections among all of these laws in Tigay, *Deuteronomy*, 455-56.

[31]See the discussion of the "standard triad of domestic activities" in Tigay, *Deuteronomy*, 456.

Edomites and Egyptians. The second half of chapter 23 becomes even more scattered in form and content, addressing nocturnal emissions, defecation, escaped slaves, temple prostitution, interest on loans, vows, and other issues. The attempts in earlier sections to link laws together in some discernable sense of organization begins to fade away as the collection brings in a wider diversity of laws which are difficult to fit into any pattern.

The lack of any discernable pattern continues throughout chapters 24–25. A few portions within these chapters, however, merit some special attention. A series of laws in 24:10-22 lists numerous provisions for the care of the poor, including the return of garments given in pledge (vv. 10-13), the timely payment of wages (vv. 14-15), and leaving behind grain, olives, and grapes for the poor to glean after the harvest (vv. 19-22). This sequence has much in common with the laws found in Leviticus 19:9-16.

Deuteronomy 25:5-10 provides the legal foundation for the practice often called "levirate marriage," an issue that arises in the narrative about Tamar in Genesis 38. This passage in Deuteronomy places an obligation on the brother of a man who dies childless to marry the widow and produce an heir for the dead brother. The social repercussions for one who fails to fulfill such a duty are expressed in subtle fashion but seem severe. Oddly, both narratives in the Old Testament concerning this custom break down for various reasons, Genesis 38 because the second brother also dies, leaving only one remaining brother and threatening to annihilate the whole family,[32] and Ruth because there is no living brother, so the process must be negotiated among other relatives.

Finally, Deuteronomy 25:11-12 offers the only case in the entire Pentateuch where bodily disfigurement is prescribed as punishment for an infraction other than the strict retaliation of "an eye for and eye and a tooth for a tooth." In this case a woman is to have her hand cut off if she assists her husband in a fight by grabbing his opponent's genitals.[33]

Deuteronomy 26 opens with the significant phrase, "When you enter into the land," which duplicates an introductory phrase used earlier in the

---

[32]For a story in which multiple deaths of brothers who marry the same woman are attributed to a type of curse, demon possession, see Tobit 6:10-18 (6:9-17 in KJV, RSV, et al.). This story of seven consecutive dead husbands is apparently the one to which Jesus refers in Matthew 22:23-33, Mark 12:18-27, and Luke 20:27-40.

[33]See the discussion in Tigay, *Deuteronomy*, 484-85. This text presented obvious problems for Talmudic interpreters because of the misfit between punishment and crime, and perhaps because of a general distaste for physical mutilation.

Deuteronomic Code at places such as 17:14 and 18:9 and resembles the similar, "When YHWH brings you into the land," of 6:10 and 7:1. So, this chapter is tied to both the early parts of the book of Deuteronomy and the Deuteronomic Code which it brings to a close. The list-like character of the past few chapters has come to an end, and chapter 26, though it still provides legal regulations of a kind, is quite different in form from what immediately precedes it. The instructions for offering the firstfruits of the ground include a recital, or confession of faith, in vv. 5-9, which recalls the grand review of Israel's story in Deuteronomy 1–3.

This is an appropriate point at which to emphasize the work of Gerhard von Rad, whose writings on Deuteronomy, and particularly this passage, have dominated the discussion for the past three-quarters of a century. Von Rad famously labeled 26:5-9 the "little creed," and argued that it constituted one of the earliest traditions around which Deuteronomy and the Pentateuch grew. His central observation was that this creed is limited in its elements. It includes Jacob (the "Wandering Aramean"), the Egyptian bondage, the deliverance from Egypt, and the entry into the Promised Land. This brief recital lacks any mention of the earlier ancestors, Mount Sinai and the legal tradition, or the wilderness period.[34]

The recital of Israel's past is followed by a declaration of obedience to the commandments of YHWH in vv. 12-15. This includes a pledge from the worshiper that offerings have been made and handled properly, so that Israel might enjoy the blessings of the land to which YHWH has brought them. There is great theological significance to the request in v. 15 to "bless the ground," the ground which YHWH had cursed because of human beings (Genesis 3:17).

The Deuteronomic Code concludes with an "agreement" between YHWH and Israel, that Israel will keep YHWH's commandments and thus be YHWH's people (26:17-19).

---

[34]Von Rad argued that Israel's earliest profession of its faith did not include these items, but they accrued to later expressions which appear elsewhere in the Old Testament. Joshua 24:2-13, e.g., expands the description of the ancestors and includes a reference to the wilderness tradition, and Nehemiah 9:6-31 finally adds Sinai to Israel's creedal tradition. See Gerhard von Rad, *Deuteronomy: A Commentary*, trans. Dorothea Barton (Philadelphia: Westminster Press, 1966) 157-59.

Moses Proclaims the Blessings and Curses of the Law

Interpreters of Deuteronomy generally agree that chapter 27 begins a new section of the book, after the Deuteronomic Code in chapters 12–26 is finished. The most prominent feature of chapter 27 is the list of twelve curses that appears in vv. 15-26. These curses are preceded by a curious set of instructions in which the Israelites are commanded by "Moses and the elders" to construct an altar and a set of stones covered with plaster on Mount Ebal. On the stones they are to write "all the words of this law." It is not clear what the text considers "this law" to be. Moreover the building of an altar and conducting of sacrificial rituals at a place other than Jerusalem does not fit well into the theology of Deuteronomy. Mount Ebal is in northern Israel, very close to Shechem and Mount Gerizim. For those readers aware of Israelite tradition, it would be impossible to deny the existence of such places as important centers of worship in the past. Some interpreters explain this text by calling it "pre-Deuteronomic,"[35] but while this explains its contradictory content, it does not explain its inclusion in the book of Deuteronomy, where it rests so uneasily. Another possibility is that Deuteronomy is attempting to deal with these places, whose past significance is unavoidable, by placing a major, one-time-only event there. The story also has a potential etiological function. If the stones were there, and their presence was widely known, then Deuteronomy needed to explain their existence and incorporate them into its own view of Israel's faith. The presence of the "levitical priests" with Moses (v. 9) helps to link the Ebal story to the curses which are to be pronounced by the Levites on Mount Gerizim.

The list of curses in 27:15-26 contains twelve distinct elements. It is introduced by the placement of two groups of Israelite tribes on the two mountains, Ebal and Gerizim (vv. 11-14). Comparisons of the ways the tribes are listed have already appeared in tables 3.1 and 5.3. A few features of this list are worth noting. First, the placement of two groups on two different mountains necessitates the division of the twelve tribes into two groups of six, a division that places the two eldest sons of Jacob, Reuben and Simeon, at the beginning of the two separate lists. Second, Levi is included within the list, creating the need to list Joseph as a single tribe in order to keep the number at twelve. Third, while it is not easy to determine

---

[35]Von Rad, *Deuteronomy: A Commentary*, 164-65.

a clear pattern in the division and placement of the tribes, those which have the most persistent and distinctive sense of identity within the biblical tradition (Levi, Judah, Joseph, and Benjamin) are placed on Mount Gerizim and associated with the blessing rather than the curse. Finally, the Levites are given a special role in v. 14, even though the tribe of Levi is also included among the others in v. 12. The twelve curses follow a fairly consistent form, "Cursed be anyone who commits Act X. All the people shall say, 'Amen.'" The two most significant diversions from this pattern are the first and last commandments. The first curse is in v. 15 and addresses the making of idols. It is longer than all of the others and varies in its wording from all the others. The last curse is summary in nature, referring to no specific act, but speaking of "this law" in a manner that connects it back to 27:3. Some interpreters have raised the possibility that these two are later additions to an ancient list of curses, and that they were added for various reasons, including a desire to bring the list to twelve.[36] All of the first eleven curses are related to prohibitions that appear elsewhere in the Pentateuch. Elizabeth Bellafontaine has made a major attempt to discuss these relationships and the construction of the curse list.[37]

The introduction to the curses (27:11-14), which places six tribes on Mount Gerizim "for the blessing of the people," and six on Mount Ebal "for the curse" would seem to anticipate the list of blessings in 28:3-6, yet there are only four statements of blessing here, and they are matched and balanced by four additional curses in vv. 16-19. The blessings are followed by a more detailed description of the gifts YHWH will bestow upon an obedient Israel in vv. 7-14. This description is overwhelmed, however, by the disasters described following the curses. A stunning forty-nine verses provide details about the results of disobedience to the covenant.

By the end of chapter 28 it is plain to see that Deuteronomy knows the story of Israel ends in defeat. The description of an invasion in vv. 47-57 looks like the Babylonian destruction of Judah and Jerusalem in the sixth century. The "iron yoke" of v. 48 resembles the story in Jeremiah 27–28 and the poetic lines of Lamentations 1:14, and the portrayal of besieged

---

[36]For a more extensive discussion of these and other issues related to the curse list, see Elizabeth Bellafontaine, "The Curses of Deuteronomy 27: Their Relation to Prohibitives," in *A Song of Power and the Power of Song: Essays on the Book of Deuteronomy*, ed. Duane L. Christensen (Winona Lake IN: Eisenbrauns, 1993) 259-60.

[37]Bellafontaine, "The Curses of Deuteronomy 27," 260-68.

Israelites eating the bodies of their children (28:53-57) reflects a similar image in Lamentations 4:10. By the end of the chapter, the ultimate fate of Israel is described as a return to Egypt (28:68), and the passion of these descriptions seems too great to be merely an explanation of a potential threat.

The division between chapters 28 and 29 provides a point of interest and difficulty. The verse designated as 29:1 in most English translations is labeled as 28:69 in the Hebrew text, so "the words of the covenant" of which this verse speaks may be understood in relation to either what precedes or what follows, but it seems more natural to understand the verse as a summary of what has gone before. When Moses "summons all Israel" in 29:2 this sounds like the beginning of a new event. The ceremony described here in 29:2-29 is reminiscent of Moses' hortatory speeches in the early part of Deuteronomy, as vv. 2-9 review God's deliverance of Israel from Egypt and care for Israel in the wilderness. Though not as harsh initially as the curses and their aftermath in chapter 28, 29:18-20 begins to describe the consequences of failing to keep the covenant with YHWH. The threat here becomes more severe, however, when the specter of Sodom and Gomorrah is raised (v. 23) and the curses are recalled (v. 27).

The purpose of this section is revealed in 29:22-23 when people are portrayed asking why YHWH has afflicted Israel in such a way, and v. 28 becomes more precise with its hypothetical conclusion: "YHWH uprooted them from their ground in anger, and in wrath, and and in great rage, and he cast them unto another land, as it is this day." These verses appear to be addressed to the generation *after* the Exile, which would be attempting to understand that event and to prevent it from recurring.[38]

Deuteronomy 30 continues to address the aftermath of the Exile, but takes a decidedly positive turn. Verse 5 assumes that the curses of the previous chapters, enacted as punishment, have accomplished their purpose, and that the Israelites are now ready to reenter the Promised Land. The covenant renewal language in v. 6 points back to the great commandment, the *Shema*,

---

[38]It should be noted that some interpreters resist an exilic reading of these texts, either by assuming that Deuteronomy is making prophetic predictions about events in the distant future, or by arguing that events at another time, such as in the seventh century BCE, provide an adequate sense of national destruction to serve as the context for such language. For an example of the latter, see Robert Alter, *The Five Books of Moses: A Translation with Commentary* (New York: W. W. Norton & Co., 2004) 1025. Elsewhere, however, Alter asserts that Deuteronomy 30:1 "assumes the condition of exile as an accomplished fact" (1027).

in 6:4-5, and provides the Israelites a new opportunity to be obedient to YHWH. The highly emotional language of this covenant renewal, with its emphasis on the heart in vv. 6 and 17, and an expressed sense of intimacy between Israel and YHWH in vv. 11-14, is often closely connected to the book of Jeremiah, particularly chapters 30–33. Despite this positive turn, however, the notion of blessing and curse still hangs over the text as Deuteronomy 30 comes to a close with a final exhortation to "choose life" (v. 19) by being obedient to the commandments.

Preparing for Moses' Departure

Moses continues to speak in Deuteronomy 31, but this speech takes on a different tone when he reveals his age and his declining abilities (vv. 1-2). This is the point at which the looming death of Moses begins to dominate the book of Deuteronomy. Moses' death has been implied earlier at Numbers 20:12, as a result of the Meribah affair, and has appeared to be imminent on another occasion at Numbers 27:12-23. As Moses prepares for his death in Deuteronomy, he reiterates his commissioning of Joshua (31:7-8), writes down "this law" (v. 9), and provides a procedure for the regular public reading of the law (vv. 10-13).

At 31:14 YHWH becomes a direct speaking character as the text provides speech from YHWH to Moses. After telling Moses that he is about to die, YHWH tells him about the future failure of the Israelites and the resulting punishment. Oddly, the response to this in v. 19 is a command for Moses to write a song. The song, mentioned again in v. 22, refers to the poem in 32:1-43, commonly called, of course, "The Song of Moses." Before the text of the song appears, however, Moses speaks again in the final verses of chapter 31. The primary subject of his speech to the Levites in vv. 26-29 is the upcoming disobedience of the Israelites after his death.

The impending death of Moses, which is everywhere in chapter 31, is forestalled by the presentation of the text of the Song of Moses in chapter 32. This is a remarkable poem, which speaks of Israel's past and future, from Israel's own perspective.

Perhaps the most surprising element of the Song of Moses is the understanding of the relationship between YHWH and Israel. The unusual name for God, *'Elyon*, is used alone only here and in Numbers 24:14 (see table 1.6). In Deuteronomy 32:8-9, YHWH and *'Elyon* seem to be presented as separate beings, with *'Elyon* as the high god who assigns groups of people to various lower gods, including YHWH, to whom Jacob/Israel is assigned. This issue is complicated by a textual problem in v. 8, which in most versions and manuscripts reads "He set the boundaries of the peoples according to the number of the children of Israel." This nonsensical reading was clarified with the discovery of a Deuteronomy scroll at Qumran which read "gods" in place of "children of Israel." Of course, the polytheistic assumptions of such a reading create difficulties, but the text itself in the Qumran scroll makes good sense, and it was easy to see why scribal traditions would have been inclined to change it. This element, along with others, leads many interpreters to consider the Song of Moses an old poem which has been embedded here in Deuteronomy.

The calling of the heavens and earth to hear the song in 32:1 connects this song with other texts in Deuteronomy, like 4:26 and 30:19, where heavens and earth are named as witnesses to the covenant between YHWH and Israel. The poem reviews Israel's past, with references to the wilderness in v. 10, and emphasizes YHWH's care for Israel like a child. The middle of the poem describes Israel's worship of other gods and YHWH's jealousy, leading to disaster and defeat. By the end of the poem YHWH has restored Israel and taken vengeance on those who destroyed it. So, the Song of Moses covers the entire sweep of Israel's story from election to deliverance to disobedience to destruction and exile to restoration and return. Placed in the mouth of Moses, such a song assures Israel of God's ultimate intention to care for the chosen people, which embraces temporary periods in which Israel's fortunes rise and fall.

At the end of chapter 32, the subject of Moses' death reappears and, again, it seems imminent. In 32:48-53 YHWH instructs Moses to climb Mount Nebo to view the land before his death. Joseph Blenkinsopp has argued that in the original P narrative Moses died on the journey to Canaan, and the record of this event is still present in Numbers 27:12-23. The attachment of Deuteronomy onto the end of the Pentateuch required that Moses be kept alive, even though this creates some awkwardness in subsequent texts.[39] In Deuteronomy the death of Moses is delayed a second time by the insertion of another long poem, the "Blessing of Moses," in chapter 33. The reluctance of the Pentateuch as a whole to let go of Moses is, therefore, reflected in Deuteronomy as well.

The end of the book of Deuteronomy very much resembles the end of the book of Genesis. In Genesis 50 Jacob and Joseph, the two major

[39]See Blenkinsopp, *The Pentateuch*, 229-32. Blenkinsopp also demonstrates that the material dealing with the death of Moses in Deuteronomy 32 and 34 is an expansion of the text in Numbers 27.

characters of the second half of the book, die. In Deuteronomy 34 Moses, the primary character of Exodus through Deuteronomy, dies. The death of a main character becomes a significant way to end a book, and will be used again in the Old Testament in Joshua and 1 Samuel. One chapter back into both Genesis and Deuteronomy, long poems appear, which have a great deal in common. The "Song of Jacob" in Genesis 49 and the "Blessing of Moses" in Deuteronomy 33 are both a composites of smaller poems about the sons of Jacob and the tribes of Israel which bear their names. Much is revealed by a comparison of these two long poems.

First, the simplest difference is the disappearance of Simeon, leaving only eleven tribes in Deuteronomy 33. Second, the order in which the tribes are presented changes. In Genesis 49 they appear in their birth order, as reported in Genesis 30. Thus, the Song of Jacob begins with the four prominent sons of Leah (Reuben, Judah, Simeon, and Levi) and ends with the two sons of Rachel (Joseph and Benjamin). The most noticeable change in order in the Blessing of Moses is the upward movement of the two youngest, with Benjamin moving into the fourth position and Joseph moving to fifth.

With the last of the delays out of the way, Deuteronomy is now prepared to face the death of its hero in the final chapter. The story of the death of Moses in Deuteronomy 34 is a remarkable text. No other passage in the Old Testament brings so many monumental things to an end. The end of the Pentateuch, the end of the book of Deuteronomy, the end of the wilderness period, the end of the giving of the Law, and the end of the life of Moses all coincide in this brief story. The subject of Moses' death has been raised a number of times in the Pentateuch. In Exodus 32, when Moses was also alone on a mountain, the people of Israel wondered what had become of him as they asked Aaron to make gods for them. Did they think he might be dead? In Numbers 11:15, Moses asked God to kill him so that he would no longer have to suffer as the leader of the Israelites and the mediator between them and God.

The second story of the "waters of Meribah," in Numbers 20:1-13, predicts the death of Moses and Aaron and tries to give a reason for why Moses died before entering the Promised Land, though the reason is difficult to determine with precision. Aaron dies in the wilderness immediately following this episode (Numbers 20:22-29), and it seems that Moses' death should follow. As described above, Deuteronomy 31–33 have already begun to approach this difficult subject.

Several important tasks are accomplished in chapter 34. First the Promised land is defined and fully imagined in the gaze of Moses (vv. 1-3). Second, the end of the Pentateuch is tied to its beginning with the recitiation of the names of the great ancestors (v. 4). Third, Moses dies without looking diminished in any way (v. 7), though this contradicts the report in 31:2. Fourth, any thought of Moses' grave becoming a sacred site to which Israelites might make pilgrimages is dismissed in vv. 5-6. This is an enormous act of forgetting, perhaps equal to the lost recollection of the precise location of Mount Sinai, but is in keeping with Deuteronomy's desire to promote Jerusalem as the one and only sacred site for Israel. Fifth, the status of Joshua, as Moses' successor, is reaffirmed in a voice other than that of Moses (v. 9). Finally, Moses is eulogized in powerful, glowing terms (vv. 10-12), with no recall of any negative aspects of his life.

Despite earlier explanations of the death of Moses—tying it to the Meribah event—there is no hint in chapter 34 of Moses' death being any kind of punishment. That the Pentateuch can proceed even in this small way beyond the death of Moses is a sign that Israel can continue beyond his death. After thirty days, according to v. 8, "the days of weeping, the mourning of Moses, were complete."

History and Deuteronomy

The connection of the book of Deuteronomy with the reform movement sponsored by King Josiah in Judah during the late seventh century has received attention earlier in this volume. The opening chapter discussed de Wette's identification of Deuteronomy with the book found in 2 Kings 22:8 as a formative moment in the development of the Documentary Hypothesis. The general consensus that at least an early form of Deuteronomy is connected to Josiah provides a specific context for parts of the book, but little is known about this period of time outside of what appears in the Bible. Further, this can hardly be understood as the context that produced the book in its final form.

Further work on Deuteronomy in the twentieth century, most importantly by Martin Noth, Gerhard von Rad, and Moshe Weinfeld, has developed the notion of a "Deuteronomic School," widely considered responsible for the book of Deuteronomy, much of the Deuteronomistic History (Joshua–Kings), and parts of the prophetic books, particularly the "prose sermons" of Jeremiah. This understanding has generated a number of defining characteristics of this Deuteronomic School, which is assumed to have been active in shaping Israel's traditions from the seventh through at least the fifth centuries.[40] The editing influence of these tradents may extend back into the earlier books of the Pentateuch in passages like Exodus 12:26-27, 19:3-9, 23:20-33, and 32:9-14. Identification of sources in the Pentateuch is always problematic, but if these assignments of texts to D are correct, then it means that the Deuteronomic School had a significant hand particularly in the shaping of Exodus, and especially the Sinai story within it, much of which Deuteronomy retells.[41]

The close connection between Deuteronomy and the Deuteronomistic History that follows it is one of the broadest areas of consensus within Old Testament scholarship, although, naturally, there are significant disagreements about the details of this relationship. Perhaps the primary task of the books of Joshua, Judges, Samuel, and Kings is to present a portrait of the origins of the Israelite monarchy. First Samuel 8 describes a pivotal moment in that portrayal when the Israelites demand of Samuel: "Place over us a king to judge us, like all the nations" (1 Samuel 8:4). Deuteronomy's awareness of this issue is betrayed in the midst of the Deuteronomic Code itself in a remarkable text at 17:14-20 which envisions a future Israel saying: "I will put over me a king like all the nations" (17:14). Deuteronomy 17:15-16 goes on to express some of the same reservations about royal power as 1 Samuel 8:10-18. Deuteronomy offers a remedy for royal abuse in 17:18 when it commands that the king make a "copy of this law." This is the very phrase that the Greek version of Deuteronomy translated as a "second" (*deuteron-*) law, leading to the eventual title of the book. The final form of Deuteronomy seems to look forward to the reestablishment of the Israelite monarchy after the Exile, and offers a program that will prevent the kinds of royal excesses that helped lead to Israel's destruction and the end of its monarchy.

While the Josianic reform may be reflected in the earliest layers of Deuteronomy, the book also demonstrates an awareness of the Exile in passages like 28:47-57. Such awareness has often led to an understanding of at least two important stages of Deuteronomic literary production and editing—one before the Exile and one after. This would make the ultimate concern of the book of Deuteronomy the reestablishment of Israel and its

---

[40]For a thorough list and description of the literary characteristics that identify this group of writers and editors, see Weinfeld, *Deuteronomy and the Deuteronomic School*, 320-65.

[41]See the discussion of this and related issues in Blenkinsopp, *The Pentateuch*, 186-89.

worship in the second temple, in a rebuilt Jerusalem. The renewal of the covenant with each new generation, emphasized in chapter 30, and the instructions to read the law publicly in Jerusalem every seventh year, in 31:9-13, define a new horizon for an Israel that has suffered the curses of 28:16-68 but has survived.

Key Terms

Shema
Moab
Josianic Reform
Deuteronomist
Song of Moses
Deuteronomic Code
suzerainty treaty
Blessing of Moses

Questions for Reflection

1. What is the relationship between the "second law" and the first law, in historical, literary, and canonical terms?
2. Why is Deuteronomy so concerned with centralization of worship? What are the advantages and disadvantages of such an effort?
3. What light might Ancient Near Eastern treaties shed on the structure and contents of Deuteronomy?
4. What different understandings of the death of Moses are present in Deuteronomy? In what ways are they in conflict with one another and the traditions in the Book of Numbers?

Sources for Further Study

Biddle, Mark E. *Deuteronomy*. Smyth & Helwys Bible Commentary. Macon GA: Smyth & Helwys Publishing, 2003.

Brueggemann, Walter. *Deuteronomy*. Abingdon Old Testament Commentaries. Nashville: Abingdon Press, 2001.

Christensen, Duane L., editor. *A Song of Power and the Power of Song: Essays on the Book of Deuteronomy*. Winona Lake IN: Eisenbrauns, 1993.

Clements, Ronald E. "The Book of Deuteronomy: Introduction, Commentary, and Reflection." In *The New Interpreter's Bible*, edited by Leander E. Keck et al., 2:269-538. Nashville: Abingdon, 1998.

Nelson, Richard D. *Deuteronomy: A Commentary*. The Old Testament Library. Louisville: Westminster/John Knox, 2002.

Olson, Dennis T. *Deuteronomy and the Death of Moses: A Theological Reading*. Overtures to Biblical Theology. Minneapolis: Fortress Press, 1994. Reprint: Eugene OR: Wipf & Stock, 2005.

Polzin, Robert M. *Moses and the Deuteronomist: Deuteronomy, Joshua, Judges*. Part 1 of *A Literary Study of the Deuteronomistic History* (4 volumes). Bloomington IN: Indiana University Press, 1993. Original: New York: Seabury Press, 1980.

von Rad, Gerhard. *Deuteronomy: A Commentary*. Translated by Dorothea Barton. The Old Testament Library. Louisville: Westminster/John Knox, 1966.

Tigay, Jeffrey H. *Deuteronomy. The Traditional Hebrew Text with the New JPS Translation*. JPS Torah Commentary. Philadelphia: Jewish Publication Society, 1996.

Weinfeld, Moshe. *Deuteronomy and the Deuteronomic School*. Oxford: Clarendon Press/Oxford University Press, 1972. Reprint: Winona Lake IN: Eisenbrauns, 1992, ©1972.

Chapter 7

Concluding Issues

The Pentateuch and the Deuteronomistic History

Readers have often found the ending of the Pentateuch most unsatisfying, leading to proposals of Tetrateuchs and Hexateuchs. It is difficult to imagine that this story could be told without the gigantic figure of Moses at its center, but the power of Moses' monumental stature comes at a price. By the end, he overwhelms the story, and tradition knows this collection not as the "Books of Israel" or the "Books of the Covenant" or the "Books of Deliverance" or any other of a dozen possibilities, but as the "Books of Moses." Moses has done all of the heavy lifting in this story and he must be compensated, so the Pentateuch must spend its final chapter burying and memorializing Moses, while all of its other goals are set aside for another story.

That second story is told in the books of Joshua through Kings, a collection that has multiple identities. Martin Noth was correct and very helpful when he labeled these books the "Deuteronomistic History," because they clearly flow out of the book of Deuteronomy, which could play a transitional role once this collection of books was added onto the Pentateuch within the biblical canon. There is enough cohesion between the two collections for contemporary scholarship to use the moniker "Primary History" to refer to Genesis-Kings and its continuous story, which runs from Creation to the Exile. Such a move wrests Joshua–Kings away from its traditional role within Judaism as the so-called "Former Prophets," four scrolls (Joshua, Judges, Samuel, and Kings) which are balanced by the four scrolls of the "Latter Prophets" (Isaiah, Jeremiah, Ezekiel, and the Book of the Twelve).

The previous chapter on Deuteronomy gave some attention to that book's emphasis on the centralization of worship in ancient Israel, characteristically expressed in the phrase, "the place where I [YHWH] shall cause my name to dwell." Of course, the book of Deuteronomy must refer to Jerusalem cryptically in order to stay true to its narrative, but that phrase also provides the Deuteronomistic History its primary assignment: to tell the story of how YHWH's name came to dwell in Jerusalem, and the ultimate fate of this location.

Like the Pentateuch, the Deuteronomistic History is composed of a vast array of materials from different locations and time periods. It appears to have gone through a preexilic formation process and then one or more significant exilic or postexilic stages of editing. The Pentateuch addresses the monarchy directly in two places, Genesis 49 and Deuteronomy 17, and is clearly aware of many traditions that underlie the Deuteronomistic History. At the same time, the Deuteronomistic History is dependent upon many traditions expressed in the Pentateuch, including the ancestors (2 Kings 13:23), the Egyptian bondage and deliverance (1 Samuel 4:7-9), and the Sinai legal tradition, including the tabernacle and the ark of the covenant (1 Kings 8:1-9). It is difficult to say whether the Deuteronomistic History expects its readers to have read the Pentateuch, but it certainly assumes familiarity with the major areas of its content.

The story lines of the Deuteronomistic History follow the contours established in the Pentateuch. The character of Joshua is transformed by the events of Joshua 1–5 into a new Moses figure, complete with miraculous water crossing and mysterious divine encounter, just as the early part of the book of Exodus transformed Moses into Jacob. In Judges the Israelites are repeatedly taken into captivity and enslaved, only to be delivered by YHWH after they cry out for help. As 1 Samuel opens, a favored, but barren, wife reminiscent of Sarah and Rachel appears and miraculously gives birth to a son. Israel's greatest king appears in 1 Samuel 16 in the familiar figure of a youngest son herding sheep, who must eventually flee into the wilderness to escape his pursuers, before finally returning and assuming his rightful place. Finally, Solomon constructs the great temple in Jerusalem following the pattern of Moses' tabernacle, and the descent of the glory cloud in 1 Kings 8:10-11 matches the event in Exodus 40:34, signaling YHWH's presence in temple and tabernacle. In all of this is difficult to deny that the Pentateuch establishes the shape and tone of the Bible.

The Pentateuch and Chronicles

One additional purpose of the label, Primary History, for Genesis–Kings is to distinguish the narrative collection it represents from the "Chronicler's History," contained within the book of Chronicles, which also traces Israel's story from creation to the Exile. The purpose of the book of

Chronicles has been the subject of much debate.[1] In the Hebrew canon, Chronicles comes at the very end, providing a parallel account of the story of Israel as a closing frame after the prophetic books and the remainder of the Writings. It is evident that Chronicles was written after the Pentateuch and the Deuteronomistic History, so was its purpose to replace them, correct them, or supplement them? Chronicles begins with the barest of genealogies: "Adam, Seth, Enosh, Kenan, Mahalel, Jared, Enoch, Methuselah, Lamech, Noah, Shem, Ham, and Japheth" (1:1-4). The reduction of the Pentateuch down to a few chapters of genealogical material at the beginning of 1 Chronicles is a striking feature of this book. It is hard to imagine that the writer of Chronicles did not expect the reader to know and recall the stories behind these names, so the replacement option is untenable. The other two options, corrective and supplementary, are not mutually exclusive.

The most striking differences between the Primary History and the Chronicler's History are the ways in which the latter revises the images of David and Solomon and magnifies their actions which led to the completion of the temple in Jerusalem.[2] This creates some distance between the Pentateuch and Chronicles, in terms of the former's distrust of the monarchy. Chronicles also spends much more space emphasizing the processes of worship, and particularly the role of the Levites. In this aspect, Chronicles goes beyond the Pentateuch and reveals something of its position in the political environment of the second temple.

Like Deuteronomy and the Deuteronomistic History, Chronicles is concerned with the Exile, its causes, and its lessons for Israel's future. The activities of the great reforming kings, Hezekiah and Josiah, are presented in the Deuteronomistic History, but these portrayals are significantly expanded in Chronicles by the presentation of grand, national Passover celebrations, sponsored by each of these kings. The celebrations of Passover in 2 Chronicles 30 and 35 show affinities with Deuteronomy 16, describing

---

[1]The book called Ezra-Nehemiah is often understood to be a continuation of Chronicles. The placement of two different versions of the decree of Cyrus at 2 Chronicles 36:22-23 and Ezra 1:1-4 surely ties them together, but a near consensus has developed over the past three decades that they were not produced by the same author. See the discussion in H. G. M. Williamson, *Ezra-Nehemiah*, Word Biblical Commentary 16 (Waco TX: Word Books, 1984).

[2]While the stories of David and Solomon comprise approximately 15% of the Primary History, they make up about 45% of the Chronicler's History.

Passover as a pilgrimage festival for which all of Israel travels to the central sanctuary in Jerusalem, and with Numbers 9, which makes allowance for who must celebrate late because of purity issues.

An additional point of contact between Chronicles and the Pentateuch is the reference to land sabbath in 2 Chronicles 36:20-21, which connects this explanation of the Exile to the prophecy of Jeremiah. There is no clear dependence on the particular land sabbath texts in Exodus 23:10-11 or Leviticus 25:1-7, but similar assumptions seem to lie behind all of these texts.

Future Directions in Pentateuchal Studies

The dissolution of the source-critical consensus which governed Pentateuch studies for a century has hardly brought an end to source-critical scholarship. In some ways, it has provided a greater sense of urgency to this approach. Source-critical studies must now compete with other, very different approaches for the attention of those who produce and consume biblical scholarship. This method will never again achieve such a grand consensus, which raises serious questions about its purpose. We would do well to recognize here the most lasting gift of source-criticism, that is, its painstaking attention to every detail of the text.[3] Like any exegetical method, its value lies in its ability to focus the reader's attention on the text and keep the reader and the text in intimate contact for as long as possible. Contemporary literary approaches can function effectively on many different levels, from describing the shape of an entire biblical book to analyzing the intricate details of smaller portions of text. These approaches will continue to be fruitful for a long time to come, but, by their nature, they will never lead to a grand synthesis. Such a scheme should, therefore, not be our goal, but rather careful attention to the Bible "one text at a time,"[4] allowing those texts to speak for themselves.

---

[3]On this point, see the comments of Phyllis Trible, *Rhetorical Criticism: Context, Method, and the Book of Jonah*, Guides to Biblical Scholarship (Minneapolis: Fortress Press, 1994) 101.

[4]For a more thorough description of this phenomenon in literary approaches to the Bible, see Walter Brueggemann, *Theology of the Old Testament: Testimony, Dispute, Advocacy* (Minneapolis: Fortress Press, 2005, ©1997) 55-56.

The Pentateuch and Contemporary Society

Two aspects of the role of the Pentateuch are worth mentioning here and, in both, it proves to be a force which can either unite or divide. The first involves the conflicts that arise between different faith communities who consider this text sacred. Can this literary collection belong to two different religions? It has been my goal throughout this book to read and present the Pentateuch on its own terms, but there are some inherent tensions and limitations involved in such an effort.[5] Perhaps this limitation is simplest and most visible as it relates to language. I read the text of the Pentateuch in both Hebrew and many of the modern English translations, but even the former is not quite the language of the text. For the most part, I read the Pentateuch in the biblical Hebrew language presented by the Masoretic Text, which is closely related to but not equivalent to the ancient Hebrew language in which it was first written. Another aspect of this limitation is that much of the Pentateuch was written by ancient Israelites and the final form was produced by Jews living in the Persian period, and I am a Christian living in the twenty-first century. Therefore, my religious experience can stand in the way of reading the text on its own terms. The Pentateuch is part of my "Old" Testament and, therefore, part of the Christian Bible. It has long been Christian practice to read the Pentateuch with questions specific to Christianity in mind. Laying these questions aside requires a deliberate effort and can never be fully accomplished. As communities of readers, it is vital that we be honest about our religious convictions.

Walter Brueggemann has set an important agenda for study of the Old Testament with his articulation of "four insistent questions."[6] One of these questions involves the "Jewishness" of the text. It has been a Christian tendency to ignore, or at least downplay, this quality. The problem of how to read such a text in Christian contexts will not go away. Platitudes about how the New Testament must be read in light of the Old Testament and the Old Testament in light of the New Testament are insufficient. What Christians call "the Old Testament" existed long before it became part of the Christian Bible. It even existed within Christianity for a couple of cen-

---

[5]For a helpful discussion of this issue, see Johanna W. H. van Wijk-Bos, *Making Wise the simple: The Torah in Christian Faith and Practice* (Grand Rapids MI: Eerdmans, 2005) 7-14.

[6]Brueggemann, *Theology of the Old Testament*, 102-14.

turies before it became part of a two-testament Christian Bible. This identity of the text must be given priority, and I have tried to do that as best I can in two important ways. First, I have minimized references to the New Testament, in order to make myself stay in the Pentateuch. Second, I have tried to interact with Jewish voices throughout the book and to let them speak whenever possible.

The second issue involves how we read and use the Pentateuch, particularly in reference to some of the issues surrounding "literal reading," which were explored at the end of the first chapter of this book. Arriving at a clearer understanding of what the Pentateuch is and is not may help avoid some of the contention surrounding these issues, but questions about whether it should be determinative in our thinking about science, human history, and/or the structure and content of contemporary legal systems will likely persist. The best antidote to an overemphasis on literal reading is a fuller awareness of everything that is in the text. Rigid systems that rely on this literalist approach to the text tend, necessarily, to be quite selective in the texts that are used. I certainly hope that the close attention to all of the Pentateuch in the preceding pages might be part of a remedy to that.

I also hope that this is not merely a negative exercise. Freeing the Pentateuch from what it is not is also an act of freeing it to what it is, a text that keeps on relentlessly bringing us back to the central questions of human existence, and with its own inadequate answers, driving us toward seeking better answers of our own.

Indexes

Author Index

Subject Index

Scripture Index